The National Review College Guide

AMERICA'S TOP LIBERAL ARTS SCHOOLS

Edited by
Charles J. Sykes and Brad Miner

Introduction by
William F. Buckley, Jr.

A Fireside Book

Published by Simon & Schuster

New York   London   Toronto   Sydney   Tokyo   Singapore

FIRESIDE
Simon & Schuster Building
Rockefeller Center
1230 Avenue of the Americas
New York, New York 10020

Designed by Irving Perkins Associates, Inc.
Manufactured in the United States of America

10   9   8   7   6   5   4   3   2   1

Library of Congress Cataloging-in-Publication Data
The National review college guide : America's 50 top liberal arts schools / edited by Charles J.
Sykes and Brad Miner ; introduction by William F. Buckley, Jr. — [2nd ed.]
   p. cm.
"A Fireside book."
  1. Universities and colleges—United States—Directories. 2. Education, Humanistic—
United States—Directories. I. Sykes, Charles J., 1954– . II. Miner, Brad.
III. National review.
L901.N3485 1993
378.73—dc20   93-1707
                                                       CIP

ISBN: 0-671-79801-4

Contents

PART I *The National Review College Guide*

Contents

PART II *The Academic Gulag*

PART III *The Art of Learning*

Introduction

by William F. Buckley, Jr.

The impulse behind this book is one part political, as might be expected. Under the aegis of *National Review*, colleges apparently conscripted to ideological biases against God or man are not recommended. But readers will quickly see that there is no sense in which the editors of this survey have been guided by sectarianism. Their uniform concern throughout has been the search for quality education. And such education, they are convinced, requires not merely that graduates of an institution emerge technically qualified to handle the machinery of the modern world; they must also learn something about its evolution. And they must be exposed to some of the reasons why bias gradually crystallized in favor of human freedom, and why freedom of the marketplace is essential to that basic liberty.

The editors and their advisers warn against fashionable developments in many colleges and universities of illustrious name and influence. Most are missing from this selection, not because you cannot get a good education at Harvard, for example, but because you *can* graduate from Harvard without getting a good education. That observation is simply not true of the institutions here described.

As stressed in the preface, and indeed throughout the book, a heavy accent is also placed on the *art* of teaching. For many students, the hunger to learn is only latently there, and the maieutic hand of the teacher becomes indispensable. Graduate students and teaching assistants may one day grow into masterly teachers, but they should not be practicing on students who might go through college without any contact with a great teacher—who happens to be off doing research.

And then there is much activity among certain colleges that engage in currying favor with, and drawing in, Big Academic Names. I wrote about this phenomenon some years ago in *The Atlantic Monthly*, commenting on the strange compulsion that drove Yale to go into deep hock in order to lure the illustrious historian C. Vann Woodward from Johns Hopkins. It raised the question: Why? It wasn't as though the academic contributions of Mr. Woodward were only now to be made possible; at Johns Hopkins he had a library as extensive as any he'd need, the students were of roughly the same caliber, and the fellowship necessary to stimulate and provide encouragement existed equally in both institutions. Among the guarantees made to Professor Woodward was a trimmed-down teaching load, so that in fact he would probably face fewer students in New Haven than in Baltimore during his first few years. And, incidentally, he would see no students at all in year one, because one of the perks was for the first year to be a complete sabbatical.

Many of the five dozen colleges recommended by Messrs. Sykes and

Miner have distinguished faculty, and several induce a greater percentage of their graduates to earn Ph.D.s than Harvard does. But they are, by and large, less interested in Fifth Avenue academic shopping than the famous showcases we are all familiar with. The student and the student's parents—concerting to find a college that will offer a first-rate education and insist incontrovertibly that the student has indeed gotten a first-rate education before handing that student a diploma—are left with a great deal of choice. There is almost infinite variety, within the stated boundaries described, in the schools here honored.

I close by making a personal observation. Many parents wrote to me throughout the more than thirty-five years that I edited *National Review* asking that I recommend a "good" college for their sons and daughters. This book is an open letter to all such inquirers. And many other parents have written asking if I could help their son or daughter get into Yale, Harvard, Columbia. The answer to that question has always been entirely truthful: No. These fortresses have, over the years, constructed near-impregnable barriers to matriculation-by-pull. Sometimes the parents I speak of are driven by traditional loyalties to their own alma maters. Others are driven by social ambition, and sometimes this ambition is removed from mere snobbery. It is generally thought that by attending Harvard a student's opportunities are maximized—to meet the banker who will hire him, or the banker's daughter who will marry him (in the spirit of the day, reread this reversing the genders). In one of his *Making of the President* books, the late Theodore White passed his finger over the profiles of the twenty or thirty most prominent men in New York City, revealing the variety of their geographical and academic backgrounds. Whereas it is probably true that if you go to Harvard (I am using Harvard here as a synecdoche, purely for convenience) you will end up meeting more corporation presidents than if you attend some of the colleges here listed, it is worth noting that this is very much less predictable than it was back when the college population was a tenth of what it is now. And the critical counterweight to the advantage of Harvard is that its graduate might find himself diploma in hand but ignorant of important elements of history and philosophy and culture—the stuff that is grist for the mill of Western civilization. It is in respect of this point that the editors of this guide show so fine an eye, doing honor to more than fifty institutions that, over the years, have growled back at the cultural hurricanes and williwaws of the past century, baring teeth refined by years and centuries and millennia of unearthing and defending the sources and inspirations of Western civilization.

Preface

A Few (More) Good Schools

We say it again: American higher education is in crisis. Admissions standards continue to be lowered (an action justified as making colleges more accessible, but which has the effect of making education less valuable), curricula continue to be debased (along with the *inclusion* of so many "nontraditional" students has come the *exclusion* of most requirements), and courses continue to be trivialized (at one formerly prestigious liberal arts school there is even a biology course that uses books about witchcraft). The many professors who have put aside teaching in favor of research and writing may have begun to give lip service to the notion that they ought to spend more time professing, but at too many schools they are still leaving their students in the hands of graduate teaching assistants (TAs), who have little more education than undergraduates and no classroom experience (let alone tested skill). And the restrictions on free speech that have been so widely publicized (thanks in part to books such as Dinesh D'Souza's *Illiberal Education*) have not been abandoned at some schools, with the result that the educational environment remains PC, that is, "politically correct."

As we wrote in the preface to the first edition of this book, one might be able to live with this crisis if students were still managing to get well educated, but in many cases they are not. A 1989 Gallup Organization survey reported that 25 percent of America's college seniors cannot tell the difference between the words of Stalin and Churchill; cannot distinguish the language of *Das Kapital* from that of the U.S. Constitution; cannot even recall that Christopher Columbus first reached the New World before 1500. (No doubt the 1992 *quinto centenario* has changed this last fact. Students now know 1492 as the first year of American *Eurocentrism*.) That Gallup report concluded: "Using the standard 'A' to 'F' scale . . . 55 percent of the students would have received a grade of 'F' and another 20 percent a 'D.' "

How on earth can this be? How can students spend four years in an institution of higher learning and fail to understand the historical, economic, and political concepts fundamental to a democratic society?

The simple answer is: You cannot know what you are not taught. The National Endowment for the Humanities (NEH) funded another survey (included in its 1989 report *50 Hours: A Core Curriculum for College Students*), which found educational programs to be so unstructured in America's colleges that it is possible to graduate from:

· 78 percent of the nation's colleges and universities without ever taking a course in the history of Western civilization;

· 38 percent without taking any history course at all;
· 45 percent without taking a course in American or English literature;
· 77 percent without studying a foreign language;
· 41 percent without studying mathematics;
· 33 percent without studying natural or physical sciences.

So the headlines have told us, and so it is.

And yet this crisis is not the whole story. There are fine schools (big and small, urban and rural, religious and secular) that still educate students in the liberal arts tradition, and, like the Marine Corps in its search for fighting men, *National Review* went looking for—and found—a few good schools. There were fifty such schools in our first edition, and we are happy to report that the number has grown to fifty-eight in this, the second.

The response to the first edition of *The National Review College Guide* was both gratifying and surprising. We heard from many readers who used the book as an adjunct to their college searches, and we heard from admissions directors at some of our profiled colleges that more than a few applicants told them they first considered the campus in question because of what we wrote.

What was surprising was the criticism. We were accused of "politicizing from the Right," which would certainly be a valid animadversion if it were true, but it is not. As our publisher remarked: "This is a guide to schools that teach you *how* to think; not *what* to think." And one commentator wondered why we were so admiring of schools to which we would *never* send our own children. We gather that this latter criticism was occasioned by the religious affiliations of some of the schools we profile. Since neither Mr. Sykes nor Mr. Miner is, for instance, a Mormon, it apparently taxes the credulity of certain pundits that we express admiration for Brigham Young University; or, since we are not Evangelicals, they imagine that we cannot really admire Calvin College. (Or, we suppose, because we come from big cities and attended large universities ourselves, they assume we would never send our sons and daughters to tiny Thomas More.) Phooey. This book and its profiles describe colleges and universities that are worthy of consideration by Americans who value the liberal arts tradition, and this is not, as just about every college seems compelled to proclaim, "regardless of religious affiliation," but *because* of it. It seems to us that those who object to a religious presence on a campus do so because they assume: (a) that students ought to go to a university to be disabused of the old pieties; and (b) that a religious affiliation necessarily subsumes academic freedom. As we note below, this is rarely true, and those who wonder at our admiration of so many religiously affiliated schools ought to examine their own prejudices.

Our Criteria

Many of America's highly rated, elite colleges and universities are not recommended by us, and in Part II (new in this edition of the *Guide*) we explain why. In some cases we passed over them because we believe they do not deserve the reputations they still maintain; but in most cases these famous schools simply do not measure up to our criteria.

We invite the reader to reflect on the criteria outlined below: if they seem to describe a sound approach to higher education, then our profiled colleges will be appropriate choices; if our criteria do not strike a chord, the reader will do well to look elsewhere. The telephone book–thick college guides (we think the best is *Peterson's Guide to Four-Year Colleges*) list up to 1,500 schools, but the criteria used to evaluate them are almost uniformly quantitative, and the books make no recommendations. To recommend is to discriminate—to believe that standards and practices do matter.

Broadly speaking, there are three styles in American higher education: the "land-grant" universities, originally chartered to emphasize some technical expertise important to a particular region (especially agriculture and engineering); the "German" universities, oriented to highly technical research; and the "English" universities, designed to graduate well-rounded scholar-citizens. The schools we prefer are almost universally on the English model.

Foremost, we looked for schools that, overall, achieve academic excellence. How do we measure that? Primarily, according to three criteria:

1. By the quality and availability of the faculty;
2. By the quality of the curriculum, with special regard for schools with a liberal arts "core" (sometimes called a general education program) that respects the tradition of the West;
3. By the quality of the intellectual environment, that elusive interaction among students, faculty, administrators, alumni, and townspeople—the entire university community.

Faculty

The importance of good teachers is obvious. Less obvious is the degree to which good teachers actually teach undergraduate students. (See Mr. Sykes's book *Profscam* for a detailed indictment of the flight from pedagogy.) At some schools, the emphasis on research and writing—the old "publish or perish" pressure—has taken many of the best faculty out of the classroom and replaced them with graduate students. To become a teaching assistant is every graduate student's wish, but is it good for undergraduates? At Princeton recently half of all general education courses were taught by graduate students. Is this what parents think they are paying for? In Pennsylvania's colleges, the poor level of English spoken by foreign TAs led the state legislature to pass, and the governor to sign, a bill requiring all college teachers to be fluent in English. A Carnegie Foundation for the Advancement of Teaching survey found that more than half the faculty members at research institutions believe that "pressure to publish reduces the quality of teaching."

And just what are they publishing? Mostly articles for academic journals. Back in the 1970s, there were as many as 8,000 scientific periodicals. During the 1980s, nearly 30,000 new ones were started. Articles for these unread, frequently unreadable journals are produced in academia at the rate of about 3,000 each day. Do the math: that's more than a million articles per year. No wonder teachers have no time for teaching! (An interesting sidelight: a minor industry has emerged to count the number of times a professor's work is cited in academic journals, and one such enterprise, *Social Science Citation Index*, actually ranks the names it collates. You will not be surprised to learn that a frequently cited expert in many papers is the author himself. Unfortunately, the *Index* does not provide a ranking of 13 those most frequently citing themselves.) And we are talking here of articles such as "Evolution of the Potholder: From Technology to Popular Art," and such subjects as high school cheerleaders, in whom the professor saw religious symbology: "polysemous, affective, and prescriptive signs, deriving their power from their multireferential or multivocal nature and their ability to encode a special model of reality." Rah-rah.

We look favorably upon a school that puts its best people between its underclassmen and a chalkboard, and values faculty teaching ability above other measures of performance. (Thomas Sowell has half humorously observed that at too many institutions a "Teacher of the Year" award is the kiss of death.)

Core Curricula

Imagine a sinking ship that attempts to stay afloat by actually taking on water as it scuttles its lifeboats. That's the way many colleges appear to us when they eliminate traditional core curricula in favor of the various "studies" fads. A core is not, in and of itself, enough to satisfy (no doubt there's a "core" at Beijing University), but we think the best schools are those that put emphasis on Western civilization and demand prerequisites for further study. Our interest in the humanities is so strong that we have not included "technical" schools—even the most prestigious ones, such as M.I.T., Cal Tech, or West Point. Technical expertise is the heart of America's economic and scientific innovations, but knowledge of the Great Books and other sources of traditional wisdom is the soul of *citizenship*, and these days it seems clear we educate more than a sufficient number of technicians but far too few citizens.

Professor Donald Kagan, former dean of Yale College, has remarked that although he favors the core-curriculum idea, he would not press to see a program of requirements return to Yale. For one thing, he'd fail if he tried—such a notion is considered terribly old-fashioned in New Haven. But the main reason he would hold back is for fear of succeeding! Imagine, he says, what kind of core requirements the left-wing faculty, given the chance, would inflict upon Yale's students.

Indeed, the only Ivy League schools with core curricula are Columbia (see our profile of that endangered program) and Harvard. The latter leaves a lot to be desired. In "Harvard's Hollow Core" (*Atlantic Monthly*, September 1990), Caleb Nelson analyzed the Harvard program and its emphasis on "intellectual skills" rather than specific *knowledge*. According to one Harvard dean, *skills* rather than *facts* are the core's appropriate emphasis because we live in a revolutionary age in which "theories and facts can be crammed in, but ten years later, you'll forget them." Aside from apparently arguing against the very existence of the university as an undergraduate institution, the dean's comment—and this applies to the argument of the core itself—is made vacuous by its supposition that, in Mr. Nelson's phrase, it is possible to "think like a physicist without knowing physics." Mr. Nelson goes on to wonder why knowledge of the *nature* of history should be more important than knowledge of history itself:

> Students certainly should recognize that history is the testing ground of public policy, and that it can reveal much about the psychology of people and nations;

as Santayana's famous aphorism goes, those who cannot remember the past are condemned to repeat it. But this lesson *about* history is useless unless one also learns the actual lessons *of* history—an accomplishment that requires careful attention to the facts themselves. When Harvard suggests that its mission is finished once students learn that historical study can be useful, the college abdicates its educational responsibility at a crucial point: it lets students decide for themselves whether to study the actual substance of history, beyond the incidental amount that they find in their core courses. Regardless of their decision, Harvard willingly certifies their educational attainments by awarding them diplomas.

That means Harvard graduates do not have to read the literature, study the science, or learn the history required of nearly all the students attending the schools profiled in this guide.

A good core curriculum is not simply a collection of humanities courses. Ideally, it should embrace the seven-discipline sequence of what was traditionally called the *trivium* and the *quadrivium*. The trivium is the language arts: grammar, rhetoric, and logic—today encompassing all of what we call the *humanities*. The quadrivium is the sciences: arithmetic, geometry, music, and astronomy. In such a list one senses the ageless character of the liberal arts. (Music may seem an odd accompaniment to numbers and stars, but its structure is mathematical.) Emerging first in the Middle Ages, the liberal arts were designed to educate a new class of freemen. The trivium led to a bachelor of arts degree, the quadrivium to a master of arts. Since as long ago as the Renaissance, the liberal arts have been understood to be opposed to vocational specialization.

A liberal arts curriculum is about connections. "Liberal" in this sense means free—free to think beyond the boundaries of a particular discipline, to think about one discipline in terms of others. In *The Great Conversation*, Robert Maynard Hutchins wrote: "The liberally educated man understands, by understanding the distinctions and interrelations of the basic fields of subject matter, the differences and connections between poetry and history, science and philosophy, theoretical and practical science; he understands that the same methods cannot be applied in all these fields; he knows the methods appropriate to each."

Writing in *50 Hours*, former NEH chairman Lynne V. Cheney identified another important aspect of a common core of studies:

A core of learning . . . encourages community, whether we conceive community either small or large. Having some learning in common draws students together—and faculty members as well. When that common learning engages students with their democratic heritage, it invites informed participation in our ongoing national conversation: What should a free people value? What should they resist? What are the limits to freedom, and how are they to be decided?

It is tempting these days to believe that specialization is the key to future success, but we think that is exactly wrong. True, for many students required courses—even in the major field—are a nuisance tolerated as a means to the end of the diploma that wins the job that begins the career. For these students a college education is, at best, an introduction to some technical knowledge, most of which will be relearned on the job, along with all the things never learned in college that make up the substance of 15 professional life. The professions themselves—grounded as they are in what we casually refer to as "the real world"—sometimes denigrate the very preprofessional graduates drawn to the field: ad agencies do not want advertising majors; newspapers and magazines will not hire journalism graduates. (There is some hyperbole here, but not much.)

We do not mean to dismiss the importance of professional knowledge. Far from it. But, forgetting for the moment the aura that often surrounds a technical degree from an elite university, companies in most fields are looking for well-rounded employees; people who can read and understand, organize and analyze, plan and execute.

The liberal arts prepare students to go forward living the "examined life." That phrase is from Socrates, and he held that the *unexamined* life is not even worth living.

As for career preparation, that is what graduate school is for. In fact, graduates from nearly every school in this book have acceptance rates in graduate programs of better than 90 percent.

University Community

If you are a high school student who has yet to visit a college, or a parent whose last days on campus were twenty years ago, you may be shocked to discover how far the intellectual environment at some schools has deteriorated; how politicized things are. Feminism (including its lesbian subspecies) and feminist studies, black studies and affirmative action, gay rights and "sensitivity" rules—these are a few of the enthusiasms that now parade in academia under the banner of DIVERSITY. As the late Allan Bloom wrote (in *Giants and Dwarfs*), this constitutes a dramatic change, a revolving door that promises:

> . . . continuing wondrous curricular variations as different specialties and groups vie for power. . . . The premise of these students' concerns is that "where you come from," your culture, is more important than where you are going. They are rather like Plato's noble guardian dogs in the Republic who love what is familiar, no matter how bad it is, and hate all that is strange or foreign. This kind of demand is entirely new. You do not go to college to discover for yourself what is good but to be confirmed in your origins.

At a few schools, things have gone so far that free speech—sometimes especially by conservatives—is repressed. "Antiharassment" codes have been established that prohibit any speech (and this includes jokes) deemed sexist, racist, or homophobic. A recent edition of the *Harper's* magazine "Index" led off with this rather stunning fact: "Number of American universities that have instituted restrictions on public speech since 1988: 137." (*Harper's* source was the American Civil Liberties Union.) This is an especially incredible number when you reflect that those initiating the restrictions were the very sixties radicals who cut their ideological teeth in the "Free Speech Movement."

And what sort of language do these antiharassment codes employ? At the University of Connecticut you can be suspended not just for run-of-the-mill nasty cracks about gender, color, or sexual orientation (the kind of dopey remarks that used to define the word *sophomoric*), but also for using "derogatory names, inappropriately directed laughter . . . [or] conspicuous exclusion [of another student] from conversation." So much for the extraconstitutional right to say "Beat it!"

Elsewhere, professors and administrators have taken to using the classroom—almost no matter what subject is supposed to be taught—as a propaganda cell. At the University of Texas at Austin, for example, the only required course in composition, English 306, was redesigned in 1990 with the intent to uplift students by focusing course readings on left-wing writing about "racism and sexism." Writing about E306 as debate about it raged, *Washington Post* columnist George F. Will delineated the attitude behind the new academic orthodoxy:

> America is oppressive, imposing subservience on various victim groups. The culture is permeated with racism, sexism, heterosexism, classism . . . so the first task of universities is "consciousness-raising." This is done with "diversity education," which often is an attempt to produce intellectual uniformity by promulgating political orthodoxy. . . .
>
> The attempt to pump E306 full of politics is a manifestation of a notion common on campuses: every academic activity must have an ameliorative dimension, reforming society and assuaging this or that group's grievance. From that idea, it is but a short step down the slippery slope to this idea: all education, all culture, is political, so it should be explicitly so.

Fortunately, the proposed changes to E306 were put on hold. Unfortunately, several other schools have already begun to redesign courses on the Texas model.

We have opted as often as possible for schools that have not supplanted education with political indoctrination, have not subverted justice in pursuit of equality—whatever that is.

Politicization has gone so far at some schools that a few "scholars"—always of the Left—have actually called for an end to certain kinds of scientific research (for example, into racial or sexual differences), and further, for the suppression of research findings that call into question the Left's political assumptions and challenge its agenda. Nobody, Left or Right, should stand for this, and we reject any university that tolerates such assaults on academic freedom.

After Thomas Jefferson, we think that the college administration is best that administers least, and we have frowned upon schools that have endless bureaucracies of deans who spend their days thinking up new ways to better promote the brotherhood of man.

Again, our intention is to highlight a few fine colleges. We have not attempted to be comprehensive, for the simple reason that comprehensiveness and selectivity are opposing, not complementary, principles. No doubt we've overlooked some schools that meet our criteria. If so, we will include them in subsequent editions. We are confident we have not included any schools that do not belong on a conservative's recommended list. That is not to say, however, that this is a guide to conservative colleges. (If it were, it would be a slim volume indeed.) We reject politicization whether of the Left or the Right.

What Makes Us Different

Most other college guides do not recommend colleges. That may seem strange, but the notion is that by simply listing or neutrally describing 17 schools, a guide provides data sufficient to aid the educational consumer in making a decision. On the surface, it is not a bad method, and seems to have the virtue of avoiding prejudicial judgments. But it seems to us that such judgments are the heart of the matter. We doubt that a guide that provides the cold data on several thousand schools will provide most students with much more than (mostly) wasted paper. After all, few students apply to more than a few schools. Because these comprehensive guides are efficiently managed by computer data bases, and because they are popular—and so are printed in large quantities—they tend to be relatively inexpensive. On the other hand, if you calculate usage (i.e., how many of a guide's 1,000-plus pages are actually employed in an individual student's college search) the books are quite expensive. More "bang for the buck" is available from the few guides that actually rate or recommend colleges.

We have explained our criteria. We do not rank the schools we admire, because we think most rankings are of questionable validity. Even the smallest college is a complex institution, with numerous departments, scores of professors, and hundreds of courses. And the only way—we believe—that one can get a handle on a school is to look specifically at the faculty and the curriculum, and judge how coherently teaching methods and course offerings guide the student through the process of educational formation. This makes us very different from, say, the *U.S. News* guide, *America's Best Colleges.*

Perhaps the most popular college guide, the *U.S. News* rankings are based on a set of spurious criteria, none of which "sees" the process from a student's-eye view. In the last three ratings Harvard has topped the list, having dethroned Yale back in 1991. What keeps Harvard on top? Primarily what *U.S. News* calls "academic reputation," which is determined by a survey of some four thousand college presidents, deans, and admissions officers. And who better to know about such things, right? Well . . . As a recent issue of *Advising Quarterly* put it: "How well can a college president in Massachusetts know the true quality of a school in Missouri or Montana?" The answer is: Not very well. But beyond that—beyond the problem of the famous looking at the not-so-famous—the truth is, the college prexy in Montana may not actually know much of real substance about Harvard. Everybody has heard of Harvard, of course, but how many people—including college administrators—have actually been to Cambridge, Massachusetts, in the last few years? How many have looked at Harvard's undergraduate course offerings? How many have scrutinized the school's faculty hirings? "Reputation" is a lofty word, but we wonder if a more appropriate one might be "celebrity."

Other *U.S. News* criteria are flatly statistical and occasionally meaningless. The "faculty resources" category is a composite of such data as faculty/student ratio (a notoriously overrated statistic), numbers of Ph.D.s, and faculty salaries—none of which tells us whether the high-salaried "doctors" are actually in the classroom teaching undergraduates. In many cases, we know that they are not. "Student selectivity," "financial resources," and "student satisfaction" are equally tenuous classification—especially the last, which is measured by retention rate (how many students stick it out) and is weighted as just 5 percent of the total evaluation. Thus Cal Tech can be ranked fifth overall, but not even place in the top twenty-five in student satisfaction. But what does this tell us about Cal Tech? That its students are not satisfied, or that Cal Tech is tough and a lot of even very bright students simply cannot cut it? *Selectivity* tells us only who gets in, not what or by whom they are then taught, and the size of the endowment (the big item under "financial resources") is an empty statistic unless you know exactly (and in each case) how the money is being spent.

A Note about Religious Colleges

When you study the histories of America's colleges and universities, you learn how many of them were founded by religious institutions, and how thoroughly philosophies of religion and education are intertwined. Indeed, you wonder how many of those founders rest quietly today, what with the traditional bond between church and college so effectively severed by their successors.

Some readers will surely be disappointed by a glance at this book's contents page. They will notice that many religious schools are missing from *NR*'s recommended list. We should explain why. (We also note that more than a few fine Christian schools are profiled herein. It pleases us to report that academic freedom is better respected at most religious schools than at many well-known secular colleges and universities.

In some cases we decided not to list a school because it has subsumed academic integrity in pursuit of doctrinal purity. Put another way, although these schools are conservative, they fail to effectively educate their students in the full spirit of academic freedom. We will not condemn them; we simply don't recommend them.

The main reason, though, for the exclusion of most Christian colleges, especially the many small ones, is similar to our reason for not discussing the great technical universities: this is, again, a guide to *liberal arts* institutions. Some Christian colleges do have liberal arts curricula, and many are certainly conservative, but it is our strong impression that for two reasons, a guide including them is largely unnecessary. First, there is little confusion among potential students and their parents about what Christian colleges teach and how they teach it. *NR*'s primary purpose in publishing a college guide is to dispel the confusion that does exist about the colleges and universities that, often despite their histories, lack the religious school's more precise identity and are not guided by the same evangelical mission. Second, the religious orientation of the Christian school is, for many who apply and attend, the criterion *ne plus ultra*. These students would not consider attending a college that is not Christian, no matter how well that secular school satisfied our criteria. Therefore, we would be telling these folks either what they already know or what they do not care to learn.

The student who thinks a Bible college or other religious school is best for him should consult his pastor. More than any high school guidance counselor (unless it is a religious high school), your local pastor will know the ins and outs of the religious university, particularly those nearby. For further information, write the American Association of Bible Colleges at 130-F North College Street, P.O. Box 1523, Fayetteville, Arkansas 72702, or call the Association at (501) 521-8164.

What We Won't Tell You

There are some things you can get from a few other guides that you will not get here. We are not going to give you a load of statistics about college   19 accreditation, racial composition, or—as *ARCO's the Right College* does—the scoop on handicapped student services. (It is not that we are unconcerned about the disabled; we just do not think any student—probably including the handicapped student—would or should choose a college simply because it offers wheelchair accessibility. What good is that if what you have access to is ill-taught propaganda?)

We are also not going to go into a lot of detail about social life. In our experience, young people manage to entertain themselves—often in quite inventive ways. It does not take much to make a party, and in any case, partying is clearly not an activity to weigh heavily in judging the suitability of a college (unless partying is your main concern; in which case, buy another guide).

We will not, as a rule, be giving imaginary campus tours. The trees and the architecture should be seen during a campus visit. Not to visit a campus before matriculating is a mistake. This is an environment in which the student will spend four years, and for which somebody (parents, are you reading us?) will invest between $10,000 and $25,000 per year. (*Fortune* magazine recently reported that tuition increased an average of 9.3 percent during the eighties.) Better go see for yourself.

But be warned: such visits are sometimes like the guided tours American tourists used to get in the Soviet Union; they are snow jobs. They can also be time-consuming and expensive, and we know wise people who think visiting before applying is actually a waste of time. All this acknowledged, we beg to differ. But do keep your wits about you, and your hand on your wallet.

Summing Up

No one has ever written more persuasively about the virtues of the university than John Henry Cardinal Newman. The idea of education was central to his life—so much so that his epitaph is *Ex Umbris et Imaginibus in Veritatem!;* that is, "From shadows and symbols into truth!" There are a great many institutions of "higher education" in the United States, but too few centers of *higher learning*—places where minds are given light to illuminate the darkness, both personal and cultural.

As a result, we believe, many formerly prestigious colleges no longer deserve their vaunted reputations. Indeed, we believe that most of the schools recommended in this book are to be preferred over, say, the renowned Ivy League institutions. After all, the body of what is to be learned—the substance of knowledge—is not hidden. Honestly presented by skilled teachers, that knowledge can be grasped and interpreted by most intelligent students. We believe, to make a painful comparison, that the undergraduate liberal arts program at Wabash College, for instance, is on balance superior to the program at Harvard. This is not an assertion made lightly, and it is based upon what has gone before; upon our sense of the critical importance of dedicated teaching and curricular common sense. Harvard's reputation for academic excellence is in many ways deserved, but we believe it fails today to provide its undergraduates with the well-rounded education that once was its hallmark. That a degree from Harvard makes a job seeker more attractive we do not deny. That's the reputation, skillfully maintained—predictably, by good public relations, and paradoxically, by Harvard's aura of tradition; a tradition we maintain it no longer fully respects.

Graduates of many prestigious universities will not wish to hear ill of their old alma mater, no matter how far gone the school. After all, when an executive at a cocktail party lets another guest know he graduated from Dartmouth, he wants to get the same old admiring reaction, not the dismissive response of an informed educational consumer. Indeed, this is not new. When William F. Buckley, Jr., was about to publish *God and Man at Yale* (1951) he received a call from "an elderly tycoon" who informed the young author that the book need not be published, because "great reforms at Yale were under way. . . ." "I gasped," Mr. Buckley writes, "at the blend of naïveté and effrontery. But although I had observed the phenomenon I was not yet as conversant as I would quickly become with the ease with which rich and vain men are manipulated by skillful educators." Well, brace yourselves, Ivy grads—the world is changing and, through no fault of your own, not entirely for the better.

The independent, courageous liberal arts colleges selected by *National Review* are doing what the Ivy League schools (and the schools of the Big Ten, Pac Ten, SEC, and every other conference and region) ought to be doing. They are educating thoughtful Americans.

Best of luck in your college search.

The Editors

P.S. We apologize for some repetition in the profiles that follow. Certain issues come up again and again. This is a reference book, one unlikely to be read cover to cover, and it is important to make those issues clear when they matter.

About the Data

Contrary to what most of the college guides, especially the larger ones, would like the public to believe, it is impossible to make *qualitative* judgments based upon *quantitative* data. Statistics can be compiled—standardized test scores, acceptance percentages, yearly costs—and compared, but there is no dependable way to draw from them conclusions that will effectively guide a student to the right school.

What *can* be gathered from our numbers, after first reading the profiles, is whether or not a given student has the probability of acceptance, the ability to pay the costs if admitted, and the possibility of receiving financial aid if needed.

As a rule, the figures we list are based on the 1992–93 academic year.

Total Cost

The vicious competition among schools for students and prestige, and the elaborate marketing schemes used by college public relations offices make "sticker price" a more appropriate term for total cost. Students are *consumers*, and college degrees are *products*. So far, competition has not forced prices down, although the shrinking talent pool may soon send prices plummeting, at what sacrifices of quality we cannot say. Throughout the last decade, tuition costs were one commodity price that rose far faster than overall inflation.

In addition to yearly tuition, our total cost figure includes room and board and any required miscellaneous fees. We have not included any estimate of typical personal expenses such as travel, parties, or even books.

Total Enrollment

Although this is a guide to *undergraduate* liberal arts colleges, many of the schools profiled are in fact universities, or are in some way linked to a university, and offer graduate programs as well. So that the reader can get a feel for the true size of each school—a community that may be home for four years—we have usually included grad students as well as undergrads in our head count.

Total Applicants/Admission Percentage

We list the number of students who applied for admission to the most recent freshman class at each school, the percentage that was accepted, and the percentage of those accepted who actually matriculated at the school.

From this you can pretty nearly determine the size of the last freshman class, which will almost always be about the same as the next.

Standardized Test Scores

Most colleges consider SAT (and/or ACT) scores to be a fair measure of a prospective student's intellectual preparedness. They may be wrong about this, but that does not stop just about every school in America from demanding to see the scores. As a result, high school juniors and seniors worry a lot about the tests. Under the circumstances, we can hardly blame them, and it would be silly of us to say, Chill! Still, SAT scores are not all-important. Schools that provide the scores of their freshman classes are begging for comparisons, and some students may count themselves out because their scores are lower or higher than an average. They should remember that an average is just that—almost everybody is either above or below it. (It is for this reason that the College Board recommends that schools list a range of SAT scores for the *middle 50 percent* of accepted freshmen.)

We present test scores three different ways—but just one way for each school—depending on the school's preference: average SAT scores, average ACT scores, or that middle 50 percent on either test.

Financial Aid

A quick look at our profiles will show that almost all the schools we have listed are private and expensive. A second look will tell you that many promise to meet the financial need of 100 percent of students who qualify—not including the scholarship money awarded for athletic or academic merit. Why is this? It is because our schools have not lowered their standards, and so must aggressively attract—and enroll—truly qualified students. Smart kids should never forget that it is a buyer's market.

For each school, we first list the percentage of entering freshmen who applied for some type of need-based aid. Then we show the percentage who were judged to have a real need for financial assistance, and finally the percentage of those who were given some type of aid. It is not possible to be more specific than this.

ROTC

The Reserve Officer Training Corp offers an opportunity for students to receive top-notch military training right on campus, as well as the possibility of some scholarship money. All this, of course, requires a commitment to a term of military service commencing at graduation (and probably including some summer camp before). Ambitious youngsters are reminded of the recent difficulties of Bill Clinton. Service to your country is not currently a legal requirement, but it will always be a moral one.

Application Deadlines

There are more deadlines than we include, such as financial-aid due dates and ROTC registration, and each deadline is only as rigid as its college makes it. Deadlines vary from school to school and can shift yearly, so early in the game students need to get a firm grasp on all the appropriate dates for each prospective choice.

We furnish the early decision, early action, and regular decision application deadlines for students applying for fall 1994 admission. The early decision plan is for students who are relatively set on one choice. They apply early and receive the school's reply early, but MUST decide early (thus the name), agreeing to void all other applications if the offer is taken. Some schools do have early action plans—for students who simply want to get a head start—that require no commitment. A school with rolling admissions will accept students in waves as they receive applications, usually until the class is full.

Some obvious advice: Be safe. Be early.

The Bottom Line

After reviewing these statistics the prospective freshman will probably still wonder obsessively: Will I get in? The most definite answer is: Maybe. As Mr. Buckley writes in his introduction to this book, the better the school, the less likely it is that any kind of "pull" will overcome competitiveness. Then again, you never know. SAT scores are important to a school, because they are one *standard* measure of success in attracting America's brightest high school grads, but some schools (we think especially of St. John's College) couldn't care less about them, and most schools know only too well that some of the very best students simply do not perform well on such measures. Men and women in admissions departments, *not their computers*, decide who will be accepted. Remember that. Seek out an interview. Write follow-up letters. Show them you know how to work. Try to discover what they are looking for, and then *demonstrate* that you have what it takes to make *them* proud that *you* have chosen *their* school.

Several enrollment officers have given us some superb advice about our "data blocks," including the suggestion to change the content, or even to dump the feature altogether. One thing emerges from the various comments we have received: our schools want to explain themselves to, and to meet with and understand, prospective students.

Be real. But don't be shy. You may not be the best student an admissions director will ever see, but you are far from the worst. As the *Christian Science Monitor* said of the first edition of *The National Review College Guide*, "It doubles as an admissions test. By virtue of its erudition, as well as its criteria for scholarship, a student able to read and understand it establishes de facto readiness for a four-year liberal arts experience."

Tell them we sent you.

Our Schools by State

Alabama
Birmingham-Southern College

California
Claremont McKenna College
Pepperdine University
Saint Mary's College of California
Thomas Aquinas College

Florida
Stetson University

Georgia
Oglethorpe University

Illinois
University of Chicago
Eureka College
Wheaton College

Indiana
Hanover College
University of Notre Dame
Wabash College

Kentucky
Asbury College
Centre College
Transylvania University

Maryland
Mount Saint Mary's College
St. John's College
St. Mary's College of Maryland

Massachusetts
Assumption College
Boston University

Michigan
Calvin College
Hillsdale College
Hope College

Minnesota
Gustavus Adolphus College
Saint John's University/College of
    Saint Benedict
Saint Olaf College

Mississippi
Millsaps College

Missouri
Northeast Missouri State University

Nebraska
Hastings College

New Hampshire
Saint Anselm College
Thomas More College of the Liberal Arts

New Mexico
St. John's College

New York
Adelphi University
Columbia College
Houghton College
Union College

North Carolina
Davidson College

Ohio
Franciscan University of Steubenville

Oklahoma
Oklahoma City University

Pennsylvania
Grove City College
Saint Vincent College

Rhode Island
Providence College

South Carolina
Furman University
Wofford College

Tennessee
Rhodes College
University of the South

Texas
Baylor University
University of Dallas
Southwestern University
Trinity University

Utah
Brigham Young University

Virginia
Hampden-Sydney College
Lynchburg College
Washington and Lee University
College of William and Mary

Washington
Gonzaga University
Whitman College

Wisconsin
Lawrence University

PART I

The National Review College Guide

Adelphi University
Garden City, New York

The Art of the Possible

That Adelphi makes our list of superb liberal arts schools should give hope to the beleaguered folks in Cambridge—at that Ivy League school known in Garden City as "Harvard, the Adelphi of Massachusetts." Okay, so the $2-million ad campaign was outrageous, every bit as controversial and feisty as the man behind it: Peter Diamandopoulos, who took Adelphi's helm in 1985, and has transformed the once-sleepy commuter college into one of the East's most dynamic universities.

He's a hero, right? To us, yes, but not necessarily to the educational establishment, or even to his own faculty. The thing about Dimo, as the president is known around campus, is that he says what he thinks, and he does what he says, and the faculty at Adelphi was used to administrators they could push around. Before Dimo, the university had five presidents in reasonably quick succession, all of whom had been forced out by the faculty. And sure enough, in 1989 the faculty voted no confidence in Diamandopoulos, and observers of higher education were confidently predicting his early retirement. The president replied that such votes are "the commonest, most ordinary, and most pedestrian routine that faculties resort to in weak institutions throughout America." And instead of jumping ship, Mr. Diamandopoulos weathered the storm.

The university's most recent ads nicely sum up the philosophy behind Adelphi's transformation:

> The premise of Adelphi is that all students (whether of nursing, psychology, business, the humanities, the physical sciences, education, the fine arts) deserve the opportunity to enrich themselves by exposure to ideas.

and

> Pre-med and pre-law are also pre-life, are they not? The doctor who knows of Aristotle and the beginnings of science, not to mention ethics, will be a

better doctor; the lawyer who knows of Hammurabi or even Draco will make a better lawyer, even for arguing against the merits of a parking ticket.

Those who suppose that colleges cannot change for the better have only to turn to Adelphi for an example to the contrary. Under the Diamandopolous presidency, just about everything about the school has been upgraded: the quality of its incoming students; the quality of its faculty (in part through stricter rules for granting tenure); and the quality of its curriculum. Appointments to the board of trustees included Boston University president John Silber, former U.S. Treasury Secretary William E. Simon, and art critic and *New Criterion* editor Hilton Kramer. And lest there be concern that Adelphi's relatively rapid transformation might represent the kind of flash-in-the-pan growth that sometimes leads to collapse, please note that the school's expansion has been accompanied by the elimination of its debts and the tripling of its endowment. Bucking the national trends, enrollment is up; SAT scores are up; every newly hired professor (more than seventy of them) has a Ph.D.; and Adelphi recently completed a new three-year contract with its faculty. If that's not enough to get the juices flowing, imagine this: more than seventy administrators were either fired or resigned, and many will not be replaced.

Adelphi University

Year Founded: 1896
Total Cost: $19,250
Total Enrollment: 8,261
Total Applicants: 2,831
  87% accepted
  24% of accepted enrolled
SAT Middle Range Scores:
  360–480V/380–530M
Financial Aid:
  72% applied
  92% judged to have need
  66% of those judged were
    given aid
ROTC Program Offered
Application Information:
  Mr. Scott F. Healy
  Vice President for
    Enrollment Planning
    and Management
  Adelphi University
  South Avenue
  Garden City, NY 11530
  Telephone: (516) 877-3050
Application Deadlines:
  No early decision
  Regular decision: rolling

The Socratic Method

The new core curriculum is now in its third year, and is definitely a work in progress. Dimo himself has stated that the core "remains today a developing enterprise, not yet fully realized, not yet a finished product." But it is so much better than the core at, say, Harvard, that it wins Adelphi a place in our book, even if you need a college education to understand the philosophy behind it. As Dimo recently told the committee that oversees it, the core "was conceived as an honestly aporetic strategy—a Socratic, *elenctic* method of rationally inquiring into contemporary knowledge and assessing its accomplishments and dilemmas." Come again? Well, what this means is that the core is about fundamental doubts and the clash of opposing arguments. The difference between Adelphi's core and the cores of the few other universities that have them is in the emphasis placed on *illustrative problems*. Many, if not most, of the books read are the obvious "great" ones, but they are not read in quite the same spirit as elsewhere. The Adelphi core approach seems determined to show that these voices of the past are not to be appreciated simply for their classical elegance, but also for the light they shed on contemporary problems. The core is divided into three segments: the freshman year's four Modern Condition and Origins of the Modern Condition courses (including a writing course coordinated with them); a five-course sequence called Modes and Versions of Knowledge in the sophomore and junior years; and a senior seminar in Values and Actions. The fall '91 syllabus for Modern Condition I is illustrative: week one—Kafka on modernity's shock; weeks two through six—Marx, Russell, Nietzsche, and Freud on the ideas that challenged the traditional worldview; weeks seven through nine—Nigerian writer Chinua Achebe, Kipling, and Gandhi on the death of imperialism, and World War I's "dead poets society" (and Paul Fussell) on the disillusion of war; weeks ten and eleven—views on our confrontation with new worlds and new ideas from Margaret Mead and Émile Durkheim, Albert Einstein, and Werner Heisenberg, Franz Marc and F. T. Marinetti; weeks twelve and thirteen—new ideas in reaction to new possibilities from a diverse list including Henry Ford, T. S. Eliot, and W. E. B. DuBois; week fourteen—Stalinist lackey Bertolt Brecht's *Mother Courage and Her Children*. Okay, so we might get the flu come the fourteenth week, but otherwise we're on the edges of our seats.

The Garden Spot

Because Adelphi is located on a seventy-five-acre greenbelt on the outskirts of New York City, concern is often raised about security. Well, everybody ventures into the city at his own peril, but amazingly the Adelphi campus is not only safe, it is the *safest in the nation* according to a 1990 *USA Today* crime-safety survey of nearly 500 schools. Dimo says this is because "the ethos of this university is not permissive."

Not surprisingly, the school's proximity to America's cultural and financial capital means that Adelphi draws many fine speakers and performers to campus, and has begun to reach out into the New York metro area for cooperative programs, such as its internship program in physics with nearby Brookhaven National Laboratory.

Education makes a greater difference between man and man than nature has made between man and brute.

—*John Adams*

Not all of the Adelphi faculty is pleased with the university's new direction, but many skeptics have been won over by the school's extraordinary progress. And whatever their attitudes about Dimo, Adelphi's faculty is committed to Adelphi's students. By our count, there are just a dozen grad students with teaching responsibilities, and most of them are in the math department where they oversee problem-solving sections in courses primarily taught by full professors.

Advising, which at most places is haphazard at best, is beautifully planned at Adelphi, and a new book—not just a pamphlet, but a 176-page workbook—for freshmen, *Academic Adelphi*, is unlike anything we've seen anywhere. Designed to guide the student through every aspect of curricular planning, it explains the core, describes how one goes about choosing a major, and then details requirements department by department. It gives the student space to record choices and to make notes, and even lists each department head's name, address, phone number, and office hours. *Academic Adelphi* contains many other savvy hints about college life, and it recently won top honors from the National Academic Advising Association.

The whole of the Adelphi philosophy can be summed up in a phrase Peter Diamandopoulos used to describe how a contemporary university strikes a balance between tradition and innovation, between spiritual enrichment and career development. The university, Dimo told us, must seek the "dynamic, dialectic middle." It is dynamic, all right, and solidly rooted in the middle of the Socratic tradition. We'll be keen observers of Adelphi's continued, astonishing growth. □

Asbury

Wilmore, Kentucky

Scholarly Faith

A s we have noted, too few of America's colleges and universities demand much of their students. In contrast, Asbury, a small, Christian liberal arts college with a core curriculum that puts many of the nation's elite universities to shame, requires all of its students to take:

- One three-credit course in freshman composition;
- Two three-credit courses in the growth of Western Civilization;
- Three three-credit courses in religion: Understanding the Old Testament, Understanding the New Testament, and Christian Theology;
- One three-credit social science course in either psychology, sociology, or anthropology;
- Two three-credit courses in literature: Masterworks: Western Classics I and Masterworks: Western Classics II
- A three-credit course in music and art appreciation;
- A three-credit course: Introduction to Philosophy;
- Six credits in a laboratory science;
- A three-credit course: Principles of Communication;
- A three-credit course: Concepts of Computer Science and Mathematics;
- Courses in physical education;

and, finally, students must:

- Demonstrate proficiency in a foreign language at a level equivalent to two years of college-level study.

The Heritage of the West

In sharp contrast to the fragmentation and incoherence of curricula elsewhere, Asbury's philoso-

Asbury College

Year Founded: 1890
Total Cost: $8,450
Total Enrollment: 1,129
Total Applicants: 912
  75% accepted
  45% of accepted enrolled
SAT Average: 950
Financial Aid:
  89% applied
  77% judged to have need
  100% of those judged
    were given aid
No ROTC Program Offered
Application Information:
  Mr. Stan F. Wiggam
  Dean of Admissions
  Asbury College
  1 Macklem Drive
  Wilmore, KY 40390
  Telephone: (606) 858-3511
Application Deadlines:
  No early decision
  Regular decision: rolling

phy of liberal learning is direct and well organized. "The college believes in the humanizing value of broad exposure to our Western cultural heritage, the 'great tradition' as a classical body of knowledge, and seeks to develop students' natural God-given potentials as physical, social, moral, rational, and spiritual beings." Says a college publication: "You'll be challenged to rethink the great issues, explore the great ideas, and read the great books."

Asbury's strength is its coherent philosophy of education in which faith is blended with academic rigor. That philosophy is cogently elucidated by Asbury philosophy professor Michael L. Peterson, who dedicated his fine book, *Philosophy of Education: Issues and Options*, to the Asbury faculty.

Describing the role of rational thought in the development of faith, Professor Peterson quotes C. S. Lewis's *Screwtape Letters*, in which the senior devil advises his apprentice that the worst possible tactic—from the Satanic point of view—is to "awaken the patient's reason," since, "once it is awake, who can foresee the result?" Turning that advice around, Professor Peterson remarks that genuine Christianity "does not offer an end to intellectual hard work," but rather "calls us right back to it." Thus the restoration of the Socratic search for objective and rational truth must be a central goal of Christian education. "Until our age recovers a regard for higher level truth and the intellectual process of seeking it," Professor Peterson writes, "calls to genuine religious commitment may fall on deaf ears." And he defines the intellectual climate at Asbury when he writes:

> Indeed, because of devotion to Christ, we should not merely endeavor to know the truth in whatever area it may be found, but to love the truth and to inspire others to love it too. . . . The whole climate of learning, including the religious and social dimensions, should be shaped and informed by the overarching desire for truth.

As good as that sounds to us, we should point out that Asbury is clearly not for everyone. Even by the standards of this book, Asbury is a conservative institution, which describes itself as "providing education guided by the classical tradition of orthodox Christian thought." For Asbury that includes "a high view of scripture as God's infallible word" and its declaration that "every facet of college life is shaped by the Wesleyan-Arminian understanding of sin, grace, and the possibility of full salvation." Attendance at chapel is mandatory. (Although Asbury is officially nondenominational, many of its faculty members are Methodists who follow the teaching of John Wesley. *Arminian* refers to the tradition that follows the Dutch theologian Jacob Arminius, who emphasized free will in contrast to the deterministic approach of John Calvin.)

"We have a structured environment," says one professor. "Some students find that somewhat oppressive at first, but when they find that they like the students and classes, they are willing to put up with it." Part of the reason for student acceptance is an outstanding freshman orientation program. "They feel that this is home for them after the first week," says a faculty member. For many students, the edge is taken off the rules and regulations both by the sense of community and by what one faculty member calls the "spiritually charged" atmosphere on campus.

Focus on Faith

While most universities recall 1970 as the year of nationwide student strikes that paralyzed most schools, Asbury's experience was strikingly different. Beginning with campus prayer meetings on the Asbury campus in 1970, the school became the center of a nationwide student evangelical revival that Billy Graham was to call "an eruption of the spirit," one that gave evidence of "what the Holy Spirit is ready to do." A significant presence on campus is the Salvation Army. Asbury is the only school officially approved by the Salvation Army for the education of its leadership, and is thus a center of the army's activities.

But this focus on faith does not come at the expense of academic excellence. Classes are small and uniformly taught by professors rather than graduate students. A majority of Asbury graduates go on to graduate school in a wide variety of fields.

One of Asbury's strengths appears to be its president, Dennis Kinlaw. While it has often been our experience that schools are good *in spite* of their administrations, Dr. Kinlaw was described to us as both academically solid and beloved by the students. "He is highly respected and greatly appreciated," one professor told us.

All education should be directed toward the development of character. Sound character cannot be achieved if spiritual development is neglected. I do not like to think of turning out physical and mental giants who are spiritual pygmies.

—*Walter C. Coffey*

Asbury has recently begun to attract increasing numbers of students from outside Kentucky, and has always described itself as national, even international. And well it should: A significant number of students have been drawn from Ohio, Pennsylvania, Florida, Michigan, Georgia, and New Jersey, and the student body now includes representatives of more than forty-five states and twenty-five foreign countries. The attraction is obvious. Located in the heart of Kentucky bluegrass country only fifteen miles from Lexington, Asbury offers the advantages of a southern atmosphere—a gorgeous rural setting amid Kentucky's rolling hills (without being isolated from urban amenities)—and an institution devoted to faith (without sacrificing academic quality). Asbury obviously deserves a serious look from students searching for a quality liberal arts education. □

Assumption College

Worcester, MA

Wherever Truth Is Found

When the Augustinians of the Assumption founded their college in 1904, its curriculum was bilingual (French and English), and its students were mostly French-American. One imagines it must have been a tight-knit community. Today, the French character of the college is gone, although interest in things French is carried on by the French Institute, an academic and cultural center on campus. The community, however, remains as unified as ever—even in its more typically American diversity. Assumption is a place where innovation is in service to tradition, not the other way around.

A fair number of the school's administrators (nearly a quarter) and faculty (15 percent by our count) are Assumption grads. Many others have come from as far away as Holy Cross, Clark University, Anna Maria College, and several of the other schools located in and around Worcester. It's a nice place to stay put.

A sense of maximum flexibility within a rigorous

structure pervades Assumption's academic programs. Assumption students have access to the Worcester Consortium, a ten-college and private-sector course and internship program, that allows, say, an Assumption art major to take engineering courses at Worcester Polytechnic, the better to understand architecture. Select sophomores may participate in one of America's most exciting educational experiences, the Rome Program of the University of Dallas. Similarly, Assumption students can participate in nearby Stonehill College's Irish Studies Program at University College in Dublin. Assumption is unafraid to send its students out to acquire the best other institutions have to offer. It knows it will not suffer by comparison.

Curricular Highlights

Assumption is also confident that its students will enhance its good name, an expectation based on the solidity of its liberal arts program. Assumption's "general education" curriculum features most of what we look for in a core. Assumption students must take the following: in philosophy, a standard introductory course, and then one of five specified follow-up courses; ditto for theology. In the humanities, there is a wide choice for the satisfaction of a single-course requirement in art, music, and theater, then more narrowly specified courses in literature and in history, where students are encouraged to take Western civ or modern European/American sequences, for a total of three courses. In the various social sciences, three courses—any three at the introductory level (and it pleases us to report that even in the department of sociology and anthropology there are very few silly offerings.) If there is a weakness in the Assumption program, it is probably in its requirements for "mathematics, natural sciences, and foreign languages," an odd juxtaposition of disciplines. Students are required to take math, biology, chemistry, physics, *or* a language, but appear to be able to avoid studying a foreign language altogether; either in the basic general ed program or in the "depth requirement" that solidifies the core studies. We're not prepared to say an educated man or woman *must* be fluent in a second language, but the Assumption approach is simply not as strong in this regard as some others we've seen. And given its rootedness in French, and the array of superb French courses offered, you might

Assumption College

Year Founded: 1904
Total Cost: $15,710
Total Enrollment: 2,896
Total Applicants: 2,225
　76% accepted
　26% of accepted enrolled
SAT Averages: 830–1040
Financial Aid:
　67% applied
　60% judged to have need
　60% of those judged were
　　given aid
ROTC Program Offered
Application Information:
　Dean of Admissions and
　　Financial Aid
　Assumption College
　500 Salisbury Street
　Worcester, MA 01615-
　　0005
　Telephone: (508) 752-
　　5615
Application Deadlines:
　Early decision: 11/1
　Regular decision: 3/1

think the college would give more weight to that part of its tradition. (Of course, nothing prevents students from diving deeply into French at Assumption, and, in fact there may not be a better school anywhere for students who want to master that language.)

We mentioned the Worcester Consortium and the study-abroad programs Assumption shares with Dallas and Stonehill, but they are only the beginning of the interesting array of special courses and programs offered, many of them developed with the assistance of our friends at the National Endowment for the Humanities. One of the best— and it is unique in all of higher education—is the foundations program. It is a two-year interdisciplinary program in art, politics, philosophy, and religion. In year one, the integration of disciplines is focused on cities, men, and art, to wit: Athens, Pericles, and the Parthenon; Rome, Caesar, and the Forum; Paris, King Louis, and Notre Dame; and Washington, D.C., the Founders, and the Capitol. Year two concentrates on religion, philosophy, and ideas of the good life, and authors studied include Plato, Augustine, Bacon, and Marx. An extension of the foundations concept, a major in liberal studies, will be introduced at Assumption sometime after the 1992–93 academic year.

> Read not to contradict and confute; nor to believe and take for granted; nor to find talk and discourse; but to weigh and consider;
>
> Reading maketh a full man; Conference a ready man; and Writing an exact man.
>
> —*Francis Bacon*

City Life

Another team-taught, interdisciplinary venture is the community studies program, which employs the tools of geography, history, and sociology in the "hands-on" study of Worcester itself. The philosophy behind the course seems to be one we treasure: subsidiarity. (Pope Pius XI in his encyclical *Quadragesimo anno* summarized the principle: "[I]t is . . . unjust to turn over to a greater society of higher rank functions and services which can be performed by lesser bodies on a lower plane.") The heart of American federalism is the local community—not, as recent history would suggest, Washington, D.C.—and students in Community Studies at Assumption get their insights right from the heart of the heart: from Worcester's parishes and ethnic neighborhoods.

It is worth noting that the notion of the city, of *civis* or *civitas*, which is the Latin root of our "civilization," animates much of Assumption's best thinking. What we mean by *civilization* is the life lived in cities: the rest is *culture*. It is, in fact, a very Augustinian concept, although the number of institutions of higher learning that actually grasp it—and order pedagogy around it—can be counted on the fingers of one hand.

Assumption's Native American and third world studies programs prove that a college can handle the thornier aspects of past and present without resorting to glib political correctness and bitter abstraction. And the recent scenes of starvation in Somalia should remind conservatives that business and politics face no greater challenge than solving the problems of the poor—exactly the premise behind Assumption's third world studies program.

Of course, Assumption College is not a perfect school, and it is haunted by many of the same problems that plague most other schools. Not all the faculty are enthusiastic about liberal education, and many of its students are rather narrowly interested in the kind of pre-professional curricula that produces technicians and not citizens. Still, we think this is a school with a sense of mission strong enough to endure the barbarian assaults on its integrity.

The expansion of professional possibilities through the deepening of spiritual resolve is what Assumption is all about. As Professor Patrick Powers, director of the foundations Program, puts it: "When you apply for a job, the most important thing is that you know how to think, how to speak, how to write; and that you understand human beings and how to deal with them. You learn these things from courses in philosophy, literature, history, theology; not from technical career courses."

We couldn't agree more.   □

Baylor
Waco, Texas

Two-time Winner

In 1987, the Baylor University debate team beat Dartmouth College to win the American Forensics Association National Championship—clearly a triumphant moment in the long struggle for Western civilization. (It won again in 1989, defeating the University of Michigan.) For our purposes, it serves as a signal reminder that much of the quality associated with the Ivy League can, in fact, be found elsewhere.

First Among Equals

Consider: Baylor now ranks first among seventy-three doctorate-granting private universities in the number of its baccalaureates who have earned doctorates in their fields during the past decade. This is in part a reflection of the quality of the students Baylor is attracting. In the 1980s, nearly 600 National Merit Scholars chose Baylor, which now ranks twenty-eighth among the nation's more than 3,000 institutions of higher learning in the number of such scholars. The same years also saw impressive growth in enrollment (although the total is capped at approximately 12,000), the size of its library (which more than quadrupled its book holdings), the school's endowment (which has tripled), and its total assets (which have grown from $149.5 million to more than $435 million in the last decade).

Such growth would mean little had Baylor's growth had not taken place within a context of a firm commitment to traditional academic and moral values. A Baptist institution founded in 1845, Baylor takes its religious affiliation quite seriously and explicitly states that its goal is "to become the foremost Christian university in the world in order to demonstrate to people everywhere that it is possible for a university committed to Christ to be a leader in the best of learning and the best of living."

About 1,150 students at Baylor University are actively preparing for the ministry, while more than 6,000 are involved in Baptist Student Union activities ranging from Bible study to church-building projects.

The Program

But the real attraction is the excellent academic program. Although Baylor is a full-fledged university, its focus remains on undergraduate teaching, and that commitment is reflected in the requirements of the core curriculum, which make up well over half of a student's undergraduate career.

"While other universities have faltered or succumbed to trends," one university publication declares, "Baylor has steadfastly provided a liberal arts education noted in eternal values." True to its status as a full-fledged university, Baylor offers 125 fields of study—but all students, even those in pre-professional programs, must spend their first two years in the College of Arts and Sciences, fulfilling the liberal arts core requirements.

Although the overall requirements differ for some of the degree programs, a candidate for the bachelor of arts must take courses in Thinking and Writing and Thinking, Writing, and Research. Building on the strong base of writing, the students are required to take a course in English Literature before Burns, which must be followed by a second English survey course, chosen from among English Literature Since Burns, American Literature: Masterpieces, and Western World Literature: Masterpieces in Translation.

Baylor students must also take American Constitutional Development and must select two courses from among Western Civilization through the Seventeenth Century, Western Civilization Since the Seventeenth Century, Introduction to Asian Civilization, and two surveys of American history. And they take two religion survey courses as well: the Old and New Testaments. Other requirements include four semesters in physical education (a rarity among core curricula); six credits to be divided among at least three of the following fields: art, journalism, Latin, music, drama, and speech; one to four semesters of a foreign language, depending on a student's high school record; three credits in math; twelve credits

Baylor University

Year Founded: 1845
Total Cost: $10,990
Total Enrollment: 12,185
Total Applicants: 4,787
  88% accepted
  56% of accepted enrolled
SAT Middle Range Scores:
  960–1160
Financial Aid:
  58% applied
  68% judged to have need
  100% of those judged
  were given aid
ROTC Program Offered
Application Information:
  Mr. Herman D. Thomas
  Director of Admissions
  Baylor University
  P.O. Box 97008
  Waco, TX 76798-7008
  Telephone: (817) 755-1811
Application Deadlines:
  No early decision
  Regular decision: rolling

43

in a laboratory science; and at least nine hours in the social sciences, including three credits from at least three of the following fields: anthropology, economics, philosophy, political science, psychology, and sociology. Only a handful of specially designed introductory courses will satisfy both the social science and science requirements. In addition, students must attend Chapel-Forum for two semesters.

Taken as a whole, the Baylor curriculum is a comprehensive and thorough introduction to the liberal arts. Students who graduate from Baylor are assured of having been exposed to the history, literature, and thought of the West, and will have received a coherent introduction to the sciences. It is a measure of Baylor's commitment to the liberal arts that even its engineering students must take the basic courses in English literature and writing, as well as courses in religion, American constitutional history, and foreign language.

Other options for students include the University Scholar program, which draws on the classic tradition of British universities by affording highly motivated freshmen the chance to design their own programs in close consultation with faculty mentors. Baylor also offers opportunities for students to study abroad, including programs in Britain, Spain, Germany, France, Austria, Italy, Mexico, Israel, Japan, and the Soviet Union. Two of the most popular programs are the Baylor in London Program, taught at the University of London, and Baylor in the British Isles, at Westminster School.

A Most Honorable Word

While some classes are large, most are small, and the emphasis remains on classroom teaching—another aspect of Baylor's distinctiveness. At many of the nation's elite universities the trend toward research and grant chasing has become so frenzied that teaching has come to be looked upon as an embarrassing distraction from the professoriat's primary activities. Not only have teaching professors become second-class citizens at many research universities, but there are indications that professors who devote themselves to making their classrooms vital centers of intellectual activity are actually regarded with suspicion and hostility by their research-oriented colleagues. Almost every major campus in the nation has witnessed cases of

> Teaching is not a lost art, but the regard for it is a lost tradition.
>
> —*Jacques Barzun*

outstanding teachers who are denied tenure (and are thus effectively fired)—a clear sign of the devaluation of teaching in institutions ostensibly devoted to education.

So it is not a trivial matter to encounter a Baylor University publication that bluntly declares: " 'Teacher' is the most honorable word in Baylor's large vocabulary." Baylor professors are scholars, writers, artists, even businessmen, "but first and foremost they are teachers." Very few classes are taught by teaching assistants.

There is little sign that Baylor has been infected by the creeping politicization that is wrecking so many other outstanding schools. In fact, *The New York Times*'s Edward Fiske quotes one student as saying that "a prospective student who views himself as a liberal, Democrat, activist, or an advocate of cohabitation should *not* go to Baylor," which seems to us a ringing endorsement. Baylor students do indeed tend to be from upper-middle-class, conservative families, to dress well, and to come from the South (although all fifty states are presently represented in the student body). And the moral atmosphere on the campus is also quite conservative. This stems, in part, from Baylor's seriousness about its *in loco parentis* responsibilities.

Officially, Baylor is dry, dry, dry and visiting hours are restricted in the campus residences. But Baylor is seldom considered a dull place. Its football team is a perennial contender, and it boasts strong teams in many other intercollegiate sports. Located in Waco, Texas, Baylor is only 100 miles from Dallas, Fort Worth, and Austin, but it is light-years away from the intellectual climate of most of Texas's mammoth-size universities.   □

Birmingham-Southern

Birmingham, Alabama

The Old South

An ambience of graciousness, a tradition of academic excellence, and close student-faculty relations have made Birmingham-Southern one of the stand-out liberal arts colleges of the South. Eschewing the temptation to emulate the rising mega-universities of the region. Birmingham-Southern tends to keep classes small, and the school still assigns each student a faculty adviser-cum-mentor, assuring individualized attention to undergraduates. As the Yale *Insider's Guide to Colleges* has remarked: "For students seeking to combine a distinctly Southern way of life with the sort of academic values formerly thought to be confined to the east coast, such a school is ideal."

The Pursuit of Excellence

The student body is overwhelmingly southern, conservative, and middle-class (although 75 percent receive some form of financial aid). We know we run the risk of being called sexist for pointing out that nineteen former Miss Alabamas are Birmingham-Southern alumnae. But we have to admit that finding a school where the feminist Zeitgeist does not insist that female students adopt the politics of Elena Ceaucescu, or the manners of Leona Helmsley, is a welcome relief from some we've looked at. That should not, however, distract our attention from the fact that Birmingham-Southern also has one of the highest rates of students who go on to earn Ph.D.s, ranking ahead of such power-houses as Berkeley, Michigan, Wisconsin, Minnesota, Texas, and Northwestern. It is also rated by the Carnegie Foundation for the Advancement of Teaching as a Liberal Arts I school, thus placing it in the same category as Amherst, Oberlin, Swarthmore, and Vassar—but without the politicized atmosphere.

That is, in part, a tribute to the seriousness of the student body as well as to Birmingham-Southern's solid anchoring in a traditional approach to liberal education. While other schools have long since drifted off into vaguely worded effulgent invocations of "diversity" as an excuse for their inability to say just what it is that constitutes a liberal education. Birmingham-Southern is quite clear on that point. "There is historically recognized a common body of knowledge and skills possessed by well-educated people," the college affirms in a mission statement. "Our degree requirements are framed with that body of knowledge and skills in mind. . . ."

A Culture of Values

Specifically, Birmingham-Southern students are expected to learn "to read critically, to write articulately, and to make coherent arguments in both written and oral form." They are required to take courses in seven major areas: Scientific Concepts, Ultimate Meanings and Values, Language and Culture, Literature, Arts, Historical Perspective, and Nature of Human Behavior and Social Relations. Students are also required to take an additional course in either natural science or mathematics; a class in social science, but not from the same department as offered Human Behavior and Social Relations; and two courses in the arts and humanities. Admittedly, this is not as tightly structured a curriculum as we would like, but the lack of a more rigorous core is compensated for by the overall culture of the school, which is unabashedly "value-centered." "This Atmosphere," a college publication says, "fosters the moral and spiritual growth of students as a central and special dimension of their undergraduate experience." In a recent annual report, Birmingham-Southern's president, Neal R. Berte, reaffirmed "that at Birmingham-Southern, the individual student remains the central focus of all we do." Within the modern academy, that is a radical commitment, and one strikingly different from the impersonality and hyperspecialization of the typical mega-university. (President Berte found himself, and the school's values, under fire in 1991, when Planned Parenthood's then-prexy Faye Wattleton was an honoree at a campus fund-raiser. But so were, among others, Anne L. Armstrong, Margaret Tutwiler, and Marilyn Quayle, and it seems clear no support of abortion was intended in Mrs. Wattleton's inclusion.)

One notable aspect of the Birmingham-Southern

Birmingham-Southern College

Year Founded: 1856
Total Cost: $12,475
Total Enrollment: 1,763
Total Applicants: 835
  73% accepted
  52% of accepted enrolled
SAT Averages: 1100
Financial Aid:
  62% applied
  53% judged to have need
  100% of those judged
    were given aid
ROTC Program Offered
Application Information:
  Mr. Robert D. Dortch
  Vice President for
    Admissions Services
  900 Arkadelphia Road
  Birmingham-Southern
    College
  Birmingham, AL 35254
  Telephone: (205) 226-4686
Application Deadlines:
  Early decision: 12/15
  Regular decision: 3/1

calendar is its January "interim term," a four-week period in which students can participate in special projects in close collaboration with faculty members, either on or off campus. In the past these projects have ranged from internships at local banks to studying the art, history, and politics of Italy—in Italy. Students are required to complete one interim term project for each full academic year of enrollment, up to four.

Hail from the Chief

Students also have the option of writing for the *Southern Academic Review*, a journal of student scholarship. While most academic journals are turgid tracts of eye-glazing dullness, the Birmingham-Southern student journal is actually readable.

A regional center of the arts, Birmingham-Southern hosts one of only two Phi Beta Kappa chapters in the state. Officially, the school is affiliated with the United Methodist Church, but there are no mandatory religion classes or church services. The moral and religious element of the college is, however, difficult to avoid, inasmuch as the school's chaplain is also its director of counseling. One aspect of the school's moral focus is its commitment to voluntarism. In 1990, President Bush visited the campus to present the Birmingham-Southern Conservatory, a student volunteer organization, with one of his "Points of Light" volunteer service awards. The school also maintains its commitment to inculcating strong moral and ethical values through its honor code, which is administered by students.

Although Birmingham-Southern's campus— known as the "Hilltop"—is in an urban area, it is one of the safest, most security-conscious colleges of its kind in the country. A formidable fence surrounds the campus, which gives the school the feel of being an enclave within the city.

Given the school's single-minded focus on academics, Birmingham-Southern surprised the world —and itself—in 1990 when its basketball team won the national NAIA Basketball championship. That feat would probably be worth only a footnote, except that five of the team's players were also on the dean's list. Ninety-five percent of Birmingham-Southern students on basketball scholarships actually get a degree—a record that puts to shame most of the big-name schools in the nation. But then, so much of what Birmingham-Southern does best is a

> To educate a man in mind and not in morals is to educate a menace to society.
>
> —*Theodore Roosevelt*

powerful critique of what the academic elite does so poorly.　　　　　　　　　　　　　　　□

Boston University

Boston, Massachusetts

Genius Loci

For the most part, the modern university president sees himself less a statesman of the intellect than what Tom Wolfe once termed a "flak-catcher." When he or she is not out shaking down alumni and foundations for cash or placating the various special interests on campus, the university prexy is busy denying the existence of these problems that can plausibly be denied, and appointing committees to study the ones that can't.

Because a university president who is actually a leader, let alone one with conservative impulses, is such a rarity in the modern academy, John Silber is a double curiosity. The brilliant, irascible, articulate, and dynamic BU president has succeeded in infuriating the Left, roiling the tender sensibilities of the faculty, and making Boston University one of the nation's academic success stories—all more or less simultaneously. A sharp-tongued critic of the abuses of the academic establishment and the politicization of scholarship, Mr. Silber is credited with the renaissance of a university that has long been overshadowed by its neighbor in Cambridge. (For a summary of his views on a variety of issues, see *Straight Shooting: What's Wrong with America and How to Fix It*—good book, silly title.) Although he has his detractors, Mr. Silber seems to have won the grudging respect of some of his most ardent faculty foes, a tribute to the force of his intellect and his forceful sense of purpose. (One of his accomplishments was the creation of a center to study disinformation—a notable counterpoint to the metastasis of "peace study" centers for Marxist apologists throughout American universities in the 1980s.)

The Reasons for the Battle

But BU is not Silber, and Silber is not BU. Neither the student body nor the bulk of the faculty shares Mr. Silber's educational conservatism. Still, he has created a sense of institutional mission that is as rare as his own leadership abilities; moreover, he has the strong support of a committed and savvy board of trustees. With that backing he has succeeded in creating an intellectual atmosphere where ideas are taken seriously, and where the Left has had to acknowledge that there are different points of view.

But most important is Mr. Silber's firm commitment to the liberal arts. After Seneca, he recognizes that "there is really only one liberal study that deserves the name—because it makes the person free—and that is the pursuit of wisdom."

Although it is hopelessly out of step to pursue wisdom rather than "diversity" these days, that seems exactly what BU's core curriculum attempts to do. The late Sidney Hook singled out the program for praise as an example of the successful blending of Western and non-Western classics without the usual tinge of politicization.

Boston University

Year Founded: 1839
Total Cost: $23,157
Total Enrollment: 28,364
Total Applicants: 18,149
  70% accepted
  30% of accepted enrolled
SAT Averages: 540V/604M
Financial Aid:
  64% applied
  93% judged to have need
  97% of those judged were
    given aid
ROTC Program Offered
Application Information:
  Mr. Thomas Rajala
  Director of Admissions
  Boston University
  121 Bay State Road
  Boston, MA 02215
  Telephone:
    (617) 353-2318
Application Deadlines:
  Early decision: 11/15
  Regular decision:
    (suggested) 1/15

The Union of Disciplines

The backbone of the integrated core curriculum is the humanities core course, a four-semester sequence organized around selected masterworks. The core's first course, The Ancient World, is taught by professors from the philosophy, classics, and political science departments, and focuses on the two seminal strands of the Western tradition: the Hebrew Scriptures and classical Greece, with intensive study of Homer, Sophocles, and Plato.

In the core's second semester students complete the study of ancient Greece through a reading of Aristotle's *Ethics* and the *Handbook* of Epictetus; and are introduced to Rome through Virgil's *Aeneid*. They study the origins of Christianity by reading the Gospels of Matthew and John and St. Paul's Letter to the Hebrews. But what makes the course distinctive is its introduction of such non-Western authors as Confucius and Lao-tzu. They are read, one professor explains, because of their "content and their power to move and enlighten, not because they satisfy some ideological requirement such as multi-culturality."

The focus of the core is ethical as well as historical. "Its concerns," the professor explains, "all center on finding a proper pathway through life." Students begin with Aristotle's logical and cognitive approach to ethics and then turn to Confucius, whose emphasis on intuition and reverence for the golden age provide a contrasting perspective. "By studying Aristotle and Confucius, students get a sense of the difference between Western and Eastern thinking, and begin to see why questions about 'the good' are important and worth thinking about. They also begin to see that the idea of the gentleman is common to two great cultures, and that there cannot be millions of subjective definitions of what a gentleman is."

In a similar fashion, students discuss the visions of God in both Dante and the *Baghavad Gita*. "The focus is on the supreme relevance of all these works to contemporary life—and on the way in which, taken together, they can give students some notion of what it means that we live in history, in time, and in place." Among the ethical questions explored by students in the class are: "How can man come to know what is good? How can man come to know anything about God or the gods? What is the proper attitude toward the dead? From whence does evil, or do evils, arise?"

To get some sense of how far this sort of approach is from much of the academic mainstream, simply compare it to Stanford's new CIV program in which professors must give special attention to issues of "race, class, and gender," and which includes such non-Western *classics* as Frantz Fanon's apologia for terrorism and revolutionary bloodshed.

BU's core course in the sciences, Evolution of the Universe and Life, again stresses the integration and commonalities among the humanities, natural sciences, and social sciences, and deals with the historical development of science and technology.

> They teach you anything in universities today. You can major in mud pies.
>
> —*Orson Welles*

Bigger Things

BU is the largest school profiled in our book. It has ten divisions, liberal arts and professional, and offers more than 5,000 courses.

While some students may be underwhelmed with BU's non-campus, which lacks many of the charms of the more traditional college settings, Boston is often called "student heaven," and indeed there are few cities more congenial to the academic lifestyle. Housing is a more difficult dilemma. In 1989, Mr. Silber attacked "institutionalized degeneracy" by ordering that all dorm rooms were off-limits to visitors of the opposite sex after 11 P.M. on weekdays and 1 A.M. on weekends. We would like to report an increase in chastity as a result of the edict, but in general the new rule has merely provided an added incentive for students to begin the hunt for off-campus housing. And rule changes now allow guests in rooms up until 1 A.M. weekdays, 2:30 A.M. on weekends, and "no overnight visitors except by permission."

One major question hanging over BU's future is Mr. Silber's probable decision to move on. He was narrowly defeated in the 1990 election for governor of the state of Massachusetts, and his candidacy was a pretty broad hint that he is interested in a wider platform for his views and his talents. Given the paucity of university presidents of his caliber, and the inevitable pressures of the academic culture to return the university to status quo ante Silber, his departure could be a major setback for BU. □

Brigham Young
Provo, Utah

Present-Day Scholars

At various times throughout this book we say, "This school is not for everybody." This time we mean it. To say that BYU is "conservative" is actually an understatement. Many students, especially non-Mormons, would find the atmosphere just a bit too restrictive. Witness:

> Beards are not acceptable. Beards are defined as noticeable growth that is beginning to look grubby, which usually means that men will need to shave daily.

Mustaches are not "encouraged," and "bushy sideburns are not acceptable." At BYU, a man's ears must be visible, and hair can't sneak over the collar. Donny and Marie, right? (Women face similar restrictions, e.g., ". . . the no-bra look is unacceptable.")

The obvious point to make is this: for most students who'll consider BYU, crews cuts and bras (although not on the same person, obviously) are *already* the standard; the admissions process at BYU is self-selective—almost everybody who studies and teaches there is Mormon, and the standards of BYU are simply the standards of the larger community. So, one must wonder, do you have to be a Mormon to attend?

Required Religion

No, but it helps. First of all, the church subsidizes 70 percent of each of its students' costs (although the price is reasonable for non-Mormons). Also, fourteen hours of religion are required for graduation, with at least four hours devoted to study of the *Book of Mormon*. For the 3 percent of BYU students who are *not* members of the Church of Jesus Christ of the Latter-day Saints, such study may be no more remarkable than a course in which a Catholic student reads the Koran or a Jew studies the *Baghavad Gita*. More to the point, it is entirely fitting that a non-Mormon who'll spend four years in Provo get to know the ethos of the university community.

The environment at BYU is defined by the church. Mormon students are divided into "stakes and wards," the second being 200- to 300-member groups around which the student's devotional life is organized. Students from the "twenty-five other religious denominations" represented in the student body are "encouraged to attend the congregation of their faith located in the Provo area" but are not otherwise required to participate in campus religious activities.

But make no mistake: to attend BYU is to participate in Mormon life, to be governed by its philosophy. All students must adhere to the BYU code of honor. That code espouses some hard-to-dispute generalities: graciousness, integrity, morality. It demands standards we enthusiastically support: compliance with the rules, no drugs, no cheating. But the BYU code goes several steps further: no alcohol, tobacco, tea, or coffee. And every winter semester each student undergoes an evaluation in order to receive "ecclesiastical endorsement." Has the student had a cup of coffee? Is his hair too long? Of course, the process is not so trivial, and its intention is to guarantee that the university fulfill its commitment to educating the whole student, including his or her moral character—part of the traditional mission of higher education that few contemporary schools take seriously. But we won't argue with those who suggest that BYU takes this role too seriously.

Brigham Young University

Year Founded: 1875
Total Cost: $5,848
Total Enrollment: 28,455
Total Applicants: 14,355
  72% accepted
  74% of accepted enrolled
ACT Average: 26.6
Financial Aid:
  93% applied
  56% judged to have need
  74% of those judged were
    given aid
ROTC Program Offered
Application Information:
  Mr. Tom Gourley
  Director of Admissions
  Brigham Young
    University
  Provo, UT 84602
  Telephone: (801) 378-2507
Application Deadlines:
  No early decision
  Regular decision: rolling

Academic Commitment

As is true of the many other religious colleges we profile, the sense of the sacred at BYU does not diminish its commitment to academic freedom nor undermine its attention to *true* cultural diversity. A new 92,000-square-foot museum of fine arts has joined BYU's three other museums (one each devoted to life sciences, peoples and cultures, and earth sciences). There is also plenty of cultural diversion, including dance, theater, and film.

There is a good general education (GE) program, with requirements in English and writing, math and language, American and Western civilization, and biological and physical science. The participation of the Latter-day Saints community, one of America's most industrious and prosperous, has allowed BYU to build a research facility that is world-class; and it has done so without vitiating its responsibility to the broad education of its undergraduates. There are no fewer than thirty-seven research centers, institutes, and laboratories, including the Center for Cold Nuclear Fusion Studies, which has recently received worldwide attention, not all of it positive.

For the Gifted

Even more impressive is the extensive honors program BYU offers. Students may choose to pursue university honors, a distinction awarded at graduation upon completion of an alternate set of requirements, or they may wish to participate in select honors classes and events. The program consists of special departmental classes, colloquia, and seminars, each extra-rigorous and taught by the best faculty. The colloquia are large, interdisciplinary courses whose more recent titles include The Great Ideas and Values of Mankind and The Sciences and History. The seminars are smaller discussion-oriented groups. To graduate with honors, students must complete, among other things, a two-semester honors sequence in the history of civilization, an independent study of "a number of the most important works of literature and the other arts," and an honors thesis. BYU takes this program seriously. Students must also finish with a cumulative grade point average of at least 3.5, and there is even honors housing, the honors center, an honors student council, and a separate honors journal, *Insight*.

Educate men without religion and you make them but clever devils.

—*Duke of Wellington*

BYU also has superb athletic facilities—its intercollegiate teams have won national championships in football and golf.

The campus is set between the Wasatch Mountains to the east and Utah Lake to the west, with Salt Lake City only forty-five miles to the north. This seems just the right place for the school to pursue its mission: "to assist individuals in their quest for perfection and eternal life."   □

Calvin College
Grand Rapids, Michigan

Shared Commitments

If the nation's politics have become, in the words of Richard John Neuhaus, a "naked public square," devoid of religious or moral content, the condition of higher education is no less denuded. Over the last century, higher education has largely succeeded in forcing issues of faith and morality to the margins of the academy. A trendy literary theoretician might well describe the status of religion in higher education today as "the presence of absence." When faith is not ignored altogether, it is trotted out as a quaint cultural curiosity, whose place has been usurped by the new "sciences" of the sociologists, psychologists, and sundry academic sorcerers of the New Age.

It is worthwhile to recall that nearly all of the early American colleges and universities began as church-related institutions, reflecting the belief that liberal learning was integrally tied to a recognition of the role of faith in history and culture. The consensus that education had a metaphysical basis was more or less taken for granted throughout higher education until it was displaced by the Germanic-style universities, which replaced faith with science as the lodestone of their ambitions.

Calvin's Way

But this is decidedly not the case at Calvin College, which continues to stress "the sovereignty of God in every part of life," including the liberal arts.

Calvin College

Year Founded: 1876
Total Cost: $12,150
Total Enrollment: 3,725
Total Applicants: 1,825
  95% accepted
  58% of accepted enrolled
ACT Average: 24
Financial Aid:
  70% applied
  60% judged to have need
  95% of those judged were
    given aid
No ROTC Program Offered
Application Information:
  Thomas McWherter
  Director of Admissions
  Calvin College
  3201 Burton S.E.
  Grand Rapids, MI 49506
  Telephone: (616) 957-6106
Application Deadlines:
  No early decision
  Regular decision: rolling

Affiliated with the Christian Reformed Church, Calvin describes itself as a "setting of Christian commitment," yet, with Illinois's Wheaton College, it is one of the finest Christian liberal arts schools in the nation.

Calvin students must complete a rigorous and extensive liberal arts core, including required courses in the history of Western civilization, an introductory philosophy course, Biblical Literature and Theology, and Basic Christian Theology. Other requirements include six courses in history, religion, and philosophy. Students must choose three courses beyond specified introductory courses in mathematics and the sciences, including at least one course in physical science and one in biology. Calvin graduates must also have completed one course in basic economics or political science and one introductory course in psychology or sociology; and three courses are required in literature and the fine arts. Students must also demonstrate competency in written and spoken communication, and in a foreign language. One course in physical education is also required.

In short, Calvin students are assured of receiving an introduction to the history, thought, and literature of their civilization; moreover, the values of their faith are acknowledged and highlighted in their study of the Western tradition. The Calvin curriculum not only reflects a commitment to the tradition of liberal learning, but places the intellectual and spiritual needs of the student at the center of its program.

One innovative wrinkle in Calvin's program is an interim term in January, during which students can choose from specially developed on-campus courses, or travel abroad as part of the college's study-abroad program. Opportunities for off-campus study include semester and yearlong programs of study in France, Germany, Austria, the Netherlands, Spain, and Wales in cooperation with Central College; a Latin American studies program administered by the Christian College Coalition; a special Netherlands studies program in Amsterdam offered in cooperation with Dordt College; study in Britain in cooperation with Oak Hill College, a theological college located in northern London; and a spring-semester language study program in Denia, Spain.

Faith Undeferred

Admission to Calvin is relatively easy, but degrees are not handed out lightly and students are expected to meet rigorous academic standards. Classes are small and contact between faculty and students appears close, as befits a Christian institution. The school is also distinguished by the sense of community that makes for a welcome relief from the intensive dog-eat-dog atmosphere of some more intensely pre-professional schools. As might be expected at an old-line Protestant school, there are a number of left-leaning faculty members who teach courses like "Diversity and Inequality in North American Society," but the atmosphere on campus is morally quite conservative; there are no Yale-like Gay and Lesbian Awareness Days at Calvin, nor is there a women's studies program (although something called a "scholars' group" does study "gender issues"). Two out of three Calvin students are members of the Reformed Church, and faculty members are expected to subscribe to the creedal positions of the church. Most Calvin students are from Michigan and the upper Midwest, but the school has recently broadened its reach.

Prospective students take note: Calvin is as scholarship-conscious as any school we've encountered. It offers literally hundreds of scholarships to incoming freshmen, ranging in yearly value from the large ($2,500) to the not-so-large ($750). There are also numerous departmental scholarships available for upperclassmen.

But as with the other evangelical institutions in our guide, Calvin is not for everyone, certainly not for students who might feel awkward at the constant references to Christianity. Calvin explains its approach to student life on campus by noting that "this matter of being totally Christian cannot be deferred until graduation." The school attempts through its regulations and counseling programs "to show students how a life of commitment can be lived in their rooms, on the athletic field, in their academic work, and in daily religious practices." For example, "students are expected to attend some chapel services during the week." Still, the emphasis is not on the rules alone. "The Calvin community has come together from wide-ranging backgrounds and places," a college publication explains. "Personal and spiritual maturity is uneven; expectations and goals, diverse. Obviously, unanimous agreement by every member in the commu-

> Education is simply the soul of a society as it passes from one generation to another.
>
> —*G.K. Chesterton*

nity's shared commitments is quite impossible. While no one is forced to acknowledge the community's Lord or to obey Him unwillingly, each one who has chosen to join the Calvin community thereby declares he or she is willing not to violate the community's values and commitments." □

Centre College

Danville, Kentucky

C6H0

Centre College is a "rising star" among national liberal arts colleges—but one that has not felt it necessary to jettison its traditional curriculum or its laudable undergraduate teaching in order to win acceptance by academia's elite. Like many of the other schools in this guide, Centre College is a living rebuke to many of the most prestigious universities in the country that are unable to fashion a coherent curriculum or provide quality classroom instruction to their students.

The evidence of Centre's success is impressive: the small Kentucky college boasts the most loyal alumni of any college or university in the nation, as measured by the percentage of alumni who give to the college. In fact, Centre broke the all-time national record, once held by Princeton, for alumni support and has gone on to set new records year in and year out. (Nearly three-quarters of the alumni support the college financially, an eloquent testimony to their recognition of the value of a Centre education.) The reason for such loyalty is obvious. Centre has produced more Rhodes Scholars and finalists than any other school in Kentucky; it is one of the smallest coeducational colleges in the country to have a Phi Beta Kappa chapter; and its graduates enjoy an acceptance rate of more than 90 percent at graduate and professional schools. (More than half of Centre's graduates go on to earn advanced degrees.)

The Little Giant Killer

Centre seems actually to revel in its giant-killer traditions. Its upset victory over the nation's top-ranked football team—Harvard—in 1921 is still the talk of the campus. (At each home game the mysterious formula C6H0 appears—commemorating the score of that game: Centre 6, Harvard 0.) Two Centre graduates have been vice presidents of the United States, one an associate justice of the U.S. Supreme Court, another, chief justice (Fred Vinson, Class of '09). Nine graduates have served in the U.S. Senate and thirty-seven in the House of Representatives; twenty-eight have served as college presidents; and fifty-two have become state or federal judges.

A nonsectarian institution committed to the Judeo-Christian tradition, Centre emphasizes its sense of community and commitment to a liberal education that provides basic intellectual skills as well as a common intellectual experience. Says a college publication:

> Centre's notion of general education goes beyond exposure to disciplines and the accumulation of facts. It is rooted in the concept of liberal education as a formative and transformative process—one that provides students with a permanent foundation for learning through the development of basic human capacities such as the ability to imagine and create, to think and reason analytically, to solve problems, to integrate and synthesize complex information, to use language clearly and persuasively, and to make responsible choices.

Ancients and Moderns

The foundation of Centre's core curriculum is a two-semester interdisciplinary humanities sequence focusing on "masterworks of literature and the fine arts." The first semester is a study of the literature, philosophy, and fine arts of Greece and Rome "with special attention given to ethical and aesthetic values." In the second semester of the sequence, students study the literature, music, and fine arts of the Renaissance, Baroque, and Neoclassical periods. In both courses, emphasis is placed on writing, analysis, and discussion.

The humanities sequence satisfies two-thirds of Centre's requirements in the Aesthetic Context, one of six areas of study demanded of all students. Students must take a third designated course intended to build upon the introductory sequence. The second "context" of the curriculum is the Scientific and Technological Context, which requires students to take designated courses including two

Centre College

Year Founded: 1819
Total Cost: $14,955
Total Enrollment: 907
Total Applicants: 972
  88% accepted
  33% of accepted enrolled
ACT Average: 27
SAT Average: 1120
Financial Aid:
  60% applied
  55% judged to have need
  100% of those judged
    were given aid
ROTC Program Offered
Application Information:
  Mr. John W. Rogers
  Director of Admissions
  Centre College
  Danville, KY 40422
  Telephone: (606) 238-5350
Application Deadlines:
  Early action: 11/15
  Regular decision: 3/1

four-credit laboratory courses, one in life science and one in physical science, followed by an approved course dealing with science, technology, and public policy.

In satisfying Centre's Cross-Cultural Context requirement, students need to take a single course in a foreign culture (n.b.: Centre does not limit this to so-called non-Western cultures), and are encouraged to take advantage of Centre's off-campus foreign study programs. Students also take two courses in the Context of Fundamental Questions concerning questions "about the possibility and limits of human knowledge, about our common nature and destiny, and about what constitutes a good life." Centre takes an unabashedly value-centered and Eurocentric approach to the subject.

Under the Social Context, Centre students are required to take three courses in the social sciences, including at least one in the analysis of social institutions and one in historical analysis. Finally, in their senior year, students take a course that seeks to integrate the various major areas of their study, choosing among topics such as the theory of justice or interpretations of language.

In addition to the above, students must also satisfy basic skills requirements, including competence in mathematics, expository writing, and a foreign language.

A Compelling Clarity

Notably, Centre's general education program is not a random assemblage of vaguely related courses thrown together under the arbitrary rubric of general education. Instead, the courses are specifically designed and selected with common goals and criteria in mind and are intended to "enhance the coherence of the educational experience."

Reviewing Centre's curriculum a few years back, Ernest Boyer of the Carnegie Foundation for the Advancement of Teaching, and a frequent critic of the curricular incoherence of American higher education, said that he had not "seen a more elegant, a more thoughtful, a more compelling arrangement for the undergraduate curriculum in twenty years."

This emphasis on integrating knowledge is in the finest tradition of liberal education. "The best possible preparation for a career—whether in medicine, law, business, government, journalism or whatever—is a well-balanced education in the arts and sciences," says English Professor Milton Rei-

> A teacher affects eternity; he can never tell where his influence stops.
>
> —Henry Adams

gelman. "The best poet is the one who knows something about physics and chemistry, and the best doctor is the one who knows something about history and poetry."

An interesting aspect of Centre's curriculum is its four-two-four schedule, under which students take four courses in the fall semester, two courses during the six-and-a-half-week winter term, and four courses in the spring term. Students in engineering can participate in Centre's three-two combination program with the University of Kentucky, Georgia Institute of Technology, Vanderbilt, Columbia, and Washington University to obtain a master's degree in five years.

Centre's other overwhelming strength is its tradition of excellent teaching by accessible faculty members. Classes are almost uniformly small, many with fewer than ten students and, says the college, "almost none larger than thirty." But most important of all is a faculty still dedicated to providing their students with an outstanding education. The climate is light-years away from what you might find at any large university, where the average senior professor is often merely a vague rumor to undergraduates who never actually see him. In contrast, one biology professor at Centre is quoted in a college publication as saying:

> I try to make a credible offer of being available outside my office, so that one of the first things I do in my courses is to put down my telephone number and my address. And I draw a map of how to get to my house and tell my students that I really expect them to call me any time if they have a problem. They not only do that for four years, they do it for the next ten years and more after they graduate. It's for real—the friendship is a lifelong friendship.

A growing regional arts center, located on a beautiful, well-maintained campus in Kentucky's bluegrass country, Centre is a school we think we'll hear more and more about in the future—and we expect all of the news to be good. □

Chicago
Chicago, Illinois

The Image of Hutchins

Robert Maynard Hutchins once defined the minimum qualifications of a university president as "courage, fortitude, justice, and prudence or practical wisdom." He did *not* include patience, which he regarded as "a delusion and a snare." He thought that administrators "have far too much of it [rather] than too little. . . ."

Those were appropriate sentiments for a man who remade the University of Chicago more or less according to his own vision. One of the rare breed of university presidents who think of themselves as leaders rather than conciliators or mediators, Hutchins became Chicago's president at the absurdly young age of thirty, and promptly began to implement a bold plan to revive the liberal arts at the university. More than half a century later, his achievement remains a standard against which other efforts are judged.

Aristotle for Everybody

His plan, which was only partially implemented, was a four-year program of completely prescribed courses: he made no allowances for electives or specialization. One of his crucial innovations was to defy the growing fragmentation of knowledge by creating an academic structure of his own that organized knowledge not along departmental lines but in broad comprehensive fields, and that acknowledged the place of metaphysics in the curriculum. While many were following John Dewey's lead and inaugurating the dogmas of "value-free education," Hutchins was focusing Chicago's curriculum on the exploration of first principles and the discernment of right ends.

It was, in fact, Chicago's forthright Aristotelianism that gave the school its distinctive personality, embodied in such figures as Mortimer Adler, Leo Strauss, and Richard Weaver, the author of *Ideas Have Consequences*, one of the seminal works of modern conservatism. The theme underlying their scholarship and, indeed, the theme of the Chicago revolution itself, was an attack on the abandonment by liberal intellectuals of the classical tradition, and the subsequent tragic failure to recognize the importance of ideas in the rise and decline of civilizations.

At the heart of Hutchins's reforms were the classics of Western thought that were to become known as the Great Books. For Hutchins these works constituted what he called the "Great Conversation" that began in pre-Homeric civilization and continues to this day.

> Whatever the merits of other civilizations in other respects, no civilization is like that of the West in this respect. No other civilization can claim that its defining characteristic is a dialogue of this sort. No dialogue in any other civilization can compare with that of the West in the number of great works of the mind that have contributed to this dialogue. The goal toward which Western society moves is the Civilization of the Dialogue. . . . [T]he Western ideal is not one or the other strand in the Conversation, but the Conversation itself.

Daniel Bell was later to characterize the Chicago reforms—like those at Columbia University—as a reaffirmation of the traditional focus of the liberal arts in Western civilization, and of the need for higher education to provide society with a unifying principle through a shared intellectual experience. It was also a reaction against the growing tendency of academia toward specialization. In place of the "religion of research," Chicago led a return to *humanitas;* and in place of the splintering of knowledge into a Babel of academic voices, the Chicago curriculum stressed integration and the "broad relationships of knowledge."

The Chicago Sequence

A distinctive element of the Chicago program was the presence of outstanding scholars who were also gifted and committed teachers, a tradition that, by and large, remains.

Although the Hutchins curriculum did not survive his 1945 departure intact—he quipped that his successors lacked "the courage of my convictions"—his influence is still clearly evident in the University of Chicago's undergraduate program.

University of Chicago

Year Founded: 1891
Total Cost: $23,461
Total Enrollment: 10,950
Total Applicants: 6,673
  42% accepted
  37% of accepted enrolled
SAT Middle Range Scores:
  570–680/620–730
Financial Aid:
  61% applied
  95% judged to have need
  100% of those judged
    were given aid
ROTC Program Offered
Application Information:
  Mr. Theodore A. O'Neill
  Dean of Admissions
  University of Chicago
  1116 East 59th Street
  Chicago, IL 60637
  Telephone: (312) 702-8650
Application Deadlines:
  Early decision: 11/15
  Regular decision: 1/15

On one occasion
Aristotle was
asked how much
educated men
were superior to
those uneducated:
"As much," said
he, "as the living
are to the dead."

—Diogenes Laertius

Even though its emphasis on the Great Books has been watered down somewhat, the university remains one of the finest in the country.

Continuing to eschew typical department structures, Chicago divides its faculty into five collegiate divisions—Biological Sciences, Humanities, Physical Sciences, Social Sciences, and the New Collegiate Division—which are responsible both for the school's extensive core offerings and its majors.

All Chicago students are required to take twenty-one courses in the "common core." Unlike many schools that define a set of essentially unrelated and highly specialized courses as a "core," Chicago has created sequences of courses designed to provide a comprehensive and progressive introduction to the humanities, sciences, and social sciences. An example is the required three-quarter sequence in the "interpretation of historical, literary and philosophical texts." Students choose from six sequences, including Readings in Literature, Philosophical Perspectives on the Humanities, Greek Thought and Literature, Human Being and Citizen, Form, Problem, Event, and Introduction to the Humanities. An additional course in the musical and visual arts is required to complete the humanities requirement.

In the natural sciences, students can fulfill the six-quarter requirement by taking an integrated two-year sequence in the natural sciences or a three-quarter sequence in the physical sciences and a three-quarter sequence in the biological sciences.

Chicago students fulfill their social science requirement by choosing among four sequences titled Political Economy, Individual and Society, Interpretations of Culture; Self, Culture, and Society; Mind; and Classics of Social and Political Thought. They must also take a three-course sequence in Civilizational Studies, which is described as "an in-depth examination of the development and accomplishments of one of the world's great civilizations through direct encounters with some of its most significant documents and monuments." We're quite sure, though, that Hutchins would never have countenanced the relativism inherent in the current option to take Introduction to African Civilization instead of History of Western Civilization.

Chicago students are also expected to demonstrate knowledge of a foreign language, and to take three quarters of physical education and two quarters of mathematics beyond pre-calculus.

Needless to say, there are few if any "guts" or Mickey Mouse courses at Chicago.

The Perils of Diversity

Can this be improved upon? Of course, as the *Chicago Crucible*, a conservative publication on campus, notes. Even though a majority of Chicago students choose to study Western civilization, "they are never exposed to much of American history, while those studying American history often by-pass the Western context of American civilization. And, of course, students can graduate with a 'liberal education' without studying either." Moreover, even at Chicago, the push for "diversity" means that there are not always clear guidelines of what constitutes a "Great Book." Notes the *Crucible:* "*The Wealth of Nations* enjoys the same 'great book' status in the Common Core social sciences course as *Color Classification in Ndembu Ritual.* And when truly great books are read, they are usually studied with the cursory rapidity endemic to survey courses."

Even so, Chicago's curriculum remains light-years ahead of most of what passes for a liberal education in the Ivies. Complementing the outstanding curriculum is one of the most distinguished faculties in American higher education, including Allan Bloom, author of *The Closing of the American Mind.* Professor Milton Friedman left to join the Hoover Institution, but not before establishing a vision of economics known as the Chicago School. Although there has been greater use of teaching assistants in recent years, and although some classes can be as large as 100, Chicago students report that faculty members are accessible, and praise the school's advising system. (Students nevertheless must still camp out the night before registration in order to get the most popular classes on campus.) It is hard to name Chicago's specific strengths because there are so many of them, but political science, sociology, and economics—where free-market economics still reigns supreme—are among the standouts.

If we have one problem with the University of Chicago it is its urban location. While security on the fortress-like campus is good, safety nonetheless remains a concern. But things are a whole lot better now than in decades past: the Hyde Park/Kenwood neighborhood was recently profiled in *Town & Country* magazine—a sure sign of gentrification—

65

and more than two-thirds of the university's faculty live in the immediate area. Still, we recommend looking four ways before crossing the street. □

Claremont McKenna College
Claremont, California

A Unique Marriage

Claremont McKenna College, founded in 1946, is one of the six Claremont Colleges (the others are Harvey Mudd, Pitzer, Pomona, Scripps, and the Claremont Graduate School). Pomona was established in 1887 by a group of settlers who wanted a "Christian college of the New England type," and the incorporation of the other schools began in 1925, with the goal of maintaining the advantages of a small college while gaining the facilities and accommodating the number of students of a large university. One specific example: the joint library, with 1.7 million holdings, is larger than those of schools like Dartmouth and Georgetown, an almost impossible reality for comparably sized liberal arts colleges.

Each of the schools in the "Claremont Cluster" is an independent institution—separate endowments, deans, professors—but their campuses adjoin, and the rules allow cross-registration for course offerings. This means you can pursue your studies at Claremont McKenna but avail yourself of the expert faculty in any one of the specialties at the other Claremonts (for instance, engineering and chemistry at Harvey Mudd). Ralph Rossum, CMC's dean of faculty, compared the cluster to a hand: the five fingers function individually, or together with the power of a fist.

CMC: Liberal Education and Citizenship

All of the undergraduate colleges define themselves as primarily "liberal arts" institutions (*U.S. News* still lists Harvey Mudd under engineering schools in its annual report), but to avoid the redundancy of five identical schools, each has its own area of specialization. CMC's curricular emphasis is in public affairs, its best departments being government and economics. Prominent conservative scholars teach in both departments, many of them disciples of Leo Strauss, Milton Friedman, and James Buchanan. But CMC steadfastly clings to the liberal arts label, and, as we learned on publishing our first edition, it just as vigorously refuses to be labeled *conservative*. Fair enough. The point is made that CMC is a place "rooted in the interplay between the world of ideas and the world of events," meaning that you get the spirit of the liberal arts and the pragmatism of specialization, without what Dean Rossum refers to as "vulgar vocationalism." Neither do you end up with "self-indulgent, otherworldly thinkers with no sense of social responsibility and citizenship." It's not a bad idea. From our standpoint, of course, Claremont McKenna would not qualify if the scales dipped too heavily on the side of specialization.

As if to underscore its belief in such a balance, the school makes a point of hiring faculty with prior "real world" experience. In the government department alone there are, among other notables, three former congressional fellows, the chairman of the Reagan/Bush California campaign, a former chairman of the President's Commission on Educational Research, a former assistant secretary of defense, and a former deputy assistant secretary of defense.

But even the most narrowly focused students (half of CMC's students end up majoring in either economics or government) are required to fulfill a rigorous distribution requirement that includes courses across the traditional trivium and quadrivium. In all, a student may easily end up taking a dozen required courses in English, math, science, and the humanities. To be specific: every student must take one of two courses (Lit. 10 or 20) in English composition and analysis; math and science course work depends greatly upon the nature of high school work (and/or performance on Claremont's proficiency tests), but most will take a one-semester calculus course and two semesters of physical or biological science; all students will take three one-semester courses in the social sciences (economics, history, government, or psychology), and a semester in one of the humanities (religion, philosophy, or literature). The foreign language requirement is interesting: either you take the Roots of Western Civilization course, which obviously has nothing to do with speaking a foreign tongue, or you pass a third-semester level course in one of the

Claremont McKenna College

Year Founded: 1946
Total Cost: $21,100
Total Enrollment: 845
Total Applicants: 1,736
  38% accepted
  12% of accepted enrolled
SAT Averages: 610V/670M
Financial Aid:
  60% applied
  64% judged to have need
  100% of those judged
    were given aid
ROTC Program Offered
Application Information:
  Mr. Richard C. Vos
  Vice President and Dean
    of Admissions and
    Financial Aid
  Claremont McKenna
    College
  890 Columbia Avenue
  Claremont, CA 91711
  Telephone: (714) 621-8088
Application Deadlines:
  Early decision: 12/1
  Regular decision: 2/1

European languages. You *can* avoid French altogether (or German, Spanish, Italian, etc.) by taking a proficiency test, but you can see that there's no way around learning something important.

Every course at CMC has a writing component, so students have ample opportunity to hone their writing skills.

Finally, everyone must take three semesters of physical education, and meet a requirement in American history and institutions by taking either Introduction to American Politics or Forging a New Nation: America to 1865. To graduate, fourth-year students must complete a senior thesis, either an extensive research paper, or a creative project of their own choosing that is not necessarily related to their major fields.

The Research Institutes

But back to the specialization. One unique aspect of the school is its group of seven separately endowed research centers that undertake the study of Individual Freedom in the Modern World, State and Local Government, Decision Science for Business and Public Policy, Political Economy, International Strategic Studies, Natural Resources, and Humanistic Studies. CMC, as one of the nation's only undergraduate research colleges, demands from its professors what to us would normally seem impossible—top-notch liberal arts teaching *and* ground-breaking research. Something has to give. But the school claims to pull it off. For one thing, there are no TAs to take over for busy profs. Plus, the research centers' directors are just about the only faculty given a break in their teaching load. And the students are included in the research, so much so that most of the graduating psychology majors leave the school with their own published work.

Other pluses for the school include a rigorous full-semester-credit internship in Washington, during which the students work forty-hour weeks (presenting a report when finished), take two weekly night courses, and undertake an independent study worth one course credit. Unlike the internships at many other schools, this one is not part-time, and the students are placed in real jobs in one of the branches of government, in political party organizations, and in journalism, giving them the chance actually to get involved with current issues rather than lick stamps. Also worth mentioning is the

> If a nation expects to be ignorant and free in a state of civilization,
> it expects what never was and never will be.
>
> —*Thomas Jefferson*

Marian Miner Cook Athenaeum, an elegant dining and speaking facility dedicated solely to the students, drawing prominent speakers throughout the year.

Well-Rounded Graduates

It seems that balance—between liberal arts and specialization, teaching and research, knowledge and worldly success—is CMC's driving philosophy, and the college's graduate success rate proves it pays. Eighty percent of the graduates "go on to advanced degrees at prestigious institutions," and about three-quarters of that number pursue degrees in either law or business. Eight percent of all CMC alumni are presently either CEOs or CFOs of major companies.

It is our conviction that what separates the successfully educated person from the unsuccessful person (period) is the ability to identify worthy pursuits and sources, sustain effective study and analysis, and present convincing arguments and conclusions. If a college does not demand evidence of this accomplishment, it cannot know if it has succeeded in its fundamental task. Claremont McKenna is properly confident that its students will graduate properly prepared to succeed. □

Columbia
New York, New York

Carved in Stone

. . . in solid letters above the columns of Butler Library, a garland of names keeps watch over the Columbia campus. Homer. Herodotus. Sophocles. Plato. Aristotle. Vergil. Dante. Shakespeare. Cervantes. Voltaire. To students at many other colleges, such a list may sketch only the fuzziest outline of the past, no more resonant than the name of any investment bank or law firm. But at Columbia these names on the library façade are not mere architectural decoration, or an emblem of a long-forgotten classical education. Here they are a roster of vital, important and familiar Columbia teachers—the authors read by every freshman and sophomore, in the famous and influential Core Curriculum.

> . . . Without the Core, Columbia might be just another first-rate college.
>
> —From *The Core Curriculum*
> by Harry Bauld, Columbia College.

Columbia College

Year Founded: 1754
Total Cost: $24,190
Total Enrollment: 3,400
Total Applicants: 6,591
  29% accepted
  44 % of accepted enrolled
SAT Middle Range Scores:
  560–680V/610–720M
Financial Aid:
  70% applied
  62% judged to have need
  70% of those judged were
  given aid
No ROTC Program Offered
Application Information:
  Mr. Lawrence J. Momo
  Director of Admissions
  Columbia College
  212 Hamilton Hall
  New York, NY 10027
  Telephone: (212) 854-2521
Application Deadlines:
  Early decision: 11/1
  Regular decision: 1/1

Indeed, long before there was a St. John's College and before Robert Maynard Hutchins began the long ordeal of transforming the University of Chicago, Columbia had placed the best that has been thought and said at the center of its curriculum. It is no exaggeration to say that the history of liberal learning in the twentieth century has largely been the story of higher education's response to the remarkable core curriculum put into place during the first half of the century by Columbia College.

In Search of Humanity

Over the last fifty years or so other schools have created core curricula that have come and gone with varying tides of fashion and politics (Harvard comes to mind). But few ever attempted what Columbia achieved seventy years ago: a curriculum that explores "what it means to be human" through the careful study of the traditions of Athens and Jerusalem—a duality that can be described as the traditions of Reason and Faith. Despite the increasingly bitter complaints of faculty radicals (about whom more later), that curriculum remains remarkably intact.

We are quick to point out that Columbia is not for the faint of heart, particularly among conservatives. No other school in this guide, we make bold to say, is more left-leaning than Columbia, which has a long and cherished tradition of radicalism. In the 1990s, we suspect that no academic outrage goes unrepresented in the Columbia faculty, from unreconstructed Marxist professors and post-structuralist feminists to sixties retreads who devote their professional lives to creating a better world—and to trashing Columbia's curriculum. Race relations are also poor at Columbia, where the tensions created by increasingly militant and separatist factions have created an environment of politically correct bullying that makes Columbia uncomfortable even (or, perhaps we should say, especially) for liberals on campus. So consider this fair warning: a conservative student at Columbia will have to call upon all of his or her talents as a guerrilla student to survive.

So why is Columbia on our list? Because for all its faults it is utterly unlike the rest of the Ivy League. Quite simply, we think the Columbia core provides students with the intellectual weapons they will need to combat the deconstruction of the West. And we think the best guarantor of the continuing stability of the Columbia curriculum is its remarkable tradition.

Erskine's List

Its great experiment dates back to World War I, when Columbia offered a War Issues course. With the end of the Great War, attention turned to creating a peacetime equivalent. In 1916, John Erskine introduced his famous Great Books course, which quickly became the model for what became Contemporary Civilization of the West, a course that was required of all Columbia students. In 1937, Columbia added a required humanities course, again based on Erskine's Great Books list.

It's ironic that Columbia's decision to create a common intellectual experience grew out of the increasing diversity of Columbia's student body in the early years of this century—ironic only because in the 1990s it is so often taken for granted that a diverse student body is an excuse for *splintering* the curriculum into a congeries of special-interest offerings. Columbia saw it differently. Far from an inducement to surrender intellectual judgment over the contents of a liberal education, Columbia saw its students' diversity as an impetus to create an educational program that would assure all of them—whatever their varied backgrounds—a common humanistic education.

Now in its ninth decade, Contemporary Civilization (known as "CC") continues to be a yearlong exploration of "the important questions of social and political thought from ancient Greece to the twentieth century: How have people made a living? How have they lived together? How have they interpreted the world they lived in?" Meeting in small classes with Columbia professors, students study the Greek and Roman worlds by reading Plato, Aristotle, Cicero, and Epictetus; the "sources of the Judeo-Christian Tradition" by reading Genesis, Exodus, Isaiah, Matthew, Acts, selected letters of St. Paul, and Revelations; the Middle Ages by reading Augustine, Aquinas, and de Pisan's *Book of the City of Ladies;* the Renaissance and Reformation by reading Machiavelli, Calvin, and modern

> I hate by-roads in education. Education is as well known, and has long been as well known, as ever it can be.
>
> —*Samuel Johnson*

71

writers Hillerbrand and Braudel; the "New Science" by reading Descartes, Bacon, and Galileo; and the "New Philosophy and the Polity" by reading Hobbes and Locke. And this is only in the first semester.

The second semester of Contemporary Civilization includes readings from Rousseau, Kant, Hume, Paine, Adam Smith, Burke, Hegel, Marx, John Stuart Mill, Darwin, Nietzsche, Freud, Lenin, and Virginia Woolf.

Columbia students are also required to take Humanities A—known as Lit Hum among undergraduates. The reading list has evolved over the years —no fewer than 130 different works have been included at one time or another—but it has consistently remained true to the spirit of the original 1937 course. In the first semester students read Homer's great works, Sappho's poems, the plays of Aeschylus and Sophocles, Thucydides' *Peloponnesian War*, Euripides' *Medea* and *Bacchae*, Aristophanes' *The Frogs*, Plato's *Apology*, *Symposium*, and *Republic*, Aristotle's *Ethics and Politics*, and Virgil's *Aeneid*. In the spring the reading list includes selections from the Bible, Augustine's *Confessions*, Dante's *Inferno*, Boccaccio's *Decameron*, Montaigne's *Essays*, Shakespeare's *King Lear*, Descartes's *Meditations on First Philosophy*, Madame de Lafayette's *Princess of Clèves*, Goethe's *Faust*, and Jane Austen's *Pride and Prejudice*.

Columbia faculty members are careful to draw the appropriate intellectual linkages between Contemporary Civilization and Lit Hum. "You may get the theory of kingship from Hobbes in Contemporary Civilization," one professor told *The New York Times*. "In the other you learn what it is like to be a king through Oedipus or King Lear."

All Columbia students are also required to take Humanities courses in Masterpieces of the Fine Arts and Masterpieces of Music.

A Grand Tradition

An indication of Columbia's seriousness about its core is its continuing commitment to close student-faculty interaction—the Lit Hum courses are limited to twenty-four students. Although some of the sections of Contemporary Civilization and Lit Hum may be taught by graduate students, known as "preceptors," they are also taught by full professors, including some of the most eminent members of the faculty. But even the most senior faculty members are tested and challenged by the courses; this in the tradition of Mark Van Doren, Jacques Barzun, and Lionel Trilling.

Another mark of the Columbia core is its exceptionally demanding pace, often requiring students to absorb 100 or more pages of a difficult classic overnight. But here again, Columbia has defined the essence of liberal education. A faculty report issued shortly after World War II noted that the goal was not to produce a specialist in Shakespeare or Cervantes. "All that can safely be said of even a great scholar," the Columbia faculty noted, "is that he got enough on a first reading to impel him to go back a second time."

Columbia's intellectual integrity and seriousness are also reflected in its remaining requirements. Students must take two science courses (from among a relatively short list of introductory offerings), must complete the second term of an intermediate language sequence, must pass a physical education course, and must take two courses that satisfy the Culture and Issues requirement. This final item is a quasi-*diversity* requirement, described in the catalog as encouraging students to take courses "dealing with, for example, human rights, racism, gender issues, and environmental problems." But in reality, the requirement can be satisfied by a number of intellectually solid courses, including Oriental Humanities, which is based on the great books of the East and was singled out by the National Endowment for the Humanities as a model for the study of non-Western cultures.

An Uncertain Future

Don't get us wrong, though. Columbia is to some extent at the mercy of its politics. Over the next decade we expect to see continued assaults *à la* Stanford on the core's emphasis on "dead white guys." One Columbia faculty member, Edward Said, says of Lit Hum: "They [younger faculty members] all loathe the course. They loathe it with a passion beyond description."

Indeed, a recent *New York Times* article about the core leads us to wonder how long Columbia will qualify for a place in our book (as many friends have told us it already does not). Have some faculty begun to use Lit Hum and CC as platforms for radical preaching? The director of Lit Hum told the *Times* that the pedagogy, as the reporter put it, "now relates the works to contemporary life." Re-

73

marked the director (English professor James Mirollo): "We stress gender. We stress class issues. We stress political issues. We apply the most modern theories." To which we say: *Sic transit gloria mundi.* We are watching the core debate closely, and further political polarization will surely lead to our disaffection with Columbia.

But we think there are grounds for optimism as well. "We now have alumni coming back and saying this was the best that happened to them as undergraduates," a former director of the humanities program has said. "That's where 50 years helps. People don't break sacred traditions." Even so, we suspect Columbia could use some reinforcements. □

University of Dallas
Dallas, Texas

Truth, Virtue . . . and Travel

Those who do not know it are surprised to learn that the University of Dallas is a Roman Catholic college; indeed, it is one of the best—in the limited scope of Catholic schools, and in the larger realm of all universities. You can believe the university's informal motto that UD is a school "where ideas still count." The University of Dallas is "dedicated to the renewal of the Western heritage of liberal education and to the recovery of the Christian intellectual tradition."

In his 1982 inaugural address the university's president, Dr. Robert F. Sasseen, explained that many of the problems in higher education arose when schools "abandoned the idea that there is a body of knowledge and understanding common to all educated persons. Without an animating, unifying belief about the qualities constituting the excellence of the human being, and so of an educated person," he said, "the university must inevitably suffer a crisis of identity. It is difficult to avoid such a crisis when one is losing one's soul."

Transcendent Standards

Obviously, we like this place, for one thing it has is soul. Few other schools see their role in quite the way UD does. Words such as "recovery" and "renewal" do not merely express nostalgia for a more venerable approach to education; they indicate a commitment, as the university's statement of purpose puts it, to a curriculum "informed by principles of learning which acknowledge transcendent standards of truth and excellence, and which affirm human nature to be spiritual, rational and free." Truth and virtue exist, get it? And to pursue the one and develop the other is the purpose of an education.

The core curriculum is based upon the continuity that is Western civilization. In the Constantin College (the university's undergraduate program, as distinct from the Braniff Graduate School), *all* students must take four courses each in philosophy, English, and foreign languages; three courses in some combination of math and art; two each in science, Western civilization, American history, and theology; and one course in economics and another in politics. There are very few choices among the courses in each discipline, making it a true core (rather than merely a set of distribution requirements) amounting to just over half the total credits required for a diploma.

Freshmen immediately find themselves reading, among other things, all of Plato's *Republic;* and whatever the major, every student is required to take all four courses of the Literary Tradition, covering many of the important works of Western literature, from the *Iliad* to Faulkner's *Light in August.* The rest of the core is equally thorough, not only in exposing the students to the great ideas but in allowing them to share the exposure.

"At the University of Dallas the strong sense of community is as much an influence on the students as anything," says Donald Cowan, the school's president from 1962 to 1977, "and the community's closeness is in part due to the core common to all students." Dr. Cowan, who helped shape the curriculum, notes that "the level of ordinary conversation is high because the students share a common background of learning."

The Rome Semester

Study hard as a freshman, because—among other reasons, obviously—you need a C average to go to Rome, which is where nearly all UD students spend one semester in the sophomore year. The university has its own campus in the Eternal City,

University of Dallas

Year Founded: 1955
Total Cost: $13,870
Total Enrollment: 2,871
Total Applicants: 625
  86% accepted
  41% of accepted enrolled
SAT Average: 1120
Financial Aid:
  78% applied
  87% judged to have need
  100% of those judged
    were given aid
ROTC Program Offered
Application Information:
  Mr. Christopher P.
    Lyndon
  Director of Admissions
  University of Dallas
  Irving, TX 75062
  Telephone: (800) 628-6999
Application Deadlines:
  No early decision
  Regular decision: 2/1

and the content of the curriculum is enriched by the students' presence in the ancient capital. The students also take side trips to other historic Italian cities, as well as a ten-day trip to Greece, that reveal cultures which, as Rainer Maria Rilke wrote, "are like eternal life, serenely new, without age, without exhaustion."

The University of Dallas sees it this way:

> The road to Rome from Dallas doubtless needs no justification. We are all of us still, in a sense, as T. S. Eliot has said, citizens of the Roman Empire, for Rome brought together the Judeo-Christian revelation and the classical wisdom to form that Europe which was the progenitor of American ideals. Thus, to be a student in the Western World—to seek one's true heritage in the liberal arts—is to follow the path to Rome.

A university is an *alma mater,* knowing her children one by one, not a foundry, or a mint, or a treadmill.

—*John Henry Newman*

The cost of study in Rome, not including travel expenses, is the same as in Dallas, and students receiving financial aid are not excluded. The Rome program is truly a unique opportunity that, unlike most other foreign study programs, fits hand in glove with the school's curriculum. "The idea is not to interrupt the core program, but to continue it," says Dr. Cowan. Over 90 percent of UD's alumni surveyed singled out their experience in Rome as the most rewarding of their college years.

Concern, Not Worry

You might think that UD's emphasis on the liberal arts would work against its students' ambitions in the so-called real world. We've encountered this canard before, but the evidence against it is nowhere more effectively presented than at UD. Sixty percent of its graduates go on to further study, and a remarkable 95 percent of all UD applicants to medical and law schools are accepted. For students concerned with the future, a career counseling program has been developed to advise on the marketability of liberal learning.

All students should be concerned about their future, but with the complete education the University of Dallas offers, UD graduates have nothing to worry about.   □

Davidson

Davidson, North Carolina

Focus on the Classroom

In his book *Choosing a College*, Thomas Sowell notes that despite its lack of a national reputation, Davidson College has produced more students who earn doctorates in mathematics than Amherst, Wellesley, Williams, or Smith—even though all of them are larger than Davidson. Law school deans, moreover, rank Davidson in the top dozen schools nationally—ahead of most Ivy League schools—for the quality of its graduates who go on to law school. Adjusting its rating for class size, a recent survey by *Fortune* magazine ranked tiny Davidson seventh out of sixty-six schools in the number of graduates who become chief executive officers of major U.S. companies. And only four schools its size have turned out as many Rhodes Scholars as has Davidson.

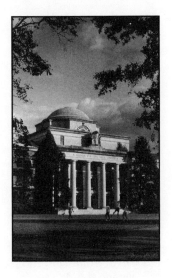

This is no news to most southerners. They have long recognized Davidson's outstanding quality. But Davidson now appears to be moving into the ranks of the nation's elite liberal arts colleges—a clear rival to the Ivy League itself. The new status is obviously good news to Davidson, but also poses some perils, about which more later.

To date, Davidson's reputation has been based on its traditions: a commitment to the liberal arts; a focus on outstanding teaching; an honor system that is regarded as the "touchstone" of college life; rigorous academic standards; and a conservatism, both social and political, reflected in the school's culture. The result of all of these factors is that students graduate from Davidson with the sort of humanistic education seldom found in graduates from the elite universities of the American academy.

An Honorable Family

Located only twenty miles north of Charlotte, Davidson's campus reflects the tradition of the school. Most of the architecture is colonial, while the campus itself is both beautiful and peaceful, conducive to the sort of scholarship and community Davidson prides itself on. One college guide quotes a student as saying, "From the moment I arrived at Davidson for freshman orientation I felt like I was being welcomed to a family, albeit one with an established way of doing things."

Reflecting its traditions, Davidson proudly points to its honor code, which it is more than willing to compare with the legendary code of Washington and Lee. "As students and alumni proudly attest, the honor system at Davidson is the touchstone of the college life, creating an atmosphere of trust in the college community." The library stacks are open and unguarded, students schedule their own exams and take tests without the presence of proctors, and it is simply understood that one's word is one's bond. Every entering student signs a pledge to adhere to the code, and by all measures, it seems to work well, clearly a legacy of the school's tradition of southern gentility.

That tradition is also reflected in Davidson's work ethic. There are few Mickey Mouse courses in the Davidson curriculum and students are expected to work long and hard. Reading lists are extensive and the faculty simply assumes that students will *read* the books assigned. The requirements are also extensive. Students must complete a composition requirement and a foreign language requirement— either to complete three semesters of a language or to demonstrate proficiency in one. Other requirements include courses in literature, the fine arts, history, religion and philosophy, natural science and mathematics, and the social sciences. Many of those, however, can be satisfied by completing Davidson's five-course humanities sequence, which includes The Classical World, The Judeo-Christian Tradition and the Medieval World, From the Renaissance to the Nineteenth Century, and The Modern World. (Because two of the courses meet more frequently than the norm, they are counted as a course and a half—thus the five courses.) The core is rounded out by a physical education requirement that insists on proficiency in four different sports.

Davidson College

Year Founded: 1837
Total Cost: $19,420
Total Enrollment: 1,550
Total Applicants: 2,245
  39% accepted
  53% of accepted enrolled
SAT Averages: 1160–1330
Financial Aid:
  40% applied
  33% judged to have need
  100% of those judged
    were given aid
ROTC Program Offered
Application Information:
  Ms. Nancy Cable Wells
  Dean of Admission and
    Financial Aid
  Davidson College
  Davidson, NC 28036
  Telephone: (704) 892-2230
Application Deadlines:
  Early decision: 12/1
  Regular decision: 2/1

Incomparable Teaching

We could wish for tighter requirements. The choices for satisfying the various distribution requirements are so broad that there is no real common intellectual experience in the curriculum, and it is in fact possible to graduate with a somewhat eccentric program. But this said, the humanities sequence reflects the underlying respect for the liberal arts that continues to dominate Davidson's culture. One Davidson graduate, parachuting into Grenada during the invasion, reportedly chanted verses of Chaucer as he dropped into combat. (We have a hard time imagining a paratrooper from Yale deconstructing Shakespeare as he dropped from the plane.)

This is no accident. At Davidson, the focus remains on the classroom, and the quality of teaching is outstanding. Between 1985 and 1989 no fewer than six Davidson professors were honored by the Council for the Advancement and Support of Education (CASE) for teaching excellence. Says a spokesman for CASE: "No other school in the country has a record comparable to Davidson's." Two of Davidson's professors have been named North Carolina Professor of the Year—one was named a national Professor of the Year. Says one of the winners, a professor of physics and the humanities (!): "If there's anything I try to do it's to give students the feeling that they and I together are discovering something wonderfully new. If you've laid out enough material in the right way then someone else in the class will discover it without your help. That's great stuff!"

As much as anything, this commitment to close faculty-student relations has defined schools like Davidson and sets them apart from the mega-universities where teaching is at best a second thought, if not completely turned over to graduate teaching assistants. But it is here that Davidson's growing national reputation seems to pose the greatest challenge. As it moves into the national spotlight, some college administrators and faculty members have been pushing for a greater emphasis on published "research" as a qualification for hiring and promoting professors. Of course, they deny that this will come at the expense of Davidson's historic emphasis on teaching, but various faculty members are skeptical. Some senior professors, who are among the school's most distinguished, go so far as to say they doubt they would be awarded tenure at Davidson today because of the shift toward research. But so far the push for academic glory has not appreciably diminished Davidson's traditional commitment to the primacy of teaching.

More troublesome perhaps is the still subtle but

> A liberal education is at the heart of a civil society, and at the heart of a liberal education is the act of teaching.
>
> —*A. Bartlett Giamatti*

growing emphasis on "diversity." Davidson's graduation requirements now include something called the "cultural diversity requirement," which is described as "an approved course exploring societies or cultures which differ from that of the United States or Europe." That nomenclature is often a harbinger of the politicization of the curriculum, although this does not appear to be the case at Davidson. The vast majority of the courses that satisfy the requirement are solid studies of Asian culture and language, including offering in Sanskrit and Vedic literature. While some schools use "diversity" requirements as a cover for overtly politicized courses, all of the courses we looked at were legitimate and appear to be well within Davidson's liberal arts tradition.

Immune by Tradition

We do, however, note with some concern that Davidson has taken a leading role in something called the Leadership South Consortium for Campus Diversity, which echoes the usual rhetoric of "multiculturalism" that has been responsible for so much of the inanity and dislocation elsewhere. At one such meeting a Davidson administrator declared: "This will take a significant modernization of the mission" of schools like Davidson. There are some signs that is already happening.

Still, this sort of thing seems to have had little impact on the education students at Davidson receive. In fact, Davidson seems to be a classic case of a school whose rhetoric is worse than the reality (the reverse of the usual situation). We think Davidson remains a solid choice, not only because of its traditions, but because of a student body and alumni whose values have been strengthened by their exposure to a genuinely fine liberal education. (That fact alone should serve as a brake on the more dangerous ambitions of the administration and faculty, some of whom seem quite open in admitting their glee in *curing* students of intellectual maladies, such as Republicanism.) Although Davidson is affiliated with the Presbyterian Church, only one-third of the students are Presbyterians. As it becomes increasingly selective, the quality of the student body will rise and become more geographically diverse, although about 70 percent of Davidson's students still come from the Southeast.

Perhaps the most important factor in Davidson's future is the fierce loyalty of its students. For more than three-quarters of its students, Davidson was their first choice. While we can't vouch for the administration, Davidson's students seem to recognize the value of the school's traditions—and we don't think they'll let anyone undermine them. □

Eureka College
Eureka, Illinois

Executive Sweet

Dutch slept here. Back in 1928 he came to Eureka College, and took the place by storm. He became a star in football, track, and swimming (he even coached the swimming team during his junior and senior years, and was a cheerleader for the basketball team); he served on the student senate for two years (becoming president in his senior year); he was a frat man (TKE) who worked in the campus dining hall all the way through college; and he appeared in no fewer than fourteen plays in four years. We assume he took a course or two in political science, since after he parlayed the drama experience into Hollywood stardom, Ronald Wilson Reagan went on to become president of the United States. (Five freshmen each year receive Reagan Scholarships, the awarding of which depends partly on academic achievement, but also on commitment to public service and leadership potential, although how one measures the latter in a teenager we couldn't begin to guess.)

Of course attending Eureka is no guarantee of future executive success, although its graduates have gone on to the presidencies of thirty-nine colleges and universities. The current president of Eureka, George A. Hearne, speaks of the college program as having been constructed upon four cornerstones: liberal education, great teaching, student involvement, and values. Our kind of school. According to Dr. Hearne, in recent years Eureka has "increased, rather than decreased, emphasis on Western civilization and culture." Although, he adds, "I can't say that our undergraduates are always enthused about being required to participate in these classes, many return as alumni singing the praises of what they resisted as students."

Eureka College

Year Founded: 1855
Total Cost: $13,655
Total Enrollment: 515
Total Applicants: 670
  68% accepted
  32% of accepted enrolled
ACT Average: 22
Financial Aid:
  97% applied
  95% judged to have need
  100% of those judged
    were given aid
No ROTC Program Offered
Application Information:
  Ms. Susan R. Jordan
  Dean of Admissions
  Eureka College
  300 College Avenue
  Eureka, IL 61530
  Telephone: (309) 467-
  3721
Application Deadlines:
  None

Tested Success

The Eureka catalog describes its core curriculum rather obliquely, delineating the program under its list of requirements for graduation. But what one sifts out of the hours-for-graduation and other campus rules is a fifty-hour core that is first-rate. The heart of the program, as suggested by Dr. Hearne's comments, is the history and English requirements. The history sequence (The Ancient World and the Middle Ages; Renaissance, Reformation and Revolution; and The Modern Age) is rigorous. But it is the school's emphasis on English mastery that is most impressive. At first the requirements seem slight: a couple of composition courses, and —perhaps—an advanced writing course. But then there is the little matter of the English qualifying examination. After fifty hours of course work, or at about the end of the sophomore year, all students are required to take a test certifying their competence in the mother tongue. As the college says in introducing its writing program, "Eureka College takes writing seriously."

Other core requirements include two courses in math; two courses in the fine or performing arts; single courses in literature, in philosophy or religion, and in phys ed; and eight hours of lab science. As seniors, Eureka students must take a senior seminar, which is the sort of liberal education summary course elsewhere referred to as a "capstone," and must pass the senior examination. Imagine: a school that actually demands that its students demonstrate comprehension of what they've been taught!

Intensive Study

At some schools a semester program will typically include five or more courses that meet three times each week. Not so at Eureka, where students study under what's called the Intensive Study Plan: eight-week terms (four in the year) in which students take two or three courses that meet five days a week. This little innovation is now fifty years old. The obvious benefits of this approach are two: closer interaction with professors and greater concentration on subjects. This approach works at Eureka because it is a small school where teaching is the *summmum bonum*.

But as with many small colleges, there are some minor drawbacks in the Eureka program. Course offerings are quite limited. If, for instance, a student really was intent on following in "Dutch" Reagan's footsteps, and so decided to major in political science (called "government" at some schools), said student would end up taking rather a lot of electives. The "departmental" requirement for a poli sci major is thirty-four hours of government and history courses, of which twenty-two hours must be in poli sci. Well, there are only nine courses offered in political science, for a total of twenty-five hours. We guess you'd take them all. We also guess you'd see quite a lot of the only two professors who teach political science. There are a dozen history courses beyond the three required in the core, and most would certainly dovetail with the government major's program, but that would still leave about twenty hours' worth of course work to meet the graduation requirement. So, one looks to economics and (gag!) sociology. It seems odd to us that a political science major would have more semester hours of credit in history than in political science, but it is a likely scenario at Eureka. And the fact is, the paucity of course offerings is even more acute in other areas. We happen to love the classics, but Eureka doesn't have a classics department, and offers no courses in Latin and only one in Greek.

On the other hand, prospective teachers will find many more offerings—especially in physical education (forty courses) or music (thirty-five)—than they could possibly take, even if there were no core requirements. The curriculum in business (accounting, economics, and management) is extensive and thoughtfully constructed.

Nearly a quarter of the Eureka faculty is part-time, and only about a third have earned Ph.D.s (although the catalog claims that 90 percent—and other publications say 85 percent—hold "terminal degrees" in their fields). And for those with a narrowly elitist view of higher education, these factors might disqualify Eureka from serious consideration. We, however, are *broadly* elitist. We *don't* believe that everybody ought to have "access" to a college education, but we *do* believe that those who go to college ought to be taught the traditional core of knowledge. Eureka's part-time teachers are just that—teachers—and are mostly employed in Eureka's teacher education programs. Subtract them from the rest of the faculty, and it is clear that the personnel leading Eureka's undergraduates through the glories of the liberal arts are almost all

The function of a university . . . is, above all, to be the organ of that fine adjustment between real life and the growing knowledge of life, an adjustment which forms the secret of civilization.

—W. E. B. DuBois

as well educated as any faculty anywhere. They are hired for their teaching ability, and are proficient enough so that a third of the school's graduates go on to further study. That may not seem a world-beating number, but—again—when you consider how many Eureka graduates go straight into business (the school's most popular major) and into primary- and secondary-school teaching, its grad school numbers are quite impressive.   □

Franciscan University
Steubenville, Ohio

Spirit First

Faced with a sullen and rebellious student body, declining enrollment, and growing confusion over its academic mission, the Franciscan University of Steubenville took a bold leap of faith and in 1974 named Father Michael Scanlan its new president. Almost immediately upon taking office, he was presented with petitions asking the school to drop its Sunday morning Mass requirement (because, they argued, no one wanted to get up that early), and demanding open coed dorms (a logical extension of the growing permissiveness on campus). It was a test of Father Scanlan's commitment, his administrative abilities, and his backbone. It was, in other words, the sort of test university presidents usually fail. But Father Scanlan is not the usual university president.

Acting quickly, Father Scanlan—a Harvard law graduate before becoming a priest—called a meeting of the entire college community, giving only three hours' notice, thus ensuring that campus dissidents would not have time to organize a boycott or other disruptive actions. Speaking to the assembled faculty and students, Father Scanlan flatly rejected the proposal to drop the Mass. In fact, he said, he would be the one celebrating the Sunday Mass from now on. And because of his emphasis on charismatic worship, Father Scanlan warned that the Mass would probably last twice as long as before.

He was no less definitive on the demand for coed dorms. Not only would the dorms *not* become coed, Father Scanlan announced, but beginning that next fall all of the school's dorms would be organized into "households" of ten to fifteen members that would set and share mutual spiritual goals. No one would be exempt.

A Remarkable Turnaround

"There was quite an uproar," Father Scanlan later told *New Covenant* magazine. "It was the most difficult thing I ever did with students, and it really was hard for them. But I was very concerned about student life at the college. In addition to the alcohol and drug problems, many students were terribly lonely. That meeting was the beginning of a system on campus to build committed relationships. Households are no longer compulsory, but the vast majority of students choose to belong to them."

They also became one of the cornerstones of the university's revival. Since Father Scanlan took over, enrollment has more than doubled, theology has become the favorite major on campus, and the Franciscan University of Steubenville has recommitted itself to the liberal arts in the Catholic tradition. And defying the national trend, the SAT scores of Franciscan's freshmen have been moving steadily up. In the most recent academic year, the composite average rose by nearly twenty points, and now stands some eighty points above the national average—this at a time when the decreasing numbers of high school grads has led most schools to lower admissions standards. Misbehavior, once a problem on a campus that had a reputation for raucous partying, has all but disappeared. In 1991 there was exactly one arrest for drunkenness; none for drugs. The remarkable turnaround can be attributed in large measure to Father Scanlan's leadership. He took the job under two conditions: that spiritual matters be given first priority and that he be given full authority to redirect the university. He has used that authority to the fullest and placed the university squarely in the Roman Catholic tradition. He has also struck the proper balance between academic standards and doctrinal purity. The Catholic college, Father Scanlan declared in an address on "Making and Keeping Catholic Colleges Catholic," must "take a stand in the classical debate between Athens and Jerusalem. How much is it of the nature of Jerusalem, called church, and how much is it of Athens, that is, the classical education beginning with Socrates, Plato and Aristotle, and

Franciscan University of Steubenville

Year Founded: 1946
Total Cost: $12,190
Total Enrollment: 1,851
Total Applicants: 1,002
  85% accepted
  50% of accepted enrolled
SAT Averages: 473V/490M
Financial Aid:
  86% applied
  95% judged to have need
  100% of those judged
    were given aid
No ROTC Program Offered
Application Information:
  Mrs. Margaret Weber
  Director of Admissions
  Franciscan University of
    Steubenville
  Steubenville, OH 43952
  Telephone: (800) 783-6220
Application Deadlines:
  No early decision
  Regular decision: rolling

continuing through the tradition of the liberal arts?"

For Father Scanlan, the answer was simple: "We have to be Jerusalem and build Athens as best we can within: build the best possible Athens, the best possible scholarship and academic standards."

Community of Scholars

With that focus, the university's general core curriculum is extensive, requiring fifteen credits in the communications core, which includes English composition, analytic philosophy, modern languages, speech, drama, mathematics, and film study; fifteen credits in a humanities core, which includes courses in art, history, literature, philosophy, and theology; six credits in the social science core, with courses in history, political science, economics, psychology, and sociology; six credits in the theology core; six credits in the natural science core, with courses in biology, physics, and chemistry; and six credits at the intermediate level of a modern foreign language.

Even more impressive, however, are the university's two honors programs: the Great Books of Western Civilization, and the Humanities and Catholic Culture Program. The first is a four-year-long series of eight seminars in Early Classical Thought (Homer to Thucydides), Later Classical Thought (Aristophanes to Seneca), Rome and the Early Fathers (Lucretius to St. Benedict), Medieval Thought (Bede to Chaucer), the Renaissance (Montaigne to Francis de Sales), the Enlightenment" (Swift to Goethe), the Nineteenth Century (Tolstoy to Newman), the Twentieth Century (Dostoevsky to John Paul II).

The program's approach to the great works is in the best traditions of liberal learning. The program description reads:

> Vigorous discussion encourages thought about the larger and ultimate questions of life. Indeed, one of the most important elements of the honors seminar class is "the community of scholars" that is formed in the love of learning. Through the seminar method, students can learn the art of analysis. . . .
>
> Finally, through contact with and vigorous discussion of these great works of Western Civilization, it is hoped that each student can come to a deeper understanding of reality itself and of his own nature, place and purpose before God, the world and the human community.

It is the duty of good education to arrive at wisdom by means of a definite order.

—St. Augustine

The second honors program, the Humanities and Catholic Culture Program, is, again, a four-year program that draws its inspiration from historian Christopher Dawson. The courses draw upon literature, history, theology, foreign languages, and the natural sciences to discuss the development of Western culture and the role of Catholicism in its rise.

Fittingly, the university's study-abroad program takes place at a Carthusian monastery in the Austrian Alps.

A Charismatic Community

Although we have stressed Father Scanlan's role, it is important to note that the success of the Franciscan University of Steubenville also rests on the solid and resolute support he receives from its faculty and trustees. Unlike many other institutions, the university has focused on "revivifying and rescuing" faculty members who "came in with a deep sense of purpose but maybe over the years have lost it or become confused." Professors who use their positions to propagate Marxism, secular humanism, lesbianism, and feminism "as a priority over a Christian commitment" have been eased out.

We acknowledge elsewhere in this book that St. John's College may be the most intellectual college in the country. But Franciscan may well be the most *spiritual*. And, like St. John's, it is clearly not for everyone. The atmosphere of the school is suffused with Scanlan's own charismatic form of Catholic worship. The school's chapel is filled twice a day; more than 60 percent of its resident students attend Mass daily. The "households" create close personal and spiritual relations among students and draft basic commitments, goals, and activities for the school year. We suspect that given this intense focus on religious life, non-Catholic students might do better to look elsewhere, but for the deeply religious student, Steubenville may prove the academic version of the city on a hill.

It surely deserves serious consideration. Against heavy odds and the dominant trends of the academic culture, the Franciscan University of Steubenville has proved that by emphasizing "the unchangeable values and norms of the college," an institution can revivify itself and reaffirm the most basic values of liberal learning. □

Furman

Greenville, South Carolina

Education and Elegance

Let us, for a moment, celebrate the South. Where else can we find a campus festooned with rose gardens, well-manicured grounds, redbrick colonial architecture, coeds who dress like fashion models, an eighteen-hole golf course, and a lake (man-made) wherein swims the noblest of birds, the swan? Add the proximity to the Blue Ridge Mountains and the nearly two dozen tennis courts, and it is not difficult to see why Furman has been called the "Country Club of the South."

Receptiveness to Beauty

But it would be a gross error to dismiss Furman as merely a julep-by-the-eighteenth-green academic throwback. Furman is the senior college of the South Carolina Baptist Convention, and, although not directly affiliated with Convention, the school takes its commitment to Christian ideals seriously. Furman, the university says, "aspires to be a community of scholars which introduces students to the methods and concepts of liberal learning and prepares them for the life-long process of becoming educated." These commitments are reflected not only in the fact that Furman is a dry campus, but also in its solid liberal arts curriculum.

A recent report by the university's president declared that "we continue to provide our students with a strong, indeed 'classical,' liberal arts curriculum, taking care to avoid the educational fads and trendiness that often occur in response to highly publicized studies that recommend reform."

Many of those trends involved replacing questions of value with an emphasis on the mere accumulation of data, the apotheosis of "fact" at the expense of thought. But as Alfred North Whitehead noted, true culture is not the piling up of useless data, but the "activity of thought, and receptiveness to beauty and humane feeling. . . . A merely well-informed man is the most useless bore on God's earth."

The Best from the West

The goal of Furman's general education program is to develop its students' skills in "thinking and communicating clearly and effectively"; "to develop a basic knowledge and understanding of the physical universe, of society and of themselves, as well as a critical appreciation of the ways such knowledge is acquired"; "to develop an awareness of the moral, aesthetic and spiritual issues inherent in life and society"; "to develop a knowledge of other cultures"; "to develop the habit of searching for relationships among the various forms of human thought and feeling"; and "to develop an awareness of the intrinsic value of thought and learning."

Students are required to take an introductory English composition course as well as a sequence of courses introducing them to the history and thought of the West. They can satisfy that requirement in one of two ways, either by taking Ideas and Institutions in Modern Western Civilization, Introduction to Biblical Study, and a English literature survey course, or by taking a three-course sequence of humanities courses: The Roots of Western Civilization, The Search for New Authorities, and "Revolution, Progress and Anxiety. They must take also an additional upper-level course in English, history, classics, philosophy, or religion.

Furman also expects its students to demonstrate proficiency in a foreign language. Other requirements include one to three courses in mathematics, two introductory courses in the natural sciences, two introductory courses in the social sciences, a course in the fine arts, one course in physical education, and a course from Furman's Asian-African program.

And lest Furman students spend too much time on the links or playing tennis, the school requires them to attend a certain number of plays, lectures, and concerts during their undergraduate careers as part of its Cultural Life Program. A student enrolled at Furman for four years, for example, would be expected to attend at least thirty-six designated events. Furman also offers options for studying abroad. The English, political science, history, and economics departments jointly sponsor a fall term in England, where students study in London and Stratford-on-Avon. The department of classics and

Furman University

Year Founded: 1826
Total Cost: $15,556
Total Enrollment: 2,474
Total Applicants: 2,667
 74% accepted
 39% of accepted enrolled
SAT Middle Range Scores:
 1050–1250
Financial Aid:
 80% applied
 67% judged to have need
 100% of those judged
  were given aid
ROTC Program Offered
Application Information:
 Mr. J. Carey Thompson
 Director of Admissions
 Furman University
 Greenville, SC 29613
 Telephone: (803) 294-2034
Application Deadlines:
 Early decision: 12/1
 Regular decision: 2/1

modern languages offers a term in Madrid, Munich, and Paris. Winter term travel in a recent year consisted of programs in the Mideast and the Galápagos islands.

The Furman Family

One distinctive program that deserves mention is the Collegiate Educational Service Corps, a volunteer program run completely by students. More than half of Furman's students work as regular unpaid volunteers in more than seventy agencies in the Greenville area, including day-care centers, children's hospitals, neighborhood centers, nursing homes, and miniparks. The program not only instills the values of voluntarism, but also provides a firsthand lesson in non-statist approaches to social problems.

As you might expect of a school of Furman's caliber, classes are small and students feel that for the most part the faculty is helpful and accessible. "Furman is like a family away from home," one biology major reports. "The administration and faculty take a personal interest in each student." Says one Furman philosophy major: "The very best thing about Furman is the relationship with your professors. They genuinely care about you. In fact, I still go by to see professors I had freshman year and they remember me."

Although Furman draws students from forty states and several foreign countries, more than a third are from South Carolina, and the overwhelming majority are from upper-middle-class, conservative backgrounds. In keeping with its southern traditions, Furman boasts one of the best-dressed student bodies around. But again, it is not all for show. Furman graduates have consistently done well in gaining admission to professional and graduate schools, with acceptance rates of 80 to 90 percent for medical, business, and law schools.

Not everything, however, is idyllic in Greenville. There are elements of the faculty that would like to see Furman become more research-oriented—more like other big-name universities, such as its arch-competitor, the University of North Carolina. Some Furman profs have begun arguing that the school should begin to require more academic "research" and publications in scholarly journals for tenure candidates. But the opinion is far from unanimous and some faculty members seem to recognize that a shift away from Furman's traditional focus is

> The school should always have as its aim that the young man leave it as a harmonious personality, not as a specialist. This in my opinion is true in a certain sense even for technical schools. . . . The development of general ability for independent thinking and judgment should always be placed foremost, not the acquisition of special knowledge.
>
> —*Albert Einstein*

a Faustian bargain. Alas, it is an increasingly common one in small and midsize schools that are caught up in academia's more virulent forms of status envy, in which every teachers' college in southern Arkansas fancies itself the next Harvard. Too often, the result of this mad scramble after academic prestige is that schools with good teaching records end up eviscerating their curriculum and devaluing the classroom—and still end up as third-rate research institutions.

At its best, however, Furman manages to marry research and undergraduate teaching in a creative and impressive fashion. Furman's associate academic dean, William M. Christie, tells us that much faculty research in Greenville, whether in computer science or linguistics, chemistry or history, is "carried on to involve and benefit undergraduate students, not as a means of achieving some abstract kind of national prestige." In fact, guidelines for grant support of research projects "state explicitly that preference is given to faculty who involve students as partners in their research." This is the way it ought to be.

Furman's strength lies in its distinctive mission and its focus on undergraduate education; to the extent it abandons that clear-sighted commitment, it could become just another in the long list of Harvard-wannabes that already litter the landscape. But as Dean Christie says, "The classroom is never slighted at Furman. . . . We are committed to the belief that good faculty research can be the very best form of undergraduate education." Point taken.

We suspect that Marcus Aurelius had other things than the university in mind when he wrote: "Occupy thyself with few things, says the philosopher, if thou wouldst be tranquil." It remains sound advice, however, especially for schools like Furman, which does the few things it does exceedingly well. □

Gonzaga

Spokane, Washington

Faith and Reason

We suspect that some of our readers might not be able immediately to identify Aloysius Gonzaga. He has never been one of the superstar saints, but he is an unusually appropriate namesake for a liberal arts university. The heir of a noble family and page at the court of Francesco de Medici, young Gonzaga entered the Society of Jesus (the Jesuits) in 1585. Moving to Rome as a seminarian, Gonzaga arrived in time to encounter a vicious plague sweeping the city. Heedless of his own health or safety, the young Jesuit worked night and day to care for the sick and dying. As a result of his efforts, he died of exhaustion at the age of twenty-three. In 1729 he was declared the patron saint of youth.

We are not sure about this, but we suspect that the young saint's influence may have something to do with the quality of education students receive at Gonzaga, the oldest Jesuit college in the Pacific Northwest. Although Gonzaga has graduate students, they do not teach in the classroom. All classes are taught by professors, and classes tend to be small.

Teaching First

Says a recent Gonzaga senior and National Merit Scholar:

> Gonzaga's reputation for good teaching is well deserved. The instruction here is excellent. In addition, both the faculty and the staff are readily accessible. . . . They are consistently willing to discuss any problems or questions with students and frequently go out of their way to accommodate students' individual needs. There is no question that Gonzaga's faculty is concerned first and foremost with good teaching.

Equally important is the humanistic tradition of the school, which suffuses all aspects of the curriculum. The school's president, Bernard J. Coughlin, S.J., describes Gonzaga as striving for excellence "by integrating science and art, faith and reason, action and contemplation." In practice that means that moral and ethical considerations are an integral part not merely of the liberal arts courses, but of the school's various professional programs as well, not excepting education, engineering, business, and law.

It all appears to work. One national survey found that Gonzaga graduates recommended their alma mater to high school students more readily than any other alumni group in the survey—90 percent said they probably or definitely would recommend Gonzaga to a student in search of a college. Significantly, the most frequently cited comment was supported for the philosophy and religious studies requirements, which graduates felt helped them in personal, moral, ethical, and spiritual development.

The Core Program

Nearly half the College of Arts and Science's curriculum is made up of the core curriculum. All students are covered by the all-university core, which is grouped into five basic areas. Under Thought and Expression, freshmen are required to take a sequence of three courses—English Composition, Critical Thinking, and Speech Communication—which are intended to be taken as a bloc in a single semester. All Gonzaga students must also take nine credits in philosophy, including Philosophy of Human Nature and a course in ethics, and nine credits in religious studies, including an introductory-level course in scriptural studies, an intermediate-level course in Christian doctrine, and an advanced-level course in applied theology. Students must also take a course in mathematics and an English literature course in Literary Genres.

In addition, undergraduates in the College of Arts and Sciences must complete a two-semester survey of the history of Western civilization (students have the option of substituting a course in American history for one of the two Western civ courses); a course in art, music, or theater; a laboratory science course; a course in British or American literature; an additional course in mathematics or natural science; two courses in the social sciences; and a course in a foreign language or a foreign culture.

From our perspective Gonzaga's curriculum is

Gonzaga University

Year Founded: 1887
Total Cost: $15,600
Total Enrollment: 5,200
Total Applicants: 1,912
  79% accepted
  41% of accepted enrolled
ACT Average: 25
Financial Aid:
  78% applied
  60% judged to have need
  60% of those judged were
  given aid
ROTC Program Offered
Application Information:
  Mr. Phil Ballinger
  Dean of Admissions
  Gonzaga University
  East 502 Boone
  Spokane, WA 99258
  Telephone: (509) 484-6484
Application Deadlines:
  No early decision
  Regular decision: rolling

both comprehensive and well designed. Students cannot graduate without studying the history, philosophy, literature, science, or religious thought of the West. There appear to be few "gut" courses, and no easy way to evade the humanistic education required of all students.

The Measure of Success

Gonzaga's rigorous humanistic approach to education appears to be paying off. The National Collegiate Debate Championship was won by two Gonzaga students in 1989. In 1990, Gonzaga's business school became only the third in eastern Washington to win accreditation from the American Assembly of Collegiate Schools of Business. Gonzaga was also recently selected to participate in an exchange program with Tbilisi State University in the former Soviet Georgia. Another exchange program sends students to the People's Republic of China, and a third is being finalized with a Japanese university. In addition, study-abroad programs are offered in Spain, England, France, and Italy, including its Gonzaga-in-Florence Program (in which juniors can spend a full year studying abroad), located in the city of Aloysius Gonzaga's birth.

Moreover, Gonzaga appears to be a school on the rise. It recently completed a successful $33 million capital-fund drive two years ahead of schedule, and subsequently raised its goal to $62 million. Gonzaga is in the process of building a $20 million, 135,000-square-foot, state-of-the-art library, which will be known as the Center for Information and Technology. There are also plans for a new center for the visual arts, and the school's president envisions an institute or center for leadership studies.

But what about Spokane? We don't think it is necessary to remark on the area's spectacular natural beauty. But it is perhaps worth noting that Spokane is not quite as backwoods as a non-westerner might imagine. The city is the hub of a four-state region (two Canadian provinces are also nearby) which relies on Spokane's business, service, and transportation facilities. Spokane's metropolitan area has a population of 355,000, which gives students ample opportunities for work and socializing, while maintaining a small-town atmosphere unusually conducive to the study of the liberal arts and the contemplation of the ends and duties of man.

> The liberally educated person is one who is able to resist the easy and preferred answers, not because he is obstinate but because he knows others worthy of consideration.
>
> —*Allan Bloom*

Grove City

Grove City, Pennsylvania

Defeating the Philistines

I t is perhaps inevitable that Grove City College is
best known for its legal battle with the federal
bureaucracy and for its doughty crusade for the
independence and integrity of small private colleges. But Grove City College is on our recommended list not because of its legal exploits, but
rather because of its solid values, the quality of its
academic program, and its outstanding new core
curriculum.

Although we hesitate to cite other college guides,
we do note that *Money* magazine has consistently
rated Grove City among the top five private schools
nationwide—ahead of Princeton, Stanford, and
Harvard among others—in its "Value Rankings," a
measure that factored in cost, student-faculty ratio,
class rank of freshmen, and SAT scores. It has also
been rated among the top twenty-five small comprehensive schools in the country by *U.S. News
and World Report*. Grove City's quality is also reflected by other objective measures. In recent
years, Grove City graduates have averaged 99 percent admission rates at the law, medical, and graduate schools to which they have applied. Would-be
teachers who graduate from Grove City's education
department have ranked first in the State of Pennsylvania's teacher's exam. And Grove City has been
selected for the John Templeton Foundation Honor
Roll for Character Building Colleges, and the Templeton list of leading colleges for free-enterprise
teaching.

Grove City's prospects for continued improvement appear promising: there are now nearly four
applications for every opening in the freshmen
class. Seventy-six percent of Grove City freshmen
finished in the top fifth of their high school graduating class (half finished in the top tenth), and the
average combined SAT score for entering students
is now more than 1100, placing Grove City among
the most selective schools in the country.

David and Goliath

This outstanding record often tends to be over-shadowed by the *Grove City* case, and in truth the school's fight with the federal government is eloquent testimony to its commitment to its bedrock principles.

In 1977 the Department of Health, Education, and Welfare (HEW) demanded that Grove City sign a government compliance form committing the school to abide by a series of regulations barring sex discrimination. Grove City had in fact never discriminated against women, and had no objection to the law itself.

But the issue was much broader. Did the federal government have the right to impose its regulations on schools like Grove City, even if they accepted no government money or aid? Grove City thought not, and refused to sign the compliance forms. Since the school received no federal aid of any kind, HEW had little leverage over Grove City itself, so it chose to retaliate against its student, many of whom received federal student aid. The government argued that because some students received Pell Grants, it had the power to regulate all of the college's programs. And it gave Grove City an ultimatum, essentially using the school's students as hostages: either sign the form, or HEW would cut off all grants to the students. To its eternal credit, Grove City refused to back down. "Our concern," the school's president declared, "is that, as history has demonstrated, even limited government control inevitably spreads like a virus to become inclusive control."

In 1980 the school won a major victory in federal court. Noting that "there is absolutely no evidence of sex discrimination" on the part of the college, the judge ruled that HEW had no power to cut off student aid or to force the college to sign the compliance forms. Sadly, subsequent legal maneuverings have narrowed the scope of the ruling.

The Value of Liberal Learning

Like Hillsdale College, however, Grove City continues to assert its independence and continues to refuse government aid of any kind. It has also moved to provide its own aid to students who cannot now receive federal grants or support. Its independence has certainly done it no harm. In fact, quite the contrary seems to have happened.

Grove City College

Year Founded: 1876
Total Cost: $7,550
Total Enrollment: 2,217
Total Applicants: 2,604
  43% accepted
  55% of accepted enrolled
SAT Averages: 509V/577M
Financial Aid:
  70% applied
  58% judged to have need
  94% of those judged were
  given aid
ROTC Program Offered
Application Information:
  Mr. Jeff Mincey
  Director of Admissions
  Grove City College
  100 Campus Drive
  Grove City, PA 16127
  Telephone: (412) 458-2100
Application Deadlines:
  Early decision: 11/15
  Regular decision: 2/15

In 1990 Grove City introduced a new liberal arts core closely modeled on the curriculum recommended by Lynne Cheney, chairman of the National Endowment for the Humanities, in her report *50 Hours*. In so doing, it reaffirmed its traditional commitment to the values of liberal learning. Said the school's academic vice president: "We are rejecting what I call political, ideological, or philosophical agendas that go against objective truth as the goal of liberal learning."

The new core (general education program) is built around a three-year interdisciplinary humanities sequence known as the Civilization Series. The new program reflects Grove City's solid grounding in the traditional principles embodied in the vision of the school's founders. Declares the course catalog:

Rejecting relativism and secularism, it fosters intellectual, moral, spiritual and social development consistent with a Christian commitment to truth, morality and freedom. . . . While many points of view are examined, the college continues to unapologetically advocate preservation of America's religious, political and economic heritage of individual freedom and responsibility.

Freshman at Grove City begin with Genesis of Civilization, a course that focuses on the ancient Middle East (including the Old Testament) and the Homeric foundation of classical Greek ideas. The next semester, students study Athens and Jerusalem, discussing the "leading ideas of classical Greece, Republican and Imperial Rome, and early Christian Europe." About half of the class is devoted to study of the New Testament. Other topics include Plato's *Republic*, Virgil's *Aeneid*, the Greek dramatists, the Hellenization of Palestine, and Roman art and architecture.

As sophomores, students take a course in the Middle Ages, Renaissance and Reformation, with topics ranging from St. Augustine's *Confessions*, Dante's *Inferno*, and Shakespeare's *Hamlet* to the Koran. In the spring students take a course in the Birth of Modernity, which covers seventeenth- and eighteenth-century Europe and America. Topics covered range from Galileo, Bacon, Newton and the birth of science, to Pope's *Essay on Man*, Molière's *Tartuffe*, and Voltaire's *Candide*. The course also includes Adam Smith, Enlightenment art, music, and architecture, and the *Federalist Papers*.

Liberal education develops a sense of right, duty and honor; and more and more in the modern world, large business rests on rectitude and honor as well as on good judgment.

—*Charles William Eliot*

In the junior year, the Civilization Series turns to Culture in the Nineteenth Century, with discussions of Kant, Hegel, Tocqueville, Marx, Nietzsche, Darwin, Melville, Dostoevsky, Freud, and Tolstoy. Students are also introduced to romantic and modern art, music, and architecture. The final course Culture in the Twentieth Century, covers Tolstoy, Michael Novak, Hannah Arendt, Aldous Huxley, Elie Wiesel, Albert Camus, C. S. Lewis, Aleksandr Solzhenitsyn, and T. S. Eliot, as well as contemporary art, music, and architecture.

In addition to the humanities core, Grove City students must take six credits in introductory social science courses (from at least two different departments), eight hours of lab science in introductory natural science courses, and six hours of mathematics. They must also demonstrate writing competency. Other requirements include two hours of physical education, and chapel credit for each semester. Although affiliated with the Presbyterian Church, Grove City is not narrowly sectarian, preferring to regard itself in general as a Christian liberal arts college.

Big Time, Small Town

Located in a small town about sixty miles north of Pittsburgh, Grove City's estate-like campus covers about 150 acres and is home to more than a hundred student organizations, sixteen varsity sports, and a quite impressive array of facilities. Its Technological Learning Center, for example, houses two mainframe computers as well as 120 IBM, Apple, and Zenith personal computers; the library has close to a half million volumes and a computerized card catalog and periodical index; and its Machine Design and Robotics Laboratory provides the unusual opportunity for undergraduate engineering students to apply their knowledge to hands-on projects. For the athletically minded, Grove City's Physical Learning Center has two swimming pools, a fitness center with Nautilus and Universal machines, an indoor track, four full-size basketball courts (which can also be used for indoor tennis or volleyball), and eight racquetball courts.

Although you may have heard of Grove City only in relation to its David and Goliath fight with the federal government, it offers quite a bit more than just moral courage (which is no small thing). Grove City College deserves a serious look from any student in search of a school that is not only conservative in orientation, but committed to the great conversation of the West in an atmosphere of academic seriousness and quality.　　　□

Gustavus Adolphus
St. Peter, Minnesota

Winning the Cold War

This is probably as good a time as any to remind our readers that this is not a guide to conservative colleges: Our top priority is the availability of a quality liberal arts education in an atmosphere free of politicization and intimidation. That brings us to Gustavus Adolphus, which is not a conservative institution. But it is an outstanding liberal arts college that deserves a closer look.

Founded in 1862 by Swedish Lutheran immigrants, this small (about 2,200 students—not so small by our standards) liberal arts school has a reputation for intimacy, friendliness, and academic quality, all of which tend to counterbalance the disadvantages of having to spend winters in the frozen North. As one recent graduate said, "I value the personal challenge here. Knowing our professors well seems to make anything possible, and everything worthwhile."

The Second Time Around

The school's literature urges students to "Surpass Your Expectations" and unabashedly acknowledges that the development of moral and spiritual values is at the center of its curriculum.

In 1985, Gustavus Adolphus made a good thing even better by introducing its Curriculum II, an integrated and well-designed liberal arts program. The new core was consistent with Gustavus Adolphus's traditional emphasis on the humanities, the development of critical thinking, and its concern for quality teaching.

Under the Curriculum II program, sixty members of each entering class take in their first semester a sequence of specially designed interdisciplinary courses, beginning with Historical Perspective I, an introduction to Western civilization from the ancient Greeks to the Middle Ages; and The Biblical Tradition, an exploration of the major contributions of the Judeo-Christian tradition. Subsequent courses include The Individual and Morality, Historical Perspective II, Quantitative Reasoning, and The Natural World.

What impresses us about this core is the acknowledgment of the centrality of the Western tradition and its roots in the great dialogue between Athens and Jerusalem (which is to say, between reason and faith), which has shaped the history and form of Western religion, philosophy, literature, politics, and law. We are also impressed by the emphasis on morality and values, too often overlooked in the highly specialized curriculums of higher education. Combined with basic courses in quantitative reason and science, the core provides a broad introduction to the best that has been thought and said in the Western tradition. Said one student: "We're really understanding the parallels between subjects, and I think it's fascinating."

For students in the regular curriculum, core requirements account for about one-third of a student's undergraduate courses. They include one course in arts appreciation; one in arts participation; a basic course in religion; four courses in Meaning and Value, the Use of Language, and the Historical Process; two courses in quantitative and empirical reasoning; two courses in Human Behavior and Social Institutions; one course in personal fitness; and two courses in foreign culture (at least one of which must be in a non-Western culture).

In addition, students must take three courses from at least two departments with a substantial component of writing. This emphasis on writing is one of Gustavus Adolphus's strengths. While a number of schools have taken to boasting about their "writing across the curriculum" programs, Gustavus Adolphus appears actually to take writing seriously. "Again and again," one educator told *The New York Times* in 1986, "I've met English teachers deeply committed to the task of getting students to write well, [but] at Gustavus Adolphus the commitment reaches across the whole faculty."

Gustavus Adolphus College

Year Founded: 1862
Total Cost: $15,860
Total Enrollment: 2,271
Total Applicants: 1,701
  79% accepted
  46% of accepted enrolled
SAT Middle Range
  Averages: 970–1240
Financial Aid:
  76% applied
  65% judged to have need
  100% of those judged
  were given aid
ROTC Program Offered
Application Information:
  Mr. Mark Anderson
  Director of Admissions
  Gustavus Adolphus
    College
  800 West College Avenue
  St. Peter, MN 56082
  Telephone:
    (800) GUSTAVUS
    (507) 933-7676
Application Deadlines:
  Early decision: 11/15
  Regular decision: 5/1

Good Students, Good Teachers

Despite the school's small size, one of its obvious strengths is its natural science programs; one tribute to its reputation is the fact that Gustavus

Adolphus hosts the Nobel Conference on science and values. The school's science facilities are the envy of other small schools in its class. "Except for some truly exotic research tools, I can't think of anything we don't have for our students' benefit, from the genetics lab to our electron microscope," says one biology professor. "And they use those facilities daily as a part of regular class assignments or through special opportunities like our Partners in Scholarship program [which grants merit-based scholarships]."

The school typically graduates more American Chemical Society–certified majors than any other similar institution in the Midwest, a fact that faculty members rather graciously attribute to the quality of the students. More than 40 percent of Gustavus Adolphus students finished in the top 10 percent of their high school graduating class. Reflecting the school's growing national reputation, those students are drawn from forty states and nineteen foreign countries. In fact, professors say the quality of Gustavus Adolphus students is one of the major draws in faculty recruiting, while students consistently cite the attention and accessibility of the faculty as the school's major asset. Another draw might well be the active international program: 40 percent of Gustavus Adolphus students take advantage of the school's opportunity to study abroad in two dozen countries in Europe, Asia, Africa, and South America.

> Education has for its object the formation of character.
>
> —*Herbert Spencer*

The Cold War

Although Minnesota's climate cannot be counted as a major draw during winter months, Gustavus Adolphus's campus deserves special mention. St. Peter is a town of about nine thousand people located on the beautiful Minnesota River—sixty-five miles from Minneapolis/St. Paul and ten minutes from Mankato. Yet campus life is anything but isolated. Dominated by the spire of Christ Chapel, which is visible throughout the valley (a symbolic reminder of the continuing role of the school's Swedish Lutheran tradition), the campus covers 294 acres and houses major facilities that include the Alfred Nobel Hall of Science, the 220,000-volume Folke Bernadotte Library, the new $11 million Lund Physical Education Center, and the Schaefer Fine Arts Center. The emphasis at Gustavus is on being involved—freshmen are even offered free music lessons. Upon finding all of this in the heart of central Minnesota, the college reports, visitors often remark, "I didn't realize it was so beautiful," and, "All this for just two thousand students?"

In our first edition we quipped:

> If we have a qualm about Gustavus Adolphus, it's because of its active Peace Education Program and its decision to sponsor an annual May Day (*that* day of all days) gathering of "peace scholars," during which all of the usual suspects gather to one-up one another in their enthusiasm for the latest rage in disarmament. The school is also known for the proliferation of consciousness-raising awareness groups—anti-nuke groups, Amnesty International, etc.—that must surely become quite nauseating over the long winter months when students are trapped in close proximity with the various New Age agonizers.

There we go again! Well, Kathryn Christenson of GA's Office of Public Affairs set us straight:

> In northern European culture, the first day of May has been celebrated as marking the return of the season of life and growth. In particular, May Day is a Swedish holiday, and Gustavus Adolphus honors its Swedish heritage. The signal MAYDAY! is the international call of distress. The founders of the MAYDAY! conference ten years ago this spring were aware of the dual significance of May Day as a celebration of life and MAYDAY! as a warning that our time on earth is not endless. They had one other object in mind as well: determination that the Communist Party not claim sole ownership of May Day.

Fair enough. Our joke has lost most of its punch anyhow, now that the only May Day parades left are in Havana and Pyongyang. And in any case, there is clearly a healthy mix of opinions at Gustavus Adolphus, and the overall balance probably still tips to a conservative student body (although the faculty remains liberal). We think every school deserves at least one lapse, and Gustavus Adolphus more than compensates by the strength of its educational program. □

Hampden-Sydney

Hampden-Sydney, Virginia

Rebel with a Cause

What happens when a college spurns every fashionable trend? The correct answer is that it becomes one of the very best, if little-known, colleges in the country. Hampden-Sydney is doing everything "wrong," and proving that it's right.

Begin with the faculty. You cannot expect high-caliber scholars, active in their fields, to be happy in a small, rurally isolated college where teaching is emphasized and professors are intensely involved in campus life. Right? Wrong. That is exactly the situation on this beautiful campus in the green, rolling hills of southern Virginia. The faculty is outstanding; their morale is extraordinarily high.

Turn next to the curriculum. No one believes that students today will tolerate a demanding set of requirements and a limited menu of courses to choose from. Wrong again. At Hampden-Sydney students know the benefit that results: a sound, coherent education that sustains an intellectually vital community. There is nothing like it at most other institutions, where dissipated intellectual energies lead to superficiality and fragmentation.

Finally, consider the student body. An all-male school, one of few to have successfully resisted coeducation, could not possibly be anything but dull. Wrong, wrong, wrong. With three women's colleges and a number of coeducational institutions within an easy drive, weekends at Hampden-Sydney can be positively exciting. But Monday thru Friday, the main effects of single-sex education appear to be a more intense classroom experience, and a spirited camaraderie outside of class.

Demanding Proficiency

The advantages of smallness are contained in a curriculum that deliberately limits itself to the best. There are very few questionable courses and no questionable majors at Hampden-Sydney. There are no "oppression studies," no courses in "popular

103

Hampden-Sydney College

Year Founded: 1776
Total Cost: $16,401
Total Enrollment: 945
Total Applicants: 850
  67.5% accepted
  41.5% of accepted
  enrolled
SAT Averages: 508V/558M
Financial Aid:
  37.4% judged to have
  need
  100% of those judged
  were given aid
ROTC Program Offered
Application Information:
  Ms. Anita H. Garland
  Director of Admissions
  Hampden-Sydney
    College
  Hampden-Sydney, VA
    23943
  Telephone: (800) 755-0733
Application Deadlines:
  Early decision: 11/15
  Regular decision: 3/1

culture." Some may feel that the curriculum is too limited: there is no department of sociology, for example, although some courses in that subject are offered by the psychology department. Others will surely not miss a discipline that tends to balance intellectual sterility with doctrinaire Marxism.

At many schools political science has suffered much the same fate as sociology, but this is not the case at Hampden-Sydney: instead of avoiding the subject, H-S has built a department solidly grounded in the history of political thought. The philosophical foundations of the American republic are emphasized, but Marxist and other critics of liberal democracy are also studied. The result is an unusually successful department of political science—at the undergraduate level, there are only two or three others like it in the United States. The departments of chemistry, biology, mathematics, and economics are also especially notable at Hampden-Sydney, but then in no department can one go seriously wrong; moreover, English, history, and classics each boasts significant strengths. Philosophy, which had been thin, acquired an additional professor several years ago, bringing it up to par.

Perhaps the most important and remarkable educational feature at Hampden-Sydney is its demanding set of graduation requirements. Of these the most distinctive is the proficiency requirement in "rhetoric," by which is meant an ability to express oneself clearly and cogently in writing. This requirement consists of a sequence of two-semester courses, from some or all of which those with demonstrated proficiency are exempted. (There is also an introductory course in grammar and composition for those who need it, and an advanced course in public speaking which may be taken as an elective.) No one graduates from Hampden-Sydney unable to marshal his thoughts effectively in writing.

In addition, there is a proficiency requirement in foreign languages and a set of distribution requirements as well that mandate 44 semester hours of courses out of the 120 hours required for graduation. These consist of four semester courses in the natural sciences and mathematics, three in the social sciences, and seven in the humanities (including the fine arts). Contrary to the common—and dishonest—practice at most institutions, there are no easy ways to satisfy these requirements. Students are given a variety of options, but one way or another they must take at least one laboratory course, at least one course in college-level mathematics, at least two semesters in the history of Western civilization or the classic works of the Western tradition, at least one course in literary classics, and at least one course in appreciation or history of one of the fine arts.

The Wabash of the South

The quality of student life outside of class is as important as what happens within the classroom. Fraternities (to which about half the students belong) and sports play their normal role at Hampden-Sydney (making H-S seem very much like Indiana's Wabash College), but it is the honor system, the close relations of faculty and students, and the high morale generally which really distinguish this college. Other institutions boast the same features, but few if any with as much right. One indirect measure of this is the level of alumni support. About 30 percent is normal, 50 percent very good; but 70 percent of Hampden-Sydney alumni maintain their interest in and offer contributions to the college. Very few colleges produce that kind of loyalty.

As at many other colleges and universities in the southern United States, relations between white and black students here are far better than they have become, in recent years, on many northern campuses. This is not to deny that there are still some strains. About 3 percent of the students are black. But they have not separated themselves from the rest of the student body, and the fraternities are integrated. A few years ago, a black student was president of the student government (he was also Virginia's only Rhodes Scholar that year). The proportion of black students will probably grow, in part through a new program the college has instituted that helps prepare undereducated high school students in southern Virginia for college work. The graduates of that program normally meet the admissions requirements of less demanding Virginia colleges, but it is hoped that some will eventually matriculate at Hampden-Sydney. One positive factor in race relations at Hampden-Sydney is that admissions requirements are not lowered for minority students.

Hampden-Sydney is the nation's tenth oldest college. It has been in continuous operation since 1776, and its colors are taken from those its men adopted as their uniform when they fought in the Revolu-

> The desire of knowledge, like the thirst of riches, increases ever with the acquisition of it.
>
> —*Laurence Sterne*

tionary War. Though the original buildings no longer stand, many existing structures date from the early 1800s. Additional buildings have been erected in more recent years, but in keeping with the style of the earliest surviving structures, and renovation of older buildings proceeds apace. The college, already set in a lovely countryside, now owns 650 acres of land, much of it wooded. Hunting is a favored pastime.

Despite its long history, Hampden-Sydney remains little known outside Virginia, from which it draws about half of its students. But it means to become better known. And as more students are recruited from other states, levels of preparation—average combined SAT scores are now about 1100—and of academic competition can be expected to rise. That would be entirely in keeping with the rigor of the college's academic program and the quality of its faculty. □

Hanover
Hanover, Indiana

Timeless and Enduring

If we believe that there are some sorts of men and women which are needed by every age we may remark that there should be permanence as well as change in education.

—T. S. Eliot

There was more than a little poignancy to the timing of Eliot's remark. Even as he wrote (in 1949), American higher education was setting off on a mad dash toward a relevancy, an up-to-dateness, and a "diversity" that would eventually drive out the "permanent things" from much of the curriculum of higher education. Two years earlier, a presidential commission had derided the emphasis on "verbal skills and intellectual interests" and urged colleges to turn their attention to developing "social sensitivity and versatility, artistic ability, motor skill and dexterity, and mechanical aptitude and ingenuity. . . ." This was the first glimmer of the ideology that would eventually result in courses such as "Ultimate Frisbee," "Dance Roller Skating," and "The Socio-Psychological Aspects of Clothing" that now lard so many college catalogs.

Transmitting Values

Some schools, however, never bought into the new fashions. It is surely a tribute to the institutional commitment of Hanover College that its new president, Russell Nichols, would cite Eliot's defense of the "permanent things" in his inaugural speech in 1987, and declare:

> A liberal arts college, indeed, must be committed to the thesis that its educational program should be timeless or as nearly timeless and enduring as possible. Therefore, we must direct our attention to those permanent things which go beyond the skills and knowledge so correctly taught in the classroom.

Before assuming Hanover's presidency, Nichols served as vice president for academic and student affairs at Hillsdale College. (He is also a graduate of Wabash College—both schools on our list.) We certainly do not hold it against Hanover (Indiana's oldest private college) that the school selected someone with such impeccable conservative credentials, or someone whose educational philosophy is so clearly grounded in the history and culture of Western civilization. Said Nichols:

> It is time for all of us to recognize that there is no such thing as a value-free education. . . . Those who would attempt to educate young men and women without transmitting values indeed are transmitting the belief that permanency and moral positions aren't important. That belief, in and of itself, is a value, an improper one, which can only lead us down the path of servitude.

Curricular Excellence

We recount all of this to give some sense of the intellectual climate at Hanover, which seems solidly rooted in traditional standards, and based on a solid curriculum. All Hanover students must complete requirements in the fine arts, foreign languages, Judeo-Christian thought, history and international studies, the natural sciences, philosophy, physical education, and the social sciences, and must demonstrate proficiency in oral and written communications. The choices for each area are

Hanover College

Year Founded: 1827
Total Cost: $10,252
Total Enrollment: 1,061
Total Applicants: 1,185
75% accepted
52% of accepted enrolled
SAT Middle Range
Averages: 450V/600M
Financial Aid:
75% applied
62% judged to have need
100% of those judged
were given aid
No ROTC Program Offered
Application Information:
Mr. Gene McLemore
Director of Admissions
Hanover College
Hanover, IN 47243
Telephone:
(812) 866-7021
Application Deadlines:
No early decision
Regular decision: 3/15

107

quite narrowly circumscribed so that there appears to be no easy way to evade introducing students to the basic elements of a liberal education. In fact, every sign indicates that Hanover will continue tightening its requirements over the next few years.

It recently created a new major in medieval-renaissance studies and added minors in both classics and computer science. Moving to close one of the few gaps in an otherwise fine curriculum, Hanover has added a course called Foundations of the Modern Age, one of two choices students can elect to fulfill the core requirement in history/international studies. The other choice is Latin American History, which no doubt reflects the fact that Hanover offers a Latin American studies major.

Obviously, we've seen more exciting collegewide requirements. The Hanover general degree requirements, comprising some thirty-plus hours, do guarantee the basics of a liberal arts education, but they lack the *gravitas* of the program offered upstate at Wabash.

There appear to be few "guts" at Hanover, and the school's overall emphasis is clearly on liberal learning in the classical sense.

A True Community

That culture is also embodied in the unusually close relationship of students and faculty members. Hanover likes to say that it provides a special interpretation of the small-college experience because 94 percent of its students and 70 percent of the professors live on the college grounds. In other words, they are neighbors in a community. Students can meet with faculty members in informal circumstances to discuss classwork or career goals; contact is not circumscribed by the few hours spent in classes. There are no anonymous students at Hanover.

All of this has made Hanover an up-and-coming school. It is frequently mentioned among the best bargains in higher education (its tuition is thousands less than comparable schools). Hanover's endowment is now so healthy that on a per capita basis it ranks in the top 10 percent of the nation's colleges. The quality of students is also improving: 73 percent of Hanover's freshman class finished in the top 25 percent of their high school graduating class, while 60 percent of Hanover's graduates eventually go on to graduate or professional stud-

> Note too that a faithful study of the liberal arts humanizes character and permits it not to be cruel.
>
> —*Ovid*

ies. Hanover is just beginning to gain a national reputation for its accomplishments. In September 1990, a *Money* magazine survey measuring quality and price of colleges ranked Hanover among the top ten private schools in the nation—ahead of such usual powerhouses as Swarthmore, Princeton, Harvard, Stanford, and Yale.

Hanover and the World

Besides a solid liberal arts education, Hanover offers its students a variety of unconventional opportunities, including a special program in conjunction with Washington University in St. Louis under which students can earn an undergraduate degree in engineering and related disciplines from both institutions. Other programs include a junior-year-abroad program, the Washington Semester Plan (in cooperation with American University), the marine science program (with Duke University's Marine Laboratory), and the Philadelphia Center Internship Program (sponsored by the Great Lakes Colleges Association). Because the school calendar is divided into three terms—two full semesters and a four-week spring term—students have additional opportunities for study abroad. Some of the mini-courses have included studying Shakespeare in England, Spanish in Spain, French in Quebec and France, and German in Germany. International studies students have visited Asia; students of art, economics, political science, and theater have taken their classes to New York; and sociology students have studied at the East-West Center in Hawaii.

In addition to its beautiful campus, Hanover offers an unusually rich cultural life for a small college. Its theater group has won a national reputation for the quality of its productions, including four invitations to perform at the Kennedy Center for the Performing Arts in Washington, D.C., as part of the American College Theater National Festival.

Located in the Hoosier Hills, Hanover College is only forty-five minutes from Louisville and within a two-hour drive of Cincinnati and Indianapolis. Most important of all, however, it is an institution with a firm sense of its identity, its purpose, and its mission. It certainly deserves a closer look. □

Hastings College

Hastings, Nebraska

Good Sports

We've more than occasionally been tempted (in the midst of some recruiting scandal) to suggest that intercollegiate athletics be eliminated from American college life. But then we cool down, remember that the excesses of a few universities touch not the schools profiled herein, and recall how much we love football on crisp autumn Saturdays. Still we might also wish that *forensics*, not football, would be the campus passion. After all, a college exists primarily to exercise the minds of its students, not to develop their bodies.

At one-thousand-student Hastings College, the speech team has brought more honor to the school than the athletic teams are ever likely to, and its success is evidence of the intellectual quality of the students Hastings attracts. We hope HC's gridders never take the field against the Cornhuskers from over in Lincoln, but then the debaters from Nebraska's megaversity must tremble at the thought of squaring off with the team from Hastings. That Hastings is number one among small colleges is accomplishment enough, but its recent ranking as the seventh-best forensics team in the overall Intercollegiate Speech Tournament Rating System defies assumptions about the size of the "talent pool." And these people are intense: the unofficial speech-team motto is "Practice or Die." (Surprisingly, one of the team's recent "stars," William Langford, was a math major. Not so surprisingly, he has gone on to law school.) Hastings president Thomas Reeves unashamedly admits he'd rather have his college at the top of the debate ratings than in any athletic Top Ten.

Independent Studies

It goes without saying that the ability to make informed and effective arguments is one of the goals of the Hastings academic program. The core curriculum requirements are solid, if not overly inspiring. For one thing, Hastings students have an option: the core program or the personalized program. The latter is unlike many "independent studies" programs we have come across in that it does not simply allow the student to meander from course to course, but demands real commitment and planning. After two semesters, a few students (only about a dozen at any one time) may opt to design their own courses of study. To do so, they must present to the personalized program board a proposal that includes a fully designed curriculum and an essay explaining the curriculum's rationale. But this is primarily a way to allow highly focused students to construct majors outside the usual departmental requirements. You can bet the programs created satisfy the liberal arts spirit of the core program.

The Hastings affiliation with the Presbyterian Church is loose enough that its core demands just one course in religion, which is part of the fifth core segment, the humanities. Students are required to take about fifty hours of core courses, as follows: social science, six hours; fine arts, and, rather oddly, physical education, six hours; communications, which includes a loose foreign language requirement and courses in speech, writing, and computers (or in other "symbolic" areas—math, logic, music, etc.), thirteen to fifteen hours total; science, including one course in either chemistry or physics, and one in biology; and, finally, the humanities, with courses in literature, history, philosophy, and, as we noted above, religion, for eighteen hours in all.

Majors are offered in twenty-five areas and many departments require independent study. Students must have a 2.5 grade point average overall and a 3.0 in the major to qualify for independent study, and it is a solid prerequisite for graduate school. But those unwilling or unable to take that step have the option of directed study, the point of which is the same: to solidify the student's knowledge in a chosen field. The latter is simply more supervised than the former.

A Pause That Refreshes

Hastings basically operates on a two-semester schedule, but has an interim term in January. Just three weeks long, the interim is an intensive, one-subject course that can, according to the student's

Hastings College

Year Founded: 1882
Total Cost: $11,730
Total Enrollment: 954
Total Applicants: 961
  78% accepted
  31% of accepted enrolled
ACT Average: 22
Financial Aid:
  99% applied
  75% judged to have need
  100% of those judged
    were given aid
No ROTC Program Offered
Application Information:
  Mr. Sam Rennick
  Director of Admissions
  Hastings College
  7th and Turner
  Hastings, NE 68901
  Telephone: (402) 461-7315
Application Deadlines:
  No early decision
  Regular decision: rolling

choice, range from Advanced Instrumental Methods, a chemistry course that has twenty-eight students in the lab six to eight hours each day and includes a week's trip to several Chicago-area facilities, including the Fermi National Laboratory; to Tracking Killers, a survey of the history, methodology, and practice of epidemiology that in 1993 focused on AIDS. About sixty courses are offered in each interim term. Travel is often a feature of interim offerings, and recent extended-tour courses included archaeology in Mexico; marketing in Washington, London, and Berlin; and Spanish culture and history in Spain. Additional fees can range from several hundred to several thousand dollars.

The question that arises is, How much learning can really be accomplished in just three weeks? Well, Hastings grads speak highly of the program, and interim director Richard Lloyd points out that one can actually accomplish more in the long, daily sessions of the interim than in the less frequent, hourlong meetings of regular semester offerings that obviously compete with three or more additional courses for a student's attention.

A Communications Giant

Another unique feature of the Hastings experience is the Artist Lecture Series (ALS) program. The title makes it sound like a series of guest performances, but it is much more than that. As one recent student chairwoman of ALS told us, the program is a campus-wide passion, although for none so much as the planning committee members, who devote fourteen months to choosing a topic and organizing speakers and symposia. Students are also given the financial reins—an especially significant fact since the college only funds a portion of the program's costs. Recent ALS topics have been "A Fragile Balance: The Survival of Our Planet," and "Poverty: Decision or Destiny." The organizing committee has already presented programs throughout the year that help focus student attention on the topic, when the big guns come to campus for a two-day shoot-out. Locking horns in "A Fragile Balance" were leading interventionist and free-market economists, and the poverty symposium included liberal Lisbeth Schorr and conservative Allan Carlson.

The Gray Center for Communication Arts, dedicated by President Reagan in 1988, testifies to the gratitude of one Hastings native, Robert Keith

---

Education is the ability to listen to almost anything without losing your temper or your self-confidence.

—Robert Frost

Gray, former chairman of public relations giant Hill and Knowlton. The center is a world-class broadcast, taping, and editing facility, and makes Hastings a good choice for students interested in media careers. (A further word about the Gray Center and the character of the Hastings approach: the center's original advisory board included Walter H. Annenberg, William S. Paley, Grant Tinker, Ted Turner, and Walter Cronkite. Don't even *think* Hastings, Nebraska, is a backwater.)

One Hastings graduate, who went on to get his M.D. at Johns Hopkins, told us, "At Hopkins I learned to be a doctor, but at Hastings I learned to be a physician." Another told us of her admiration for the faculty: "I truly believe you will not find a more caring and friendly faculty anywhere. It is not just several of them—each and every professor will provide the students with his or her phone number. And when I took calculus, I made more than one call!"

So did we. What we found is a little-known gem smack in the middle of America's Great Plains; a liberal arts college that nurtures its students by setting a standard of excellence in teaching and curricular planning, and inspires its grateful graduates to lifelong achievement. □

Hillsdale

Hillsdale, Michigan

Ideas Have Consequences

Sam Donaldson: All universities are liberal-oriented, is that your position?

George Will: Basically. Do you dispute it?

Sam Donaldson: Well, yes, I do dispute it. You haven't been to Hillsdale College recently.

—*This Week with David Brinkley*, March 20, 1983

It is surely a measure of Hillsdale College's fame that not only has Sam Donaldson heard of it, but he knows that the doughty little school is a breed apart. Much of its notoriety is due to its long fight against the encroachments of government in aca-

Hillsdale College

Year Founded: 1844
Total Cost: $12,800
Total Enrollment: 1,070
Total Applicants: 940
  79% accepted
  40% of accepted enrolled
ACT Average: 23
Financial Aid:
  70% applied
  90% judged to have need
  100% of those judged
    were given aid
No ROTC Program Offered
Application Information:
  Mr. Jeffrey Lantis
  Director of Admissions
  Hillsdale College
  33 East College Street
  Hillsdale, MI 49242
  Telephone: (517) 437-7341
Application Deadlines:
  No early decision
  Regular decision: rolling

demic affairs. For Hillsdale, the issue was one of principle. Even before the Civil War, Hillsdale had accepted both women and blacks, a practice written into the college's charter in 1844. But when most institutions of higher education eagerly acquiesced in federally mandated affirmative action requirements, Hillsdale balked at what it regarded as the unwarranted intrusion of the federal bureaucracy. While the vast majority of schools compromised both their independence and academic integrity by accepting the federal controls, Hillsdale fought back in a decade-long struggle that culminated in Hillsdale's historic refusal of all federal support, including funds from the G.I. Bill and National Direct Student Loans. Since then, Hillsdale has gone it alone, building its programs around the traditional principles of freedom, morality, free enterprise, individualism, and independence.

A Moral Revolution

The college's rejection of federal programs providing grants and loans to students has also meant that it has had to substitute its own financial aid program—which it has done with remarkable success. But the school's tough-minded independence has mostly brought rewards. "Hillsdale," the school's president, George Roche, declared in 1988, "is part of a moral revolution. We stand apart from the culture."

Hillsdale has founded its commitment to academic excellence and intellectual integrity on Richard Weaver's adage, "Ideas have consequences," a belief that animates the school's environment and curriculum. While the Zeitgeist of the modern university has been largely shaped by "the reactionary 1960s ideas," which have "politicized our classrooms and substituted value-free standards for time-tested truths," a recent Hillsdale report declares, academic excellence at Hillsdale continues to be defined as "the authoritative transmission of those traditions and ideals that transcent time and circumstance."

The obvious question is, How well does Hillsdale live up to its promise? The answer is, Very well indeed. *U.S. News and World Report,* for example, consistently ranks Hillsdale among the best liberal arts colleges in the Midwest. That is not a tribute to its politics, but a recognition that students can receive an outstanding liberal arts education at Hillsdale because its curriculum rigorously avoids either fragmentation or the filtering of subjects "through a sieve of fashionable special-interest groups, causes, or political lines."

A Solid Core

Hillsdale's degree requirements are impressive, although reading the course catalog's sly introduction, you might too quickly assume they are slight: "There are only three specific courses which every Hillsdale student must take: English Rhetoric and Composition, Composition and Literature, and the American Heritage." Right. In fact, a few more courses are required: three in the humanities, two in the natural sciences, two in the social sciences, one seminar in Hillsdale's Center for Constructive Alternatives, and two semesters of phys ed. All this in the freshman and sophomore years. In the two-semester composition sequence, freshmen are assigned readings from the Great Books, and in each course the writing requirement "includes at least five major papers exercising traditional compositional and rhetorical skills." The course in American heritage examines the political, social, economic, and cultural forces that have shaped American ideals and institutions. Consistent with the focus on ideas, the course gives heavy weight to the philosophy and religious perspectives of the Declaration of Independence and the Constitution. Students must also attend a second seminar in the college's outstanding Center for Constructive Alternatives program, which in recent years has brought to campus such speakers as Sidney Hook, William F. Buckley, Jr., Malcolm Muggeridge, Norman Podhoretz, Midge Decter, Fred Barnes, Harry Jaffa, Jeff MacNelly, John Simon, J. Enoch Powell, Lynne Cheney, Tom Wolfe, Russell Kirk, and Eric Voegelin.

Hillsdale also sponsors the Ludwig von Mises Lecture Series, inspired by the legendary champion of free-market economics who chose Hillsdale as the repository of his personal library. The von Mises series has included presentations by F. A. Hayek, Jack Kemp, George Bush, William F. Buckley, Jr., Ronald Reagan, Paul Craig Roberts, William Simon, and Thomas Sowell.

A third program run by Hillsdale is its Shavano Institute for National Leadership, which has sponsored seminars around the country attended by more than 4,000 business, media, government, and community leaders. But if at times Hillsdale ap-

> It is not the insurrections of ignorance that are dangerous, but the revolts of intelligence.
>
> —*J. R. Lowell*

pears to be a movement as well as a college, it has never lost focus on its educational mission.

Hillsdale recently introduced new academic majors in classical studies, political economy, and Christian studies. Hillsdale's English department has also toughened its requirements by adding a senior seminar, a senior thesis, and a two-hour oral comprehensive exam for all majors.

Building upon Strength

The curriculum should continue to improve as Hillsdale adds distinguished new faculty members. The school has launched a $151 million capital and endowment campaign that envisions adding ten professors in the natural sciences, nine in the humanities and fine arts, and four in the social sciences. (Other major expenditures will include improvements to the physical plant, expansion of the library, and increases in scholarship and tuition aid.)

Hillsdale has been notably successful in attracting top-notch faculty members, many of whom express a sense of joyful release at their departure from the stifling atmosphere of the official ideologies of their old schools. Few seem to regret the move. "I took the job at Hillsdale with high expectations, and so far it has not only lived up to them but exceeded them in every respect," one Hillsdale professor said. "My students are bright, energetic, and hardworking, and I am deeply impressed by the intellect and integrity of my colleagues. The contrast with Wellesley is striking: instead of the cynicism about the Western tradition, the free market, and our nation that I found at Wellesley, Hillsdale is permeated with a sense of mission to preserve and advance the institutions that give us our freedom and prosperity."

Students also have opportunities to study at universities in Spain, France, Germany, and England, including participating in a student-faculty exchange at Oxford University's Keble College. Because of its growing national reputation, Hillsdale now draws about 40 percent of its students from thirty-eight different states. Average SAT scores for entering classes have been consistently rising and now average 1066. Hillsdale students are highly motivated, ambitious, and active. The school was chosen by the W. K. Kellogg Foundation for a pilot project in community service and leadership. One of the college's newer ventures is Hillsdale

Academy, an elementary and junior high school that embodies the college's moral and educational values. Classes are taught by four accredited teachers and by interns from the college.

What is striking about Hillsdale is that its growth and success have come about without a nickel of federal money or a single helpful suggestion from the bowels of the government's educrats. In that respect alone, Hillsdale is one of higher education's most interesting experiments, and one that is unlikely to disappoint any student or parent in search of a solid Western-based liberal education. □

Hope
Holland, Michigan

Liberty and Devotion

The most striking thing about Hope College is its success in blending faith (it is affiliated with the Reformed Church in America) with academic excellence. Readers are invited to regard such claims—made frequently by small church-run liberal arts colleges—with a good deal of skepticism. The skepticism would, however, be misplaced if applied to Hope. In 1986, for example, Hope received more physics grants from outside agencies than any other liberal arts college undergraduate department in the country. A 1984 study found that Hope ranked in the top 3 percent of the nation's undergraduate colleges in the proportion of graduates who had gone on to earn doctorates. And in 1988, *Changing Times* magazine designated Hope as a "best buy" in higher education, a tribute to the academic quality it offers for a relatively modest price tag.

All told, this is an impressive track record for a school founded on the east shore of Lake Michigan in 1866 by Dutch settlers "sustained by a love of liberty and devotion to God." Although fewer than a third of the students are members of the Reformed Church (and 13 percent are Roman Catholic), the values of the founders are still evident in the culture and curriculum of the college. "There is a unity of purpose that I have not detected else-

117

where," says a professor of romance languages. "There's a general moral intention behind the Hope College student."

Hope College

Year Founded: 1866
Total Cost: $13,036
Total Enrollment: 2,755
Total Applicants: 1,602
  88% accepted
  46% of accepted enrolled
SAT Middle Range
  Averages:
  940–1180
Financial Aid:
  75% applied
  59% judged to have need
  100% of those judged
  were given aid
No ROTC Program Offered
Application Information:
  Mr. Gary Camp
  Director of Admissions
  Hope College
  Holland, MI 49423
  Telephone: (800) 468-7850
Application Deadlines:
  No early decision
  Regular decision: rolling

Across the Spectrum

Core-curriculum requirements take up nearly half of a Hope student's undergraduate career. To study these requirements is to recognize the genius of the liberal arts approach. And few other American colleges rival Hope's achievement in realizing the liberal arts ideal. Students are required to take courses in expository writing, foreign languages, and mathematics, as well twelve credits in "cultural history and language," including introductory courses in world literature; history, and philosophy. In each field, they must choose between courses in the ancient or the modern period. They must select either Introduction to Ancient Civilization or Introduction to Modern European History; either World Literature I (up to the Renaissance) or World Literature II (since the Renaissance); and either Ancient Philosophy or Modern Philosophy.

Students have the option of completing an additional course from the approved list of courses, or an intermediate foreign language course, or a course in The History of Science and Technology.

Yet another way of fulfilling Hope's language and cultural history requirement is to take special interdisciplinary courses. Some recent offerings have included Two Souls of Germany and The Golden Age of Greece.

Students must also satisfy distribution requirements in the social sciences (six credits), natural sciences (eight credits), performing and fine arts (six credits), phys ed (two credits), and religion (six credits), again focusing on basic introductory courses that provide an extraordinarily broad survey of the various fields of the liberal arts. In addition, students must take a senior seminar specifically designed to help students "(1) consider how the Christian faith can inform a philosophy for living, (2) articulate a philosophy for living in a coherent, disciplined, yet personal way, (3) understand secular contemporary values in a Christian perspective."

Open and Tolerant

Classes tend to be small, and the faculty generally takes its teaching responsibilities quite seriously. As the college insists, faculty members "serve not only as teachers, but also as counselors, advisors, and friends to the students." The anchors of campus life for the students are the residential halls, where informal "bull sessions" among faculty and students are common. "A Hope College student can hold his or her own anywhere in the world," one professor contends.

As a member of the Great Lakes Colleges Association, Hope provides students with ample opportunities for off-campus study, including extensive and well-designed foreign study programs. Recently, Hope added a new computerized library, giving a high-tech edge to a traditional school.

Surprisingly, however, Hope established a minor in Women's Studies, even though the feminist presence on campus is still somewhat muted. Its generally spare administration now also includes an assistant dean for something called "Multi-Cultural Life." (The attitude behind such an office leads to statements such as, "The work of the Office of Multi-Cultural Life is not limited to working with multi-cultural individuals, however.") Moreover, the new president is a Swarthmore (B.A.) and Yale (M.A. and Ph.D.) man, who has taken to stressing the need for Hope to emphasize "diversity."

Still, the atmosphere on campus remains mostly conservative; for the most part Hope's English professors still teach literature—and occasionally write some themselves—and have avoided the more virulent strains of deconstructionism, post-structuralism, and the other forms of fashionable nihilism that often pass for the humanities. The political science program is politically balanced, complete with full-blooded Republicans. And although religious services are not compulsory, one professor reports that "we consider ourselves somewhat conservative in theology." Student-body opinion is also strongly conservative, with little tolerance for such trendy political causes as gay rights. This is not to suggest that all professors and students are conservative. One professor told us that Hope professors tend to be theologically conservative but politically liberal. Even so, the political atmosphere appears unusually open and tolerant.

Hope may be an especially attractive choice for students looking for a school with a religious affiliation but without a heavy emphasis on denominational identity or orthodoxy. Hope's faculty and student body represent a wide range of denominations—far more so than, say, schools like Calvin or

A well-trained mind is made up, so to speak, of all the minds of past ages: only a single mind has been educated during all that time.

—Bernard de Fontenelle

119

Wheaton. (Not unlike Calvin, by the way, Hope offers an extensive scholarship program.) "We walk a fine line between commitment to the values of the Reformed Church and openness to other faiths," one professor asserted, "and we have done it with considerable success." ☐

Houghton

Houghton, New York

Unforsaken Values

Tiny Houghton College consistently attracts a student body with one of the highest proportions of National Merit Scholars in the state of New York. Although hardly uniform, its student body is also one of the more conservative around, perhaps an inevitable result of Houghton's strong affiliation with the Wesleyan Church of America. While less than 20 percent of the students are Wesleyans, the majority are evangelical Protestants.

Houghton calls itself a "Christian College of Liberal Arts and Sciences" and stresses throughout its curriculum the integration of faith and learning—but not at the expense of academic excellence. The college insists that students "be able to think critically, as well as creatively, and to apply Christian principles to life experiences from a global perspective, transcending provincial and sectarian attitudes." Don't get us wrong, there are liberal professors at Houghton, and we detect an undertow of "peace and justice" politics in some of the faculty, while some members of the community have become quite actively anti-nuke (after learning the Houghton area had been selected for a "low-level radioactivity waste facility"), but Houghton's overall commitment seems sound.

The Demands of Independence

One indication of that solid commitment came in 1990, when the college refused to apply for New York State's generous Bundy aid program, fearing state restrictions would lead to watering down Houghton's independence and religious identity.

General Education requirements are extensive

(fifty-five hours) and include courses in the development of Western civilization. Students must choose one of three sequences. The first is Ancient Civilizations to 1648, which takes them from the rise of civilization in the ancient Near East, through Greek and Roman civilization, the formation of Western civilization in the early Middle Ages, the flowering of the West in the high medieval period, and the transition to modernity in the late Middle Ages, to the upheavals of the Reformation. The second option is a two-course sequence titled Western Civilization: 1600 to the Present, which surveys the social, cultural, political, and economic history of Europe and the United States, including the rise of science, the Enlightenment, the Industrial Revolution, the world wars, and the cold war. The third option is a course in World Civilization: 1400 to the Present, which surveys the political, economic, cultural, and social history of "selected world regions." If we have any qualms about Houghton's curriculum, it is here. It is unfortunate that Houghton allows students to *substitute* this course for a course in Western civilization, rather than require it *in addition* to a solid grounding in the history and culture of the West. The result of this unfortunate compromise with "diversity" is that students can graduate with gaping holes in their knowledge of their own culture. But that concern is mitigated by the rest of Houghton's curriculum, which includes required courses in Principles of Writing, Literature of the Western World, communications, an introductory course in social science, and two courses above the beginning level in an ancient or modern foreign language.

Other requirements include two hours in physical education, three hours in mathematics, four hours in science, four hours in biblical literature, and three hours in ethics. All of these make it unlikely (although technically possible) that students will graduate without being exposed to the major traditions and debates of Western civilization. A recent study of student attitudes at Houghton concluded that students increase their moral awareness and development but are "never made to forsake their values."

Houghton is noted for its superb division of fine arts, and especially for its school of music, which offers as extensive a program as you'll find anywhere but Juilliard.

Houghton College

Year Founded: 1883
Total Cost: $12,490
Total Enrollment: 1,140
Total Applicants: 942
  83% accepted
  49% of accepted enrolled
SAT Middle Range
  Averages: 910–1160
Financial Aid:
  95% applied
  98% judged to have need
  98% of those judged
    were given aid
ROTC Program Offered
Application Information:
  Mr. Timothy R. Fuller
  Director of Admissions
  Houghton College
  Houghton, NY 14744
  Telephone: (800) 777-2556
Application Deadlines:
  No early decision
  Regular decision: rolling

Active and Mobile

Houghton is a member of the Christian College Consortium, which means that its students can spend a semester at any other school in the group, and of the Christian College Coalition, which sponsors an American Studies program in Washington, D.C.

Because of the school's size and liberal arts orientation, faculty members are accessible and classes small. Students describe the atmosphere at Houghton as being like an extended family. Now, we know that that is probably attractive in inverse proportion to the distance some students want to be in respect to their families during the college years. Clearly, Houghton is not for everyone.

While colleges' *in loco parentis* obligations are a dead letter on many campuses, Houghton takes its responsibilities very seriously. Students are required to sign a statement of "community expectations," committing themselves to abide by the school's strict ban on tobacco, illegal drugs, and alcoholic beverages. Attendance at chapel is required Tuesday through Friday mornings. (Church on Sunday is optional.)

Lest this sound too stuffy, we should add that Houghton students can participate in intercollegiate sports from basketball to soccer and volleyball. The 1,300-acre campus includes ski slopes and cross-country ski trails and also provides facilities for racquetball, an indoor running track, and more than two dozen Morgan horses available for trail rides.

About a quarter of Houghton's graduates enter the ministry, but a Houghton degree also opens doors to graduate schools in a wide array of fields, and Houghton graduates have had excellent success in winning admission. □

There is no life that is not in community.

—*T. S. Eliot*

Lawrence

Appleton, Wisconsin

Against Temptation

Wisconsin—thank God—has more than a few excellent alternatives to Madison's University of Wisconsin, the once-great university now fallen into the twin evils of giantism and trendy politics. With their solid focus on liberal education, Alverno, Ripon, and Beloit Colleges—as well as Milwaukee's Marquette University—all offer a sharp counterpoint to the impersonality, politicization, and contempt for teaching that so characterize the Madison campus. That we have chosen Lawrence University should not be taken as a reflection on any of these other schools; all deserve serious consideration and each is to be vastly preferred over UW.

One student who fled UW for Lawrence is quoted in a Lawrence College publication as saying that at Madison "I was learning academically, but I didn't feel I was growing as a person. I felt institutionalized. At Lawrence, I feel at home." The contrast between the two institutions is dramatically highlighted in the students' freshman year. At Madison, students are unlikely to see, much less talk to, a professor; many simply slip through the cracks. At Lawrence, the freshman program is at the heart of the school's program of liberal learning.

A Right Start

Lawrence's distinctive freshman studies program was inaugurated in 1945 by its president, Nathan Pusey, who went on to become president of Harvard (where he was ritually crucified by faculty radicals in the late sixties). All freshmen take a two-term seminar (with no more than sixteen students) that is intended to improve their skills in reading, writing, and speaking, as well as to introduce them to the classics. "Through the study of the classics of systematic thought or creative imagination," one college publication says, "it also raises for discussion and analysis important ideas of abid-

Lawrence University

Year Founded: 1847
Total Cost: $18,771
Total Enrollment: 1,202
Total Applicants: 1,284
  75% accepted
  34% of accepted enrolled
SAT Middle Range
  Averages: 500–620V/
  550–660M
Financial Aid:
  66% applied
  61% judged to have need
  100% of those judged
  were given aid
No ROTC Program Offered
Application Information:
  Mr. Steven T. Syverson
  Dean of Admissions and
    Financial Aid
  Lawrence University
  Appleton, WI 54912
  Telephone: (414) 832-6500
Application Deadlines:
  Early decision: 12/1, 1/15
  Regular decision: 2/15

ing concern." The seminars expose students to masterworks of Western civilization, including Plato, Einstein, Freud, Euripides, Picasso, and Mozart, exploring how each thinker dealt with such basic dichotomies as "life and death, myth and reality, rationality and intuition, truth and justice." The seminars, often cited by Lawrence students as a high point of their undergraduate education, are characterized by close contact with faculty members, "close reading, intense discussions, and disciplined writing." Having completed the freshman seminars, Lawrence students proceed to undertake Lawrence's general education requirements, which are divided into two categories: Language and Civilization, and Logic and Observation.

Under Language and Civilization (which could also be called Humanities), students are required to complete five courses, including an intermediate foreign language course, a course in English literature (which must be completed before the end of the sophomore year), one course in art, music, or theater/drama, and two upper-level courses in history, philosophy, or religious studies. Under Logic and Observation, students must also complete five courses, including one course in mathematics, one in a laboratory science, and additional courses in a natural science, mathematics, computer science, or logic. Two upper-level courses in a social science are required. In addition, students must pass a comprehensive departmental examination in their major field before graduation.

A Global Reach

That falls short of the kind of rigorously structured core we would like to see, though the freshman program does at least provide something of a common intellectual experience. But Lawrence's real strength is in the quality of its faculty and its long-standing commitment to excellent teaching. We hear some complaints that Lawrence has begun to try to enhance its prestige by pushing for more research at the inevitable expense of teaching. That would be a disaster for a school of Lawrence's quality, because it would effectively dismantle the college's strongest suit, while forcing it into competition with the multiversities that it could never win. But we've seen this before; otherwise excellent schools have gutted their programs in an ill-fated grab at academic glory. They begin by wanting to grow up to be Harvard, and end up as just another second-rate school.

But we are confident that Lawrence can resist those temptations, and thus far the Ivy-wannabes on the faculty have had only limited success in watering down what students profit from in the classroom. Indeed at Lawrence, undergraduates are often included in a professor's research, and thus gain important hands-on experience.

Lawrence's other strong suits include its conservatory of music, which offers a rigorous and extensive curriculum culminating in the bachelor of music degree, and its study-abroad programs that generally entice fully half of Lawrence's students into studying in a foreign country. Lawrence's London Study Center is widely respected, while several departments run their own foreign study programs. As a member of the Associated Colleges of the Midwest, Lawrence students also have access to an impressive array of other opportunities, including programs to study art, culture, and society at various universities in Europe, as well as programs in Latin America and Asia. Domestic programs include opportunities to engage in humanities research at the Newberry Library and scientific research at the Oak Ridge National Laboratory.

Although it would not be fair to call Lawrence a particularly conservative school, it has never been a hotbed of radicalism or political involvement. *The New York Times*'s Edward Fiske quotes one student as saying that "Lawrence takes pride in its liberal approach to education, but both students and professors are more conservative than they like to admit." Which sounds to us like grounds for hope. □

> Colleges are places where pebbles are polished and diamonds dimmed.
>
> —*Robert Ingersoll*

Lynchburg

Lynchburg, Virginia

Impressing the Ivies

Students who are willing to stray from the beaten path of the big-name universities (and we assume that the readers of this guide are at least willing to consider straying) will find that many of the traditions that have been scrapped or

deconstructed in the Ivy League are undergoing a dramatic resurgence in smaller liberal arts institutions. But few schools have been as creative as Lynchburg College, the site of one of the most intriguing experiments in higher education today. Simply put, Lynchburg has committed itself to placing the Great Books of Western Civilization, from Plato to Freud, at the heart of its entire curriculum—whether in accounting, nursing, the humanities, or the sciences.

Lynchburg College

Year Founded: 1903
Total Cost: $16,150
Total Enrollment: 2,379
Total Applicants: 2,078
  83% accepted
  30% of accepted enrolled
SAT Middle Range
  Averages: 850–950
Financial Aid:
  42% applied
  66% judged to have need
  98% of those judged
    were given aid
ROTC Program Offered
Application Information:
  Mr. Ernest Chadderton
  Dean of Enrollment
  Lynchburg College
  Lynchburg, VA 24501
  Telephone: (804) 522-8300
Application Deadlines:
  No early decision
  Regular decision: rolling

A Core of Understanding

The revival of the classical liberal arts at Lynchburg dates back to 1976 when the college began a required senior symposium based upon a ten-volume set of readings known as "Classical Selections on Great Issues." In selecting the classics, Lynchburg faculty members drew on great works that "have met the test of time in speaking with a lasting impact to more than one generation." As a whole it was an impressive survey of the best that has been thought and said in the European and American traditions. Clearly inspired by the curricular reforms at schools such as Columbia and the University of Chicago a generation earlier, the Lynchburg Great Books list was designed to provide students with readings that contained a continuing source of ideas, as well as an "understanding of, and appreciation for, the traditions and values of Western civilization." In the senior symposia students read selections from the classics, attend weekly lectures on such major themes as the "Nature of Man," "Education: Ends and Means," "Poverty and Wealth," "Tyranny and Freedom," and "Faith and Morals," and meet in small groups to discuss the issues raised. (The collection of readings—edited by members of the Lynchburg faculty—was published by the University Press of America in 1982. A revised edition will be completed by the summer of 1993.)

But by the late 1980s, the Lynchburg faculty recognized that the senior symposium alone was insufficient to compensate for the lack of reading and writing skills of some of their students or for the fragmentation and incoherence of the undergraduate curriculum in general. They concluded that the solution was to extend the symposium readings to the entire curriculum through specially designed courses, henceforth known as LCSR courses (Lynchburg College Symposium Readings). To be designated an LCSR course, at least 20 percent of a student's grade must depend on writing and speaking assignments based upon readings from the "Classical Selections on Great Issues." All students are now required to take six such courses in order to earn a degree. The result is that writers such as Rousseau, Aristotle, John Stuart Mill, Cicero, Lucretius, and Tolstoy are taken out of the liberal arts ghetto and injected directly into pre-professional courses.

Inspiring Success

The LCSR program, however, is only one aspect of Lynchburg's overall strong curriculum. In addition to the eight LCSR (Great Books) classes, the senior symposium, and a two-semester course in Western civilization, all students must take a course in World Literature, two courses in freshman English, the Introduction to Philosophical Problems, and a course in physical education. The core curriculum totals twenty-one credits. In addition, students must satisfy distribution requirements that add up to another forty to forty-three credits. Those include three credits in an intermediate-level foreign language; three to six credits in mathematics; twelve credits in the humanities; six credits in the fine arts; eight credits in physical and life sciences; six credits in the social sciences, and two credits in physical education.

How well does Lynchburg's Great Books program work? After an evaluation of the program in action, the director of Harvard's expository writing program, Professor Richard Marius, said of Lynchburg: "I have seldom in my life been so favorably impressed by an innovation in college education. I wish it could be translated to Harvard. But I suppose the highest compliment that I could pay to the program was that I wished I could teach it." Of course, Harvard is about as likely to adopt such a program as Iran is to name Salman Rushdie minister of culture. But Professor Marius's comments are interesting:

> [During the evaluation], I read an amazingly good essay from a business course in accounting using Adam Smith's *Wealth of Nations* and showing how the work of an auditor contributes to the "invisible hand" that Smith saw regulating the marketplace. *I was astonished to find a literate, thoughtful, and scholarly paper using a "classical" source emerge*

> Whoso neglects learning in his youth loses the past and is dead for the future.
>
> —*Euripides*

from a course on a subject like accounting! I was told that students would also encounter Adam Smith in courses in history, in sociology, in economics and perhaps others.

Perhaps because he has become so inured to the intellectual level at his own school, Professor Marius also expressed profound surprise over another Lynchburg accounting student's essay on Plato—it "made me believe that the writer understood something both about the *Republic* and accounting"; and when he read a paper on the Book of Job in which he "found a casual reference of Occam's razor, one so apt and "natural," he knew that "the writer understood the concept clearly, and that he had taken it into his intellectual equipment."

The program seems to have inspired Lynchburg's teachers. All students, for example, must take a two-semester course in the history of Western civilization. At some schools such a requirement might result in a mass, impersonal survey course. But at Lynchburg, Professor Michael Santos has been known to divide his classes into three groups—each one assigned to represent the views, respectively, of Socrates, Plato, and Aristotle. The students familiarize themselves with the thinkers' views by reading their various writings—Plato's *Apology* and *Crito* (for Socrates' perspective), the *Republic* (for Plato's), and *Politics* (for Aristotle's). They are then turned loose for discussion, pitting the various philosophical perspectives and ideas against one another. "The role-playing reinforces the readings," Professor Santos remarks, "and allows the students to participate in class and respond to one another intelligently."

Lynchburg's Great Books program has, in fact, proved so successful that it publishes its own journal, *The Agora*, which features student papers, discussions of the status of the classics in higher education, faculty essays, and reprints from other publications. (Recent selections included "What Did Americans Inherit from the Ancients?" by Russell Kirk, and Sidney Hook's "Civilization and Its Malcontents," reprinted from *National Review*.)

Not all of Lynchburg's faculty have bought into the new Great Books concept (the new courses require a lot of extra work and a radical departure from normal academic norms), and the program is still relatively new. But the sense of renewal seems contagious. Faculty members who have recently joined the program after an initial skepticism express enthusiasm for its prospects. And it is beginning to draw national attention. Who knows? It may even shame the Ivies into looking to tiny Lynchburg for guidance and counsel. □

Millsaps

Jackson, Mississippi

Down South, Around the World

One commentator calls Millsaps College "the best school in Mississippi," and we're not sure if he meant that as a northern, East Coast elitist backhanded compliment. For in fact, Millsaps is among the best schools in America. *Changing Times* magazine, for example, named Millsaps one of five "excellent liberal arts colleges" in the South. It is particularly well known for its business department, where it is possible to earn both a bachelor's degree and an MBA in five years, but impossible not to imbibe a liberal education as well. Millsaps is one of only 240 schools nationally which have won professional accreditation from the American Assembly for Collegiate Schools of Business for their undergraduate *and* graduate business programs. Perhaps most important of all, given the propensities of many of the schools in the region, Millsaps in 1989 graduated a higher percentage of its intercollegiate athletes than any other school in the area —an impressive 91.3 percent.

Millsaps's pre-med and pre-law offerings also get very high marks, which is not surprising when you consider that 80 percent of Millsaps graduates who apply to medical school and 98 percent who apply to law school win admission. Fully 40 percent of Millsaps graduates go on to graduate or professional study. In part that tends to reflect the high quality of Millsaps students: half of them finished in the top fifth of their high school graduating classes, and they now have an average combined SAT score of 1100.

Awareness, Tolerance, and Inquiry

Millsaps is affiliated with the Methodist Church, but wears the label lightly; fewer than half of the

129

students are Methodists, and there are no mandatory church services. But within its ecumenical tradition, the college declares that it is "an institution that is open, value-oriented, reflective, and in pursuit of truth." In the mid-1980s, the college's faculty and board of trustees reaffirmed its mission statement, declaring:

Millsaps College

Year Founded: 1890
Total Cost: $14,260
Total Enrollment: 1,333
Total Applicants: 820
  87% accepted
  37% of accepted enrolled
ACT Average: 26
Financial Aid:
  80% applied
  67% judged to have need
  67% of those judged were
    given aid
No ROTC Program Offered
Application Information:
  Ms. Florence Hines
  Director of Admissions
  Millsaps College
  P.O. Box 150556
  Jackson, MS 39210
  Telephone: (601) 974-1050
Application Deadlines:
  No early decision
  Regular decision: 4/1

As an institution of higher learning, Millsaps College fosters an attitude of continuing intellectual awareness, of tolerance, and of unbiased inquiry, without which true education cannot exist. It does not seek to indoctrinate, but to inform and inspire. . . .

Classes tend to be small, and all reports indicate that students consider their professors to be accessible and interested in their educational development. Millsaps's seriousness is reflected in its rigorous ten-course core curriculum. The core begins and ends with liberal studies, with an Introduction in the freshman year, and Reflections in the senior year. Sandwiched in between are four *multidisciplinary* (and *that* word captures the soul of the liberal arts), and four *topics* courses. The multidisciplinary courses are in the history of civilization, from the ancient world through the day before yesterday. The topics courses deal with the social sciences, natural sciences, and math. So seriously does Millsaps take the writing component of its core courses that at the end of two years students are required to present for review a portfolio of writings, and the catalog warns: "Students will not be eligible to enroll in Reflections on Liberal Studies until they have satisfied this requirement." In addition, B.A. candidates must demonstrate proficiency at the intermediate level of a foreign language, and as seniors must also pass a comprehensive examination in their major.

As many as half of Millsaps freshmen enroll in the school's Heritage Program, a yearlong, team-taught interdisciplinary program in the arts, history, literature, religion, and philosophy of the West. The program consists of large lectures (large by Millsaps standards), but students are divided into small classes of fifteen or so for discussions. The Heritage Program is known for its demanding pace—the reading list is daunting, stretching as it does from the beginning of Western history to the modern day—but it also serves to fulfill many of the core-curriculum requirements.

Small Is Mostly Beautiful

There are, however, some weaknesses in a school of Millsaps's size. The history department, for example, has only four professors, which is twice as many as in the classics and political science departments. English, though, is much stronger, as are some of the science departments. Even so, in contrast, the school of management appears quite well endowed with faculty. That's fine for business students and accounts, no doubt, for the school's accreditation, but the disparity in numbers between the business profs and the faculty in the liberal arts curriculum suggests that Millsaps's faculty resources may reflect financial priorities over educational ones. The school itself proudly cites the success of its graduates in obtaining entrance to graduate school and the award in 1988 of a Phi Beta Kappa chapter—one of only three granted in a year when ninety were considered. President George M. Harmon defends the business school's strength by emphasizing, in part, that "it fills a distinct need in Jackson, Mississippi. . . . As a result of our meeting this need . . . significant resources flow to the college as a whole and provide strong support to the undergraduate program in the liberal arts and sciences." In any case, the margin for error is awfully slim in some departments, and students interested in a specific field need to examine carefully both the course offerings and the status of the faculty.

So far, this imbalance has not affected the school's overall quality. The student body tends to be heavily southern, and quite conservative, even if the same cannot always be said of the faculty and administration. But recent innovations include a coed dorm for upperclassmen and the creation of a women's studies concentration. More recently, Millsaps was one of nineteen institutions that won grants from a new program of the Ford Foundation "to help diversify the ethnic and cultural content of their curriculum."

The school's traditionalism, nevertheless, seems solid; its future appears promising. In 1990 the college surpassed its centennial campaign fund-raising goal a full ten months ahead of schedule. Its success in garnering donations from more than 8,000 separate donors is eloquent testimony to the number of satisfied Millsaps graduates.

> 'Tis education forms the common mind;/ Just as the twig is bent the tree's inclined.
>
> —*Alexander Pope*

Pragmatic and Well-Traveled

Unlike many other small liberal arts colleges, Millsaps is neither rural nor isolated. In fact, located in the heart of a major metropolitan area (greater Jackson has a population of about 400,000), Millsaps not only has access to urban amenities but is located within a few hours of Memphis, New Orleans, and the beaches of the Gulf Coast—all tempting options for the weary student.

Millsaps students can also take advantage of a wide array of special programs, including the Washington Semester, a joint arrangement with the American University, which provides outstanding students in the social sciences a chance to work and study in the nation's capital. Millsaps students can also study abroad under arrangements between the college and the Institute of European Studies and the Institute of East Asian Studies. Students who wish to study the classics can participate in programs conducted by the Intercollegiate Center for Classical Studies in Rome and the College Year in Athens Program. Other programs include British Studies in Oxford, run by the Associated Colleges of the South, as well as programs in virtually every country of Western Europe. For those who want to stay closer to home, Millsaps offers internships in the Mississippi legislature for political science students, as well as internships in public administration in cooperation with city, state, and federal agencies. □

Mount Saint Mary's
Emmitsburg, Maryland

A Catholic Reformation

When the National Endowment for the Humanities recently handed out a two-year grant of $359,037 to help establish core curriculums in the nation's colleges, only three liberal arts colleges in the country were selected as models. Mount Saint Mary's was one of them.

If that seems extraordinary for a little-known school in Maryland, it is no less amazing than what Mount Saint Mary's has achieved by restructuring its entire curriculum into a four-year sequential study of Western and world civilization. Its curriculum is among the most thoughtful, well-structured, and comprehensive courses of study offered by any school in this guide.

A Particular Inheritance

Although it has only recently won national attention, Mount Saint Mary's is hardly a newcomer. Founded in 1808 by a French émigré priest who bore letters of introduction from Lafayette, the school is the oldest independent Catholic college in the United States. Still, it would probably remain only one of many small, relatively unknown liberal arts colleges around the country had it not been for its decision in 1988 to undertake a dramatic institutional recommitment to liberal education.

Emphasizing knowledge, skills, and moral values, Mount Saint Mary's core curriculum includes required courses in the humanities, history, theology, ethics, and literature, as well as electives in the social and natural sciences, mathematics, and a foreign language. Perhaps most distinctive of all, the sixty-one credit core constitutes more than half of all courses taken by undergraduates and spans all four years of a student's undergraduate career, no matter what his or her major might be. This commitment to the liberal arts is all the more notable, given that about half of Mount Saint Mary's students major in business, accounting, or economics.

The first two years examine the intellectual and moral heritage of the West through a series of related and paired courses; the junior year introduces students to their "particular inheritance as Americans and as people formed by Christian faith," while the senior year is devoted to the study of a non-Western culture and a course in ethics, described as a study of the "practice of moral discernment."

For students at Mount Saint Mary's College, collegiate careers begin with the freshman year program's two-step orientation. First they meet with the faculty members who will be their advisers, the deans of academic and student life, and older students who will serve as mentors and residence assistants. The second phase of orientation consists of a three-day program in the fall, built around the theme "Choices: Personal and Social Responsibility." (Unlike most universities, Mount Saint Mary's takes advising seriously—so seriously, in fact, that

Mount Saint Mary's College

Year Founded: 1808
Total Cost: $16,425
Total Enrollment: 1,320
Total Applicants: 1,196
 89% accepted
 33% of accepted enrolled
SAT Averages: 460V/500M
Financial Aid:
 52% applied
 82% judged to have need
 100% of those judged
  were given aid
ROTC Program Offered
Application Information:
 Mr. Michael Kennedy
 Director of Admissions
 Mount Saint Mary's College
 Emmitsburg, MD 21727
 Telephone: (800) 448-4347
Application Deadlines:
 Early action: 12/1
 Regular decision: 3/1

every year the school cancels a day of classes for Advising Day.)

All freshmen are enrolled in a sixteen-person freshman seminar. The professor who teaches the seminar is also the adviser to the students in the class. The seminar concentrates on improving student writing and oral communication and focuses on the critical analysis of basic texts to examine "how personal choices shape one's philosophy of life." At the same time, all students take a two-semester course in Western history (Ancient World to 1500, and 1500 to the Present) and a course in Western tradition (students can choose one in either literature or the arts). While some schools might consign students in survey courses to huge lectures, those at Mount Saint Mary's are given by faculty teams to classes of about twenty-five students. The coordination of the so-called cluster courses, the college says, "enables students to discover connections between disciplines and among the political, social and cultural developments of Western history."

The Common Core

In their sophomore year, all students take Philosophy I (Cosmos to Citizen) and Philosophy II (Self to Society) which the college describes as "a two-semester bridge between the humanistic and scientific disciplines." A college publication describes the two courses as focusing on "enduring philosophical topics such as human nature, the modes of knowing, the nature of faith and reason, determinism and free will, and personal and social well-being." This study prepares the way for the more detailed work demanded of juniors in the American and Catholic traditions. All students simultaneously take courses in theology, and in The American Experience I (The Age of Discovery to 1890) and The American Experience II (1890 to the Present).

"Students," the college explains, "explore what is distinctive in American political, intellectual, and aesthetic experiences and what is held in common with the Western tradition introduced in the first two years."

As seniors, students cap their undergraduate education by taking a course in a non-Western culture and in ethics, taught from a philosophical or theological perspective, which reflects Sir Philip Sidney's remark that "the end of all earthly learning is virtuous action."

> Education is a companion which no misfortune can depress, no crime can destroy, no enemy can alienate, no despotism can enslave.
>
> —*Joseph Addison*

But this covers only the common courses taken by all Mount Saint Mary's students. In addition, they must take further core studies, including six credits in foreign languages, six credits in social sciences, three credits in mathematics, and four credits in natural science. Because only specially designed core courses count (for example, students must select from among only four courses in the social sciences), even these elective requirements reflect the carefully thought-out and well-planned principles of general education.

Responsible Citizens

A central element in Mount Saint Mary's renaissance seems to be the strong leadership from president Robert J. Wickenheiser, who clearly and forcefully defines the basic assumptions behind the creation of the Mount Saint Mary's core curriculum. Not only is the decline of the liberal arts in American colleges and universities lamentable, Mr. Wickenheiser declares, but the fact that a majority of American students leave the university without ever having taken a course in Western civilization, American history, or a foreign language is "not only startling, but frightening." He acknowledges that the rampant specialization of academic life has undermined the humanities, and he is not afraid of insisting that the college, in fact, *does* know better than its students "what a liberal arts education entails."

Nor is he shy about challenging the academic culture that has blocked similar reforms at other schools. "Vested interests and academic turf," he says, "have no place in defining a core curriculum, a curriculum which should be first and foremost an integrating experience." He also strongly reaffirms the central role of the liberal arts in the higher learning. Says Wickenheiser:

Educating students in the liberal arts, together with a sense of real values and purpose and with a capacity to think and write clearly, best prepares students for life and for a career, and best prepares them for responsibilities as citizens of their communities, their country and the world.

Mount Saint Mary's core is solid also because it has the strong support of the faculty—the program was adopted unanimously with only a single abstention. Faculty members, moreover, have willingly undergone six-weeks-long workshops to prepare to teach the new courses. However, there is a downside to this sort of unanimity. Liberals on campus—not surprisingly—seem ready to infiltrate the core's reading lists with their favorite third world, feminist, and minority writers, and students should be warned that some professors may use their courses to expound upon the moral dilemmas of the new academic trinity: race, sex, and class. But frankly, we are not bothered much by this, because Mount Saint Mary's students inevitably receive a thorough grounding in the best that has been thought and said in Western culture. Properly inoculated, the body rejects the virus.

Moreover, Mount Saint Mary's appears to have a solid grasp of its moral responsibilities. One litmus test for the moral health of an institution of higher learning is its approach to "safe sex." A distressing number of schools have followed the trend established at Dartmouth of distributing graphic literature about allegedly "safe" sexual practices (which we will not enumerate here), even giving condoms and rubber dams to its undergraduates at orientation. In sharp contrast, Mount Saint Mary's published a twelve-page AIDS-prevention pamphlet that actually stresses basic moral values (influenced no doubt by the on-campus presence of Germain Grisez, one of the world's leading moral theologians), rather than touting condom use. "The idea that a condom allows 'safe sex' is an overstatement," the brochure reads. "The whole 'safe sex' mentality produces, quite frankly, a false security, and is destructive of a person's well-being." The pamphlet has proved so successful that it has drawn praise not only from the Vatican's representative to the United States, but also from Maryland state health officials, and has been eagerly distributed by Catholic and other liberal arts colleges across the country.

We expect that Mount Saint Mary's will continue to play a leading role in the reformation of higher learning well into the next decade. □

Northeast Missouri

Kirksville, Missouri

The Courage of Conviction

In an obscure corner of the academic world, an unheralded school marches to a different drummer.
It's a march that other schools may want to join.
While higher education's bigger names have been
chasing fame and fortune, Northeast Missouri State
University in Kirksville has remained faithful to the
undergraduate.

—*The Chicago Tribune*

Northeast Missouri may be unheralded for now,
but we suspect that will change soon enough.
It is no exaggeration to say that Northeast Missouri is one of the nation's most innovative public
universities—a school that has remade itself into
an image of what a university *should* be. Increasingly, it is winning national recognition for its high-
quality undergraduate teaching, its rigorous liberal
arts core curriculum, and its comprehensive system
for evaluating how much its students are actually
learning.

None of this would have seemed conceivable a
decade ago. Like many smaller public universities,
this one-time regional teacher's college faced tightening budgets, a declining student base, and the
pressure to try to grow up to a research university.
If it had followed its counterparts, Northeast might
have ended up as yet another fourth-rate research
university offering a third-class undergraduate education. Instead, it decided to be reborn.

In 1985, the Missouri legislature designated
Northeast Missouri as the state's public liberal arts
and sciences university, with a specific and unapologetic emphasis on undergraduate teaching. "We
wanted to offer the best undergraduate education
in the land," vice president of academic affairs Jack
Magruder told *The Chicago Tribune*. "We knew we
couldn't do that if we spread ourselves too thin in
graduate studies and research." Noted the *Trib-*

Northeast Missouri State University

Year Founded: 1867
Total Cost:
  Residents: $5,536
  Nonresidents: $7,416
Total Enrollment: 5,925
Total Applicants: 4,988
  75% accepted
  36% enrolled
SAT Average: 1050
Financial Aid:
  66% applied
  56% judged to have need
  100% of those judged
    were given aid
ROTC Program Offered
Application Information:
  Ms. Kathy Rieck
  Dean of Admissions and
    Records
  McClain Hall 205
  Northeast Missouri State
    University
  Kirksville, MO 64152-3975
  Telephone: (816) 785-4114
Application Deadlines:
  Early decision: 11/15
  Regular decision: 3/1

une: "While administrators at other schools trumpet a long menu of degree-granting programs, Northeast's officials proudly tick off a list of how many they've killed—120 in the last five years." One of the programs to get the ax was the undergraduate major in education, a decision that speaks volumes about the administration's good sense. Today, Northeast is known for its close student-faculty involvement and its high academic standards. Entering ACT scores for first-time freshmen have risen from 20.3 in 1985 to 25.5 in 1992—making Northeast more selective than the state's flagship state school, the University of Missouri. Dr. Peter Ewell, a senior associate for the National Center of Higher Education Management Systems, says of Northeast Missouri: "The experience that this university has had is astonishing in terms of the amount of change which has occurred in a small period of time. I know personally of no other institution—and I work with about 120 at this point—which has changed so much so consciously, and so successfully."

Taking Liberal Education Seriously

While other schools were eviscerating their curricula, Northeast was crafting an unusually well thought out course of study. The seventy-two-hour core curriculum is designed to follow the guidelines of the American Association of Colleges 1985 report, *Integrity of the College Curriculum.* Almost universally ignored by colleges, the report defined the essential intellectual, aesthetic, and philosophic experiences that all undergraduates should share. They included abstract logical thinking, critical analysis; literacy; the understanding of numerical data; historical consciousness; familiarity with science, values, and art; international and multicultural experiences; and study in depth.

Reflecting such a commitment, Northeast Missouri insists that "the belief that liberal learning is the cornerstone of the undergraduate experience is reflected in every facet of the university." And they seem to be as good as their word. All Northeast students are required to complete a common core of forty-nine to fifty hours and an additional ten to eleven hours of liberal arts and science courses, determined by the individual academic program. Within that curriculum, courses are designed to provide the cumulative exercise of such skills as writing, quantitative analysis, problem solving, and critical thinking. Students must take nine hours in communication skills, including two semesters of composition and a course in fundamentals of speech. The core also includes a minimum of three hours of math and eight hours of science, plus an additional three to four hours of either math or science; fifteen hours in the humanities (from four different areas, including foreign languages, art and music, literature, and religion and philosophy); nine hours in the social sciences (from a short list of courses, including World Civilization and other introductory courses); and two hours of health, exercise science/military science.

Candidates for bachelor of science degrees must take an additional twelve hours in science and math; and a candidate for the bachelor of arts degree must take an additional twelve to fourteen hours in a foreign language. As seniors, students must also complete a "capstone," or culminating experience, in their major field of study. This can include a recital for music students, an internship for journalism students, or a thesis for students in religion or philosophy.

Making the Grade

Perhaps the most unusual aspect of Northeast's system is the way it measures how good a job it is doing in educating students. In higher education it is virtually unheard-of for schools to measure what value is added to a student's knowledge. At Northeast, however, students are tested throughout their undergraduate careers to measure their progress. Starting with entering students' ACT or SAT scores, Northeast administers another standardized test during their first week on campus. Sophomores take the test again, and scores are compared with entrance scores "to determine whether you have improved during your first 1½ years of college." Seniors also take a nationally normed test in their majors. Since 1989, students must also put together portfolios of their work—including essays, research papers, and other projects—which are included as a part of the overall assessment program.

What is striking about this effort is the school's commitment to measuring the comparative effectiveness of its own academic programs and to using those measurements to provide guideposts for continuing improvement. The payoff is demonstrable. An example: three years after upgrading its busi-

> The sole true end of education is simply this: to teach men to learn for themselves; and whatever instruction fails to do this is effort spent in vain.
>
> —*Dorothy L. Sayers*

ness courses as part of the school's "Value Added Initiative," Northeast students were leading the nation in their rate of passing a national CPA exam (85 percent).

The assessment program may also be one of the reasons Northeast Missouri is winning so much attention these days. It is frequently listed among the nation's most innovative schools and regularly makes lists of the "best buys" in higher education. Ninety percent of Northeast's graduates who wish to continue their educations win admission to graduate or professional schools. Martin Nemko, in his book *How to Get an Ivy League Education at a State University,* calls Northeast "one of the best places in the Midwest to get a top-flight liberal arts education. Here the student, not research, is king, with a faculty hired and promoted primarily on teaching ability." IBM's corporate magazine, *Viewpoint,* called Northeast Missouri "one of the nation's hottest small public schools." And *The Chronicle of Higher Education* reported that Northeast "attracts a steady stream of educators and political leaders" to study its innovations.

The irony here, of course, is that all for all the talk of "innovation," Northeast has essentially undertaken a *restoration*—of the curriculum, of the commitment to undergraduate education, and of the respect for the "ancient, high art" of teaching.

Teaching and Research

While the focus of Northeast Missouri is squarely on undergraduate education, the school has not turned its back on research. Indeed, it takes great pride in involving undergraduates in research projects as part of its emphasis on active, hands-on learning. Religious groups are popular on campus and the school actively encourages students to get involved in service projects and volunteer activities. Northeast students also have access to an extensive program of internships. Opportunities for studying abroad include programs in Costa Rica, Canada, Germany, England, Spain, France, Taiwan, and the former Soviet Union. Since Northeast is also a member of the College Consortium for International Studies, students can also study in Cyprus, Denmark, Ecuador, France, Greece, Israel, Ireland, Italy, Mexico, Portugal, Scotland, Spain, Sweden, or Switzerland.

Although located in out-of-the-way Kirksville, Northeast offers a full plate of extracurricular activities, including active athletic and fine arts programs and a thriving Greek system. The university's Lyceum series also brings in cultural events —free of charge to students—ranging from concerts to comedians. Campus speakers appear to be selected on an evenhanded basis; recent speakers include Alexander Haig, William F. Buckley, Jr., William Raspberry, Geraldine Ferraro, and Jeane Kirkpatrick. Given all of this, and its extraordinarily low tuition, we do not hesitate to say that Northeast Missouri represents one of the finest values in higher education today.   □

Notre Dame

Notre Dame, Indiana

Tall among the Giants

The first striking feature about Notre Dame is that it's small—or, rather, that it isn't as big as you may have imagined. The Fighting Irish play football and basketball against true giants like Michigan and UCLA (each with 36,000 students), but the total enrollment at Notre Dame is under 10,000. Not surprisingly, it is quite selective—only about half of the applicants are accepted (as opposed to more than 95 percent at, say, Oklahoma or, on the other extreme, about 15 percent at Harvard).

An obvious first question for non-Catholics is, How Catholic is Notre Dame? the simple answer is, Very. Many administrators and professors are members of the Congregation of the Holy Cross, 90 percent of the student body is Catholic, and two semesters of theology are among the requirements for a diploma. Still, ND is hardly uncongenial to students of other faiths.

A Good Beginning

What's more, it manages to balance its reputation as a football factory with an academic program that we consider one of the best in the nation, beginning with the Freshman Year of Studies.

Notre Dame freshmen have no majors. They are required to take a group of survey courses designed

University of Notre Dame

Year Founded: 1842
Total Cost: $16,000
Total Enrollment: 9,700
Total Applicants: 7,700
   49% accepted
   24% of accepted enrolled
SAT Middle Range
   Averages: 1170–1370
Financial Aid:
   75% applied
   93% judged to have need
   100% of those judged
      were given aid
ROTC Program Offered
Application Information:
   Mr. Kevin M. Rooney
   Director of Admissions
   University of Notre Dame
   Notre Dame, IN 46556
   Telephone: (219) 239-7505
Application Deadlines:
   Early action: 11/1
   Regular decision: 1/4

to ensure an intellectual grounding for further study. There are five courses in the freshman curriculum plus, we're happy to report, the further requirement of either phys ed *or* ROTC. These courses are a kind of shock treatment for students whose most challenging high school reading consisted of Judy Blume and *Animal Farm*. English 109, for instance, "emphasizes the composition of expository essays through formal classroom instruction in Aristotelian rhetoric, through frequent short in-classroom writing exercises, through classroom discussion and workshops, through occasional conferences between teacher and student, and through the careful written evaluation of the writing done by the student inside and outside of class." Thirty pages of written prose are required of each student.

In the Humanities Seminar (an alternative to 109 for better students) the reading list may include Genesis, Job, and St. John's Gospel; the *Epic of Gilgamesh*, the tragedies of Sophocles, and Whitman's *Leaves of Grass;* various works by Hawthorne, Melville, and Cather; Dostoevsky, Beckett, and Freud; a little of Plato, and some Shakespeare.

The freshman course of studies is not limited to literature and writing. All freshmen are also required to take two-semester courses in math, and either a foreign language or a natural science, and at least one semester of history or another social science. (All students must have completed two semesters of a natural science before the end of their sophomore year, and students in the Arts and Letters College must study a foreign language.) Counseling and tutoring are available and encouraged.

The Upper-Class Challenges

Notre Dame has four colleges beyond the Freshman Year of Studies: Arts and Letters, Business Administration, Engineering, and Science. Each has a core program, the weight of which (outside the area of specialization) is in theology and philosophy. The most extensive core requirements are, not surprisingly, in Arts and Letters, and especially in that college's Program of Liberal Studies —Notre Dame's Great Books sequence. It's as "structured" as any program around—only eight elective courses are taken in four years, allowing just enough room for a dual major. The heart of the program is the Great Books Seminars, I through VI—each of which is required. In addition to literature, natural science, philosophy, theology, and history courses, the liberal studies major must complete two semesters of either of the classical languages, Latin or Greek.

The classical tradition and other things Catholic and traditional are upheld by Notre Dame's conservative magazine, *Dialogue*. Board members include author Michael Novak and Congressmen Henry Hyde (R., Ill.) and Robert K. Dornan (R., Calif.). Another board member, J. J. Carberry, of Notre Dame's chemical engineering faculty, is a perceptive observer of the campus scene. Concerning one of the university's more important areas of study, he has observed: "If St. Paul were a member of the Theology Department, he would not be offered tenure."

Back to the Future

And the future of the Notre Dame curriculum must be considered at some risk. Near the end of his tenure, the Reverend Theodore Hesburgh, Notre Dame's former president (never considered a conservative), remarked:

> The name of the game in the 1980s is quality. We must get back out of the wild growth of the curriculum and get back into some core of knowledge— history, philosophy, theology, language, literature, mathematics, science, art and music.
>
> Otherwise we are just graduating trained seals.

And Notre Dame is not a zoo. Not yet, anyway, although Father Hesburgh's successor, the Reverend Edward A. Malloy, seems to be encouraging the barking for fish. He declared 1988–89 the "Year of Cultural Diversity," and has stepped up recruitment of minorities and women (an activity that is superficially benign but almost always creates malignant results, especially for minority students). The year 1990–91 was the "Year of Women." And in our first edition we wondered, What's next? "The Year of the Planet"? "Father Malloy," we observed, "seems to be reading *Time* magazine"— which had just honored Earth in its annual "Man of the Year" issue. "And the new head of the Freshman Year of Studies has been suggesting feminist innovations that threaten the program's integrity." Well, we spoke too rashly. Well-intentioned acts of politicization continue, but they are simply not a serious matter. Notre Dame's integrity remains se-

Never before has there been so much education and never before so little coming to the knowledge of the truth. We forget that ignorance is better than error.

—*Fulton Sheen*

143

cure. And, again as we noted the first time around, liberal theologian Richard P. McBrien, head of Notre Dame's theology department, has complained that Father Malloy may even "reassert and restore" the "presence" of the Holy Cross order in the university's life—a fact that Father McBrien finds worrisome but which we, admiring fidelity to tradition, would consider a positive sign. With the school's sesquicentennial (1990–91), Notre Dame ceased designating each year thematically, which may represent a wise step back from the precarious perch of faddish enthusiasm. In the end, *our* enthusiasm for Notre Dame remains undiminished. Where else can the prospective student find the same confluence of forces: curricular excellence, a teaching faculty, world-class facilities, championship athletics, and a sense of tradition so strong that nothing is likely to dislodge it?   □

Oglethorpe
Atlanta, Georgia

The Nine Commandments

A s noted in the preface, the American college and university have, by and large, been shaped by three disparate and often contentious models of higher education: the English college, the German university, and the land-grant college. The great research universities, with their emphasis on graduate and professional education, have drawn their inspiration from the German ideal; the state universities, distinguished by the proliferation of specialized and practical studies in fields such as engineering and agriculture, are the progeny of the Morrill Act of 1862, which inaugurated the land-grant movement.

But it is the English tradition, articulated most effectively by Cardinal Newman, that has shaped and guided the development of Oglethorpe University. The university was founded in 1835 and named for General James Edward Oglethorpe. Its structure and priorities were inspired by the general's alma mater, Oxford University's Corpus Christi College. As a recent Oglethorpe publication describes the tradition, the English-style college emphasizes "broad education for intelligent leadership" rather than narrow specialization or vocational training. Such schools encourage close student-faculty contact, because "the most important function of the teacher is to stimulate intellectual activity in the student and to promote his or her development as a mature person." Says an Oglethorpe publication: "Factory-like instruction, conducted in large classes, is the very antithesis of the English tradition."

Finally, the English college recognizes that an education is more than a mere collection of academic courses, that it must also involve the development of leadership skills.

At Oglethorpe that tradition persists. The goal of the university remains "the preparation of the humane generalist." Such training, Oglethorpe believes, is ideally suited for a rapidly changing society. "Rigid specialization, with its training in current practice, ill prepares the graduate for responsibilities in such a society. The broadly educated person, schooled in fundamental principles, is better equipped to exercise leadership in a world that is being transformed by high technology and new information."

What impresses us about Oglethorpe is that this commitment is accompanied by an exceptionally strong sense of institutional identity and mission, and is embodied in one of the most thoughtful, comprehensive, and well structured curriculums we have seen. Unlike many of its counterparts in the Ivy League, Oglethorpe has no difficulty in describing what the ends of a college education should be. Call them the Nine Commandments: (1) "The ability to comprehend English prose at an advanced level." (2) "The ability to convey ideas in writing and in speech. . . ." (3) "Skill in reasoning logically about important matters." (4) "An understanding of the values and principles that have shaped Western civilization and of the methods employed in historical inquiry." (5) "A knowledge and appreciation of great literature, especially the great literature of the English-speaking world." (6) "An appreciation of one or more of the arts and an understanding of artistic excellence." (7) "An acquaintance with the methods of inquiry of mathematics and science. . . ." (8) "An understanding of the most thoughtful reflections on right and wrong and an allegiance to principles of right conduct." (9) "A basic understanding of our economic, political, and social systems and of the psychological and sociological influences on human behavior."

Oglethorpe University

Year Founded: 1835
Total Cost: $15,050
Total Enrollment: 1,195
Total Applicants: 1,123
  84% accepted
  23% of accepted enrolled
SAT Middle Range
  Averages: 1050–1280
Financial Aid:
  70% applied
  63% judged to have need
  100% of those judged
    were given aid
ROTC Program Offered
Application Information:
  Mr. Dennis Matthews
  Director of Admissions
  Oglethorpe University
  Atlanta, GA 30319
  Telephone: (404) 233-6864
Application Deadlines:
  Early decision: 12/1
  Regular decision: 8/1

The Means to the Ends

Oglethorpe backs up those ambitious goals with an extensive core curriculum of eleven courses required of all students. Effective with the 1992–93 academic year, all students must take the following: Philosophical Conceptions of Reality and Human Life; Analytical Writing; The West and the Medieval World and The West and the Modern World; Human Nature and the Social Order I and II; and Psychological Inquiry.

In addition, students must select either Music and Culture or Art and Culture; one of four year-long courses in English, American, or world literature; one of four lab courses in the physical sciences; one of two lab courses in the biological sciences; and one of four courses in calculus, statistics, or computer programming.

In other words, whatever may be happening at other schools, it is impossible for a student to graduate from Oglethorpe without at least some exposure to the history, literature, and thought of the West. Equally impressive is the extent of the common intellectual experience provided by the curriculum. While students at some research multiversities are quickly and hermetically sealed into the specialties of the faculty, students at Oglethorpe *actually have something to talk about with one another*, even if they do not have the same majors.

> To train a citizen is to train a critic. The whole point of education is that it should give a man abstract and eternal standards, by which he can judge material and fugitive conditions.
>
> —G. K. Chesterton

A Bright Future

The English tradition is also apparent in the classroom itself. Most classes are small, there are no teaching assistants, and even the most senior faculty members teach freshman-level courses. Beyond that, students work one-on-one with a faculty member in developing their undergraduate programs.

All the signs for Oglethorpe's continued growth are optimistic. Oglethorpe's recently completed a $3 million project that tripled the size of the university library. Meanwhile, Oglethorpe is beginning to win recognition for its efforts. Its Writing across the Curriculum program won a major grant, as well as a national Excellence in Teaching award, given by the English-Speaking Union in 1989.

The quality of incoming Oglethorpe students has risen consistently in recent years as the school has become increasingly selective. Most entering freshmen graduated in the top 10 percent of their classes; 10 percent were their high school's valedictorian or salutatorian. About half of the student body is from Georgia, and two-thirds are from the Southeast, but the rest come from throughout the country. Twenty-five states and thirty foreign countries are typically represented in the student body. About one-third of Oglethorpe's graduates pursue graduate or professional degrees, and typically they have considerable success winning admission to their first-choice schools.

1991–92 was Oglethorpe's first year in what must be (perhaps after the Ivy League) the nation's most intellectual conference, the CAC. The seven-member College Athletic Conference includes six schools profiled in this book. Besides Oglethorpe, they are Centre, Millsaps, Rhodes, Trinity, and University of the South.   □

Oklahoma City University

Oklahoma City, Oklahoma

Acts of Recovery

One of the most heartening stories in higher education is Oklahoma City University's resurgence over the last decade. Faced with daunting financial problems in the 1970s, this independent Methodist university embarked on an ambitious plan to make itself into one of the region's most noteworthy schools. Because it could not rely either on massive wealth or a stellar reputation, it chose instead to emphasize excellence in its teaching, its curriculum, and in its commitment to liberal education. In that respect, this fast-growing school is swimming against the tide. Consider:

· Instead of watering down its curriculum in the name of "diversity," Oklahoma City has instituted a classical core curriculum known as the Foundation Curriculum, "which has been specifically designed to initiate the student into those disciplines and traditions of Western culture which have proven to be valuable resources in the individual search for meaning and understanding."

Oklahoma City University

Year Founded: 1904
Total Cost: $9,330
Total Enrollment: 4,450
Total Applicants: 1,083
  83% accepted
  22% of accepted enrolled
SAT Average: 949
Financial Aid: N/A
ROTC Program Offered
Application Information:
  Mr. Keith Hackett
  Dean of Admissions
  Oklahoma City
    University
  2501 N. Blackwelder
  Oklahoma City, OK 73106
  Telephone: (405) 521-5050
Application Deadlines:
  Ongoing

· While other big-name schools in the Southwest are drifting into impersonal giantism, Oklahoma City boasts: "There are no teaching assistants employed at the University; lower as well as upper division courses are taught by senior faculty. There is no 'warehousing' of students in large lecture-hall courses. Enrollment in lower division courses is kept to a maximum of 25 (20 in writing courses); most upper level major courses average 12 to 15 students." On a walk across campus, the university's president seems to know every student by name.

· When other schools talk about "multiculturalism" and the need to globalize their curriculum, they too often mean adding Frantz Fanon or Rigoberta Menchu to their reading lists. Oklahoma City, on the other hand, actually reaches out to what's best in the Pacific Basin and Eastern Europe. The school's well-regarded Asian studies program offers instruction in the Chinese and Japanese languages, as well as classes in Asian culture, literature, and religion. The program culminates in a yearlong internship in Asia. In addition, OCU runs accredited MBA programs in Singapore and Kuala Lampur, Malaysia, and a master's of higher education administration program in the People's Republic of China. It was one of only three American universities to be selected by Soviet educators to develop a special management education program for the former Soviet Union. OCU is also establishing similar programs for the new governments in what used to be Czechoslovakia.

· While the administrators of other schools see themselves as protectors of the faculty's fiefdoms, OCU's leadership is aggressive and committed to undergraduate education. From president Jerald C. Walker (himself an OCU graduate, Class of 1960) on down, OCU's administrators seem acutely aware of the need to make the school distinctive by flouting many of the conventions of the academic establishment.

· Best of all, OCU seems to recognize that the only way it can compete with bigger and better-known schools is to turn out students who are better read and better educated than their counterparts.

Firm Foundations

Oklahoma City has accomplished this goal by making the undergraduate program and the curriculum student-centered. Larry Eberhardt, the division coordinator for the social sciences, explains that this sets OCU apart from other schools because it offers a "balanced curriculum geared to the needs of students, as opposed to the faculty." The program emphasizes quality teaching and a solid grounding in the liberal arts. "Pre-professionalism is not our main focus," he explains. "We resist too much narrow specialization at the undergraduate level."

The heart of the school's program is its Foundation Curriculum. The university explains: "This is not a 'cafeteria style' curriculum; courses are chosen not merely because they are 1000-level [entry level] courses to the discipline, but because they contribute to the student's critical writing and thinking development and nurture an appreciation for the history of ideas." Oklahoma City is explicit in setting out the goals of the curriculum. After four years, a student should be able to communicate clearly, "have an informed sense of their cultural traditions. . . . have an appreciation of shared beliefs and values . . . have an understanding of the Scientific Method . . . cultivate his aesthetic sensibility . . . have an informed sense of contemporary economic, social and political problems . . . develop the necessary tools of research, logical thinking, and critical inquiry. . . ." The Foundation Curriculum requires candidates for the bachelor of arts to complete fifty-eight credit hours and the bachelor of science majors to complete fifty-two hours. Requirements include six credits in Fundamentals of Written English; a course in Classics of Western Literature; a course in speech; six credits in Shared Beliefs and Value Systems, which includes an introduction to biblical literature and an additional course in religion, English, or philosophy; a course in the Social, Intellectual and Cultural History of the United States; a political science course in American government; Principles of Economics; and one of four designated courses in studies in human behavior and culture, which include two courses in the history of world civilization, a psychology course in Motivation and Human Conduct, and a sociology course in The Structure of Society. Students must also take seven credits in natural science; a course in Mathematics, Models and Com-

That man, I think, has had a liberal education, who has been so trained in youth that his body is the ready servant of his will.

—*Thomas Henry Huxley*

puters; a course in Fine Arts and Human Values; two credits in phys ed; and twelve credits in a foreign language. Throughout its curriculum, OCU emphasizes writing. In the business school, for instance, former dean Willis Wheat notes the school's policy against true-false and multiple-choice exams. "We wanted all of our exams to be of an essay nature," he says. "We wanted the students to be able to write." An outspoken skeptic of the unread and unreadable academic goobledygook that passes for "research" in too many business schools, Dean Wheat forged close ties with the local business community and has emphasized practical, real-world approaches to business education. That seems to be paying off; OCU's graduates are sought-after and well regarded in business circles.

Real-World Recognition

One token of the regard for Oklahoma City University was AT&T's decision to select the campus to install a state-of-the-art campus communication system, including a campus-wide fiber-optic network linking together all the computers and terminals on the campus. Although the campus is relatively small, it offers an unusually active cultural life. The school's Oklahoma Opera and Music Theater Company is nationally recognized and presents four productions a year. The American Spirit Dance Company also performs on and off campus. In addition to an active theater, chamber choir, and orchestra, OCU has brought in such entertainers as Bill Cosby, Bob Hope, Luciano Pavarotti, Cary Grant, and Placido Domingo. But its strength remains its commitment to its students and to the liberal arts.

Unlike some of the other schools in this guide, whose time-honored traditions are under attack from their own administrators and faculty, and whose future is therefore questionable, we are optimistic that OCU will continue to grow in stature and quality throughout the 1990s. □

Pepperdine
Malibu, California

Sand, Surf, and Substance

Nobody ever said the liberal arts had to be drab. And Pepperdine, located in the rolling hills of Malibu on the Pacific coast, will never be accused of lacking style. But the sun, sand, and surf image of this southern California school could not be more misleading.

Affiliated with the evangelical Church of Christ, Pepperdine combines a rigorous and well-structured liberal arts curriculum with a strict moral atmosphere that includes a ban on drinking on campus, required religion courses, and mandatory attendance at weekly convocations. Although fewer than one out of five Pepperdine students is a member of the Church of Christ, the religious and moral atmosphere of the school permeates the campus.

The university's mission statement is in the form of an affirmation:

THAT GOD IS.
That He is revealed uniquely in Christ.
That the educational process may not, with impunity, be divorced from the divine process.
That the student, as a person of infinite dignity, is the heart of the educational enterprise.
That the quality of student life is a valid concern of the University.
That truth, having nothing to fear from investigation, should be pursued relentlessly in every discipline.
That spiritual commitment, tolerating no excuse for mediocrity, demands the highest standards of academic excellence.
That freedom, whether spiritual, intellectual, or economic, is indivisible.
That knowledge calls, ultimately, for a life of service.

Given that ringing creed, we should not be surprised to learn that Pepperdine students are conservative—one estimate puts the proportion of registered Republicans at three out of four. But they are not stuffy. Surfing is, predictably, a popular sport, and the school boasts a top-ranked volleyball team. Admittedly, some students are attracted less by the curriculum than by the location and amenities of Pepperdine's 830-acre campus, but all students must complete the school's extensive liberal arts core. Those requirements take up more than half the students' undergraduate course loads.

Pepperdine's Nucleus

Pepperdine's undergraduate division, Seaver College (itself divided into seven divisions: business, communications, fine arts, humanities, natural science, religion, and social science/teacher education), requires two courses in English composition and literature and a sequence of three courses in Western heritage that constitutes a historical survey of the development of Western civilization from the early Greeks to contemporary Europe and the United States. The courses are interdisciplinary, drawing on the study of history, literature, religion, philosophy, art, and music. Students are also required to take one course in non-Western heritage. At some schools, this might be a covert way of introducing a politicized third world element into the curriculum, but that does not seem to be the case at Pepperdine, where the requirement can be satisfied with only a handful of designated courses, among them: Sources of Asian Tradition, The Religions of the World, Israel Excavation, California Archaeology and Pre-European Cultures, Culture and Personality, Intercultural Communication, and Pre-Columbian Civilizations of North America.

Additional requirements include two courses in American heritage, an introductory course in either psychology or sociology, a foreign language course at the second-year level, an introductory-level laboratory science course, a mathematics course, a course in Fundamentals of Public Speaking, as well as courses in The History and Religion of Israel, The History and Religion of Early Christianity, and Religion and Culture. Rounding out the requirements are a freshman seminar and *four years* of physical education.

The virtues of this rigorous curriculum are many, but foremost are its careful design and its provision to students of a common intellectual experience. At many schools that boast a core curriculum, so many choices are offered that there is no guarantee that any two students in the university will have read

Pepperdine University

Year Founded: 1937
Total Cost: $23,300
Total Enrollment: 7,554
Total Applicants: 3,356
  57% accepted
  37% of accepted enrolled
SAT Average: 1100
Financial Aid:
  N/A % applied
  65% judged to have need
  65% of those judged
    were given aid
ROTC Program Offered
Application Information:
  Mr. Paul Long
  Dean of Admissions
  Pepperdine University
  Malibu, CA 90263
  Telephone: (213) 456-4392
Application Deadlines:
  Early action: 11/15
  Regular decision: 2/1

the same books or taken the same courses. But at Pepperdine, not only do all students take the same Western heritage sequence, but the curriculum is structured in such a way as to assure considerable overlap in areas. For example, to satisfy the two-course requirement in American heritage, students must choose from among only three options: Economic Principles, The United States of America (History), and the American Political Process.

The Great Books

Pepperdine recently inaugurated a Great Books Colloquium to complement its core curriculum. The colloquium, a limited-enrollment program, consists of four seminars taken over four semesters and is intended as an affirmation of Pepperdine's mission statement, "that truth, having nothing to fear from investigation, should be pursued relentlessly in every discipline." Over two years, the colloquium features discussions of Homer, Plato, the Greek playwrights, Aristotle, the Bible, Virgil, St. Augustine, St. Thomas Aquinas, Martin Luther, Chaucer, *Beowulf*, Shakespeare, Machiavelli, Dante, Galileo, Erasmus, Cervantes, Hobbes, Milton, Hegel, Thoreau, Emerson, Kant, Swift, Locke, Rousseau, Adam Smith, Voltaire, Goethe, Descartes, Miller, Bentham, Shaw, Darwin, Camus, Sartre, Tillich, Kierkegard. T. S. Eliot, Joyce, Marx, Faulkner, Skinner, Freud, Dostoevsky, Tolstoy, Ibsen, Twain, and Nietzsche.

The format for the colloquium is discussion rather than lectures, and the classes are kept small to facilitate close readings of the great texts. But even outside of the colloquium, Pepperdine wins high marks from students for the accessibility of the faculty.

All Seaver College students, regardless of their major, are eligible to participate in the school's extensive international study opportunities, including programs in Heidelberg, London, Florence, Madrid, and Paris. Taught by visiting faculty from the Malibu campus and Pepperdine faculty who live in Europe, the programs offer a full range of studies and are designed so that students can complete a substantial portion of their general academic requirements while abroad. The newest international program offers a yearlong course of study in Japan, reflecting Pepperdine's ever-evolving interest in California's Asian roots.

Despite its strong emphasis on the liberal arts,

In [earlier] days a boy on the classical side officially did almost nothing but classics. I think this was wise; the greatest service we can do to education today is to teach fewer subjects.

—*C. S. Lewis*

Seaver College is well known for its business administration division—by far its most popular department—and for its career center, which has an outstanding record of placing Pepperdine graduates in business. Part of the attraction of Pepperdine graduates is that they not only receive a quality academic education, but are taught the centrality of moral values in their lives. As Seaver College's dean says, "It is not enough to have the skills. It is not enough to know the world in which we live. It is crucially important to know how to determine the relative value of the competing ideas around us. We believe that the ideal Seaver graduate will not only be well prepared and well informed, but will also face life decisions with integrity and strength of character." □

Providence

Providence, Rhode Island

A Bold Reaffirmation

At the beginning of the 1970s, Providence, Rhode Island, was witness to two revolutions in higher education. In the first, Brown University put itself at the forefront of the dissolution of academic standards by abolishing all distribution requirements and watering down its grading system, thereby beginning its long slow descent into terminal academic trendiness.

Across town, Providence College, in a move that was no less revolutionary but in the exact opposite direction, defied the Zeitgeist and "boldly reaffirmed the concepts of a core curriculum and of the privileged position of the humanities in the curriculum."

The result of this *risorgimento* was the school's outstanding Development of Western Civilization program, a two-year sequence of courses taught by faculty members from the departments of history, literature, philosophy, and religious studies.

A recent college publication describes the philosophy of the program:

The study of Western civilization, in its moments of majesty and madness, glory and shame, provides a key to self-understanding because this civilization has been largely responsible for making us who and what we are, not only as we react to society but also in our most personal values. Tertullian long ago posed the famous question: "What has Athens to do with Jerusalem?" We ask students to confront similar questions honestly: What do Aristotle and Augustine, Kant and Kafka, have to do with us, or to say to us? By acquiring an understanding of the development of Western civilization, students acquire a greater ability to understand themselves and to shape their future.

From Gilgamesh to Solzhenitsyn

While students at Brown can while away their time in courses like "Rock 'n' Roll Is Here to Stay," Providence's Western civ classes meet five days a week—for a total of twenty credit hours—and are required of *all* freshmen and sophomores. During the program's first year, students discuss the roots of Western civilization from their beginnings in Mesopotamia and Egypt, through the Old Testament, the rise of the Aegean civilization, the Golden Age of Greece, the Roman Republic and Empire, the rise of Christianity, and the Middle Ages, to the dawning of the Renaissance and the Reformation. Lectures cover *The Epic of Gilgamesh*, Homer's *Iliad* and *Odyssey*, the structure of the Greek city-state, the Persian Wars, the pre-Socratic Philosophers, the plays of Sophocles, Aeschylus, and Euripides, the text of the New Testament and *The Song of Roland*, and the works of Plato, Aristotle, Virgil, St. Paul, St. Augustine, St. Anselm, St. Thomas Aquinas, Dante, Chaucer, Boccaccio, Petrarch, Rebelais, Cervantes, and Shakespeare.

During the second year, students discuss the structure and problems of the modern world, including the two world wars, and the development of modernism, totalitarianism, and existentialism. Once again the reading list is impressive: Molière, Descartes, Milton, Locke, Voltaire, Goethe, Hegel, Marx, Flaubert, Dostoevsky, Tolstoy, Nietzsche, T. S. Eliot, Sartre, Samuel Beckett, Vatican II, and Solzhenitsyn.

The Western civilization program is central to Providence's curriculum not only because it shapes the historical knowledge of students, but also because its rigorous requirements develop in the student a broad range of academic skills. Describing the goal of the program, the college says: "Effective

Providence College

Year Founded: 1917
Total Cost: $18,550
Total Enrollment: 5,771
Total Applicants: 5,106
  62% accepted
  30% of accepted enrolled
SAT Middle Range
  Averages: 950–1140
Financial Aid:
  53% applied
  85% judged to have need
  98% of those judged were given aid
ROTC Program Offered
Application Information:
  Mr. Michael G. Backes
  Dean of Admissions
  Providence College
  Providence, RI 02918
  Telephone: (401) 865-2535
Application Deadlines:
  Early action: 12/15
  Regular decision: 2/1

reading and writing and thinking, analysis and synthesis of information and concepts, and understanding of key events, forces and ideas that have shaped the Western world all contribute to the well-rounded education that Providence College seeks to provide."

Other requirements include six credits each in social science, natural science, philosophy, and religious studies; and three credits each in the fine arts and in mathematics. A particularly attractive option for superior students is the liberal arts honors program, which consists of special seminars in all four years of undergraduate study.

> By nature all men are alike, but by education widely different.
>
> —*Chinese Proverb*

Providence also wins high marks for its science and engineering programs, primarily due to the accessibility of the faculty and their involvement in academic life (unlike many schools where the science faculty is merely a rumor to undergraduates, who tend to be taught by teaching assistants.)

A Few *NR* Readers

It is important to note that Providence is not a conservative enclave. Despite the traditional orientation of the curriculum, the faculty tends to be somewhat liberal, but is pretty much a mixed bag. "We have a few live socialists, and a few who read *National Review* religiously," says one professor. Another professor describes the bulk of the faculty as "Humphrey Democrats." Although the student body is described as "socially aware," it tends to be apolitical.

In any case, the omens are good for the continuing stability of the curriculum at Providence. Although Western civilization programs are under fire from the campus Left across the country, support for Providence's program cuts across ideological lines, according to the program's director. "When these arguments [about the place of Western civ in the curriculum] began we had already committed to this program, and frankly it has worked out so well that there is no talk about radical change," says Professor Mario R. DiNunzio. "At some point you have to make a choice and we've made ours."

The school's small size (about 3,700 undergraduates) ensures close student-faculty contact, and most classes are small. Freshmen are provided an academic counselor, and are invited to a two-day orientation program the summer before they enter. Students also have numerous opportunities for constructive activism, including the Pastoral Council and Big Brothers and Sisters. The local Knights of Columbus council was recently named the most outstanding college council in the nation. Social life on campus appears healthy (the student body is divided about evenly between men and women), as does Providence's athletic program, which regularly produces winning teams at the Division I level.

Free of Restraints

Providence College also boasts an excellent record of keeping its students happy—or at least keeping them in school. Because of its close personal attention, few fall between the cracks. Fully 98 percent finish their freshman year in good standing.

Providence's religious affiliation is central to its identity as a Roman Catholic liberal arts college. It is run by the Dominican order. That probably accounts for the school's unusual eloquent and clear mission statement. "The goal of all liberal education is the freeing of the mind from the restraints of ignorance, and the elevation of the spirit to an awareness of the values which enrich human life with dignity and significance," a recent publication proclaims. "A liberal education, therefore, is necessarily concerned with enabling students to seek knowledge, to recognize beauty, and to practice virtue."

Even though classes are sometimes taught by Dominicans clad in the full regalia of their order, non-Catholics ought not be dissuaded from considering Providence. The school's charter declares that "no person shall be denied any of the privileges, honors or degrees" offered by the college "on account of the religious opinions he may entertain." After all, Providence, Rhode Island, is where Roger Williams in 1644 so boldly proclaimed American religious freedom. □

Rhodes

Memphis, Tennessee

The Search for Values

Rhodes College is a relatively new name on the scene of American higher education, although the college itself has been in Memphis since 1925. Actually, its history begins in 1837, when it was founded as Clarksville Academy. In 1855 it became Stewart College, and in 1875 Southwestern Presbyterian (Joseph Wilson, father of Woodrow, was head of the school of theology). On its move from Clarksville, the name was shortened to Southwestern, and then, in 1945, Southwestern at Memphis. Finally, it became Rhodes College in 1984, taking its new name from Peyton N. Rhodes, the physics professor and later college president (1949–65) who served the college for nearly sixty years.

"Rhodes," the college catalog says, "can be described in a few simple words: It is coeducational, undergraduate, metropolitan, private, small, well rounded, beautiful [and] church-related. . . ." That last quality allows the college to make a statement rarely heard anymore in higher education: its Christian commitment is "more than assent to a set of vague values or sentimental emotions. It is a view of existence and reality, based upon faith in God as creator, sustainer, and redeemer of life. It recognizes that the fear of God is the beginning of wisdom and that truth is God's self-revelation."

The Best Goals

As the school catalog claims, Rhodes remains private because of its belief in "the market economic system that has built this country and fostered the growth of freedom." We couldn't have said it better ourselves. Rhodes, like most of the other schools on our list, "stands as an important part of the free enterprise sector that opposes a government monopoly of higher education."

Rhodes is also quite specific about the goals of its liberal arts program ("the best education for all of life"). It seeks to develop eight skills in its students:

critical thinking, creativity, and the ability to empathize with other perspectives, communicate, research, evaluate, express, and synthesize. In pursuit of these qualities, students must fulfill certain distribution requirements. There are the usual (by our standards) requirements in writing and a foreign language, plus nine hours each of humanities, natural sciences, and social sciences, and six hours in the fine arts. A major field of study must be declared by the spring semester of the sophomore year, and in order to graduate seniors must take a two- to six-credit senior seminar, including a comprehensive exam reviewing all material in the major.

But the heart of the general-education requirement (the core of the core) is the Search for Values, a.k.a. Humanities 101-102, 201-202, a two-year, interdisciplinary survey that is subtitled "in the Light of Western History and Religion." It was Alexander Pope who said. "The proper study of mankind is man." Pope was a deistic rationalist; the folks at Rhodes are not. And yet it *is* mankind students study in the search for Values. Indeed, this requirement used to be called the "Man Course." At Rhodes, though, man is seen against a backdrop of Revelation.

A Classic Classics Course

The Search for Values is a course in the classic mold, with lectures, colloquia, the occasional special session, and, oh yes, exams. Each student works from a printed syllabus listing all lecture topics, readings, and study questions as well. Year one is divided into four units: the Hebrews, the Greeks, the Romans, and the Christians. In essence, this involves study of the history and philosophy of the West from stories (biblical and other) of Creation through the writings of Augustine.

In year two there are four tracks—religion, philosophy, literature, and history—with a common list of readings not strictly limited to each field. Students sign up for one of the four (literature and history, the more popular choices, have three class sections each) and study the great ideas from the perspective of each discipline, covering, chronologically, the periods from the Middle Ages to the present. The format is new—the present eight class sections for the four disciplines supplant what had been one large group. With no need now for the large common lecture, more time is available for

Rhodes College

Year Founded: 1848
Total Cost: $18,658
Total Enrollment: 1,414
Total Applicants: 2,086
  75% accepted
  25% of accepted enrolled
SAT Middle Range
  Averages:
  530–630V/580–670M
Financial Aid:
  84% applied
  94% judged to have need
  100% of those judged
    were given aid
ROTC Program Offered
Application Information:
  Mr. David Wottle
  Dean of Admissions and
    Financial Aid
  Rhodes College
  Memphis, TN 38112
  Telephone: (901) 726-3700
        (800) 238-6788
        (out-of-state)
Application Deadlines:
  Early decision: 11/15
  Regular decision: 2/1

the study of books within each discipline along with the common readings. For a flavor of the readings involved, let's consider just the later periods. For those skeptics supposing Rhodes's religious commitment might swing it away from "humanist" literature, consider: Kant, Franklin, Voltaire, Lessing, Rousseau, Madison, Coleridge, Wood, Schleiermacher, Thoreau, Mill, Darwin, Adam Smith; Marx, Nietzsche, Freud; Heidegger, Sartre, a colloquium entitled "Liberation of the Oppressed"; and finally Wittgenstein, Kuhn, Rorty, and Niebuhr.

Professor Doug Hatfield, the Search director, claims the purpose of the core is to give the students an "entrée into the life of the mind" by looking at history of man's longest-lasting ideas. Because the concept of such an extensive core can seem confusing to both prospective freshmen and Search students, there is a Search Advisory Council consisting of twenty-five or thirty Search graduates—juniors and seniors—who help explain the purpose and benefits of the program and assist underclassmen with papers and exams.

An alternative to the Search course is Life: Then and Now, a twelve-hour sequence that concentrates on theology and religious philosophy.

Rhodes in the World

One of Rhodes's specialties is international studies. (A new home for the department, Buckham Hall, opened in the fall of 1991. An artist's sketch of the new building shows the majestic "collegiate Gothic" style that characterizes the whole of the Rhodes campus. It's a structure that would please Prince Charles.) The department's head is John Copper, a former director of the Asian Studies Center at the Hermitage Foundation. Among other members of the department is the Polish-born Andrew Michta, who left the Hoover Institution to go to Rhodes. More than forty courses make up the I.S. program, and, true to the department's name, cover every region of the globe. "Bridge" majors wed international studies to other disciplines, such as business, economics, and language. Ninety per cent of I.S. students who apply to grad or law school are accepted.

Rhodes thinks highly of its students—so highly that it has practically no rules. It does have an honor code, and all the evidence indicates the students take it quite seriously. The code is so strong,

> The roots of education are bitter, but the fruits are sweet.
>
> *—Aristotle*

according to one insider, "that professors regularly leave the classroom when they administer a test, and so strong that the college cafeteria (we call it a *refectory*) operates solely on the honor system—no meal cards here.

Voluntarism is big at Rhodes. For thirty-two years, the Kinney Program has put students into the Memphis community in various volunteer capacities, and more recently students have been spending spring break in Mexico working with the Puentes de Cristo (Bridges of Christ) program reconstructing some of Mexico's poorest villages.

Rhodes College, with its new name and strong, focused purpose, is a good example of a school that can aim high in the competition among colleges without losing sight of its original philosophy of the goals of higher education.   □

Saint Anselm

Manchester, New Hampshire

Against the Odds

The school's patron saint may be Anselm of Canterbury, but its guiding spirit could as easily be John Henry Newman. In *The Idea of a University*, Cardinal Newman defined the value of a liberal arts education to counter the pressures that were even in the nineteenth century pushing schools toward becoming mere credential factories for the professions. Wrote Newman:

> . . . the man who has learned to think . . . to discriminate, and to analyze, who has refined his taste, formed his judgment, and sharpened his mental vision, will not indeed at once be a lawyer . . . or a statesman, or a physician, or a man of business, or an engineer . . . but he will be placed in that state of intellect in which he can take up any of . . . [these] callings . . . or any other for which he has a taste, or a special talent, with an ease, a versatility, and a success, to which another is a stranger.

Not a few schools continue to give lip service to that vision of the student as humanist, but few schools embody Newman's idea as effectively as Saint Anselm College, where students spend their first two years immersed in one of the most remarkable humanities programs we have found anywhere. So committed is Saint Anselm to postponing specialization that students normally reach their junior year before selecting a major. And why not? The school says that few students come to Saint Anselm with a firm idea of what they want to do with their lives; thus the purpose of an education at Saint Anselm is to help students make those decisions—about what they want to do professionally, and what kind of lives they wish to lead.

Saint Anselm College

Year Founded: 1889
Total Cost: $17,820
Total Enrollment: 1,857
Total Applicants: 2,331
  70% accepted
  32% of accepted enrolled
SAT Averages: 483V/519M
Financial Aid:
  93% applied
  89% judged to have need
  82% of those judged were
    given aid
ROTC Program Offered
Application Information:
  Mr. Donald E. Healy
  Director of Admissions
  Saint Anselm College
  Manchester, NJ 03102
  Telephone: (603) 641-7500
Application Deadlines:
  Early decision: 12/1
  Regular decision: rolling

Anselm and Greatness

The heart of Saint Anselm's program, of its core curriculum, is Portraits of Human Greatness. The course, the college explains, "is based on the obvious but academically unusual premise that people and the kinds of lives they choose to lead are ultimately more important than even the loftiest ideas." At any given time, as many as forty to fifty of Saint Anselm faculty will be teaching the various sections of this course, which invites students "to ponder not only the works of our civilization's great men and women but the people themselves, their values and interests, their decisions and development."

Portraits is a radical course in the modern academy, because it defies the insistence of the Zeitgeist that there is no such thing as "greatness," and indeed no standards by which to judge the questions concerning values and morals which Saint Anselm uses to measure the transcendent significance of human life. It is the often unspoken dogma of the ideology of "diversity" that all values are acceptable, because none is more worthy than any other. Thus, the saint and the moneylender, the philosopher and the ragpicker, Mother Teresa and Joseph Stalin, fade into so many pale, and ultimately meaningless, figures. Their moral indistinguishability is crucial to this academic culture, for to distinguish one from the other implies a hierarchy of values, and indeed of some measure of man beyond the academy's own etiolated standards.

In contrast, Saint Anselm draws upon 1,500 years of Benedictine tradition in asking students to "dedicate themselves to an active and enthusiastic pursuit of truth." In this respect, it reflects the patrimony of St. Anselm (1033–1109), a champion of the Church and the first of the great schoolmen of the Middle Ages. It was Anselm, defending the powers of human reason, who developed the ontological proof for the existence of God. That proof has never won universal support—Thomas Aquinas rejected it—but Anselm was nevertheless a personification of the West's restless search for truth.

The Portraits course consists of nine units, each a portrait of human greatness. In 1990–91, the portraits studied by freshmen were: "the Warrior," "the Prophet," "the Philosopher," "the Lawgiver," "the Christian Martyr," "the Feudal Lord," "the Monk," "the Knight," "the Merchant," "the Medieval Scholar." In their sophomore year, students turn to specific individuals, who are studied chronologically from the Italian Renaissance to the twentieth century. In 1990–91, the individuals studied were Calvin, Cervantes, Shakespeare, Hobbes, Jefferson, Bach, Goethe, Darwin, Lenin, Sartre, and Dorothy Day.

In each case, students are asked to ponder, concerning these individuals: "What makes them human, so inspirational? Why have they become models of 'human greatness'? What can they show us today?" There are ongoing debates about the future of the Portraits program—some faculty members question the inclusion of Lenin—but no major overhaul appears likely.

"We don't apologize for sticking to our tradition, because we think what we're doing works," one administrator says. Quips one professor, "This is a slow-moving college. We're so slow in changing that other people catch up with us."

Deeper into the Core

In addition to the Portraits program, Saint Anselm has an impressive core curriculum that includes a two-semester freshman English course, three courses in philosophy, including Philosophy of Nature and Man, and Ethics; three courses in theology, including Biblical Theology; two semesters of a foreign language beyond elementary work; and two semesters of laboratory science. Students must also pass a comprehensive examination in their major field before graduating. There are no junk courses at Saint Anselm, and each of the various programs appears strong.

Particular note should be taken of Saint Anselm's major in "Liberal Studies in the Great Books," which includes seminars and pereceptorials. How good is this program? Just consider. Students in

Character development is the great, if not the sole, aim of education.

—*William James O'Shea*

163

the first seminar—on ancient authors—begin by reading selections from among a list of authors that includes Homer, Aeschylus, Sophocles, Xenophon, Thucydides, Plato, Aristophanes, Plutarch, and Aristotle. The seminar on Roman literature exposes them to Virgil, Lucretius, Cicero, Tacitus, Seneca, Plutarch, St. John the Evangelist, St. Ignatius of Antioch, and Plotinus. Turning to medieval writers, the Great Books seminar focuses on Boethius, St. Augustine, St. Bede, St. Anselm, *Beowulf, The Cloud of Unknowing*, St. Bonaventure, and St. Thomas Aquinas. The seminar on the Renaissance draws from Erasmus, Bacon, St. Thomas More, Machiavelli, Montaigne, Shakespeare, and Milton. The seminar on modern writers chooses from among Galileo, Hobbes, Descartes, Locke, Molière, Hume, Kant, Pope, and Goethe. Late-modern writers studied include Madison, Hamilton, De Tocqueville, Hegel, Dostoevsky, Kierkegaard, Nietzsche, Tolstoy, and Newman. The seminars are rounded out by preceptorials that study a single book or author. With the help of several individual conferences with the professor, students write a long essay on a topic related to the material being studied. Recent preceptorials have included Plato's *Republic* Confucius and Lao-tzu, Dante's *Divine Comedy*, and Newman's *The Idea of a University*.

If this were not impressive enough, students in the major are also required to take a fine arts elective, two English literature courses, and five philosophy courses, including Formal Logic, Metaphysics, and Philosophy of Science.

This entire picture is all the more remarkable when one considers that while students at Saint Anselm are seeking out "what is true, what is good, and what is beautiful," students are taking The Sociology of Sport at Dartmouth, Television as Culture at Middlebury, and Women's Lives and Women's Lyrics at Amherst.

Life in the Woods

Located in Manchester, New Hampshire, Saint Anselm's campus, on four hundred rolling, wooded acres, is close to the mountains, the beach, and Boston, and offers impressively up-to-date facilities, including the elegant Dana Center (a 700-seat performing arts theater) and a new Computer Science Center. As a Benedictine school, "Saint Anselm observes and promotes Christian and Catholic standards of value and conduct." Perhaps the most notable feature of the campus is the friendliness of both the faculty and students, the true sign of a community based on shared aspirations and values.

The success of Saint Anselm in providing a quality education is evidenced by the success of its graduates in both the professions and in business. A quarter of Saint Anselm's graduates go on to law and medical schools, while a significant number enter graduate schools. Any doubts about the marketability of a classical liberal arts education should be laid to rest by considering the success of Saint Anselm's graduates, who can be found in many of the country's leading corporations, including IBM, Xerox, AT&T, American Express, Wang, and Digital.

But the ultimate success of Saint Anselm is not in its placement of graduates, but in the kind of lives they lead. The end of a truly humanistic education is the good life, well lived.　　□

St. John's College
Annapolis, Maryland, and Santa Fe, New Mexico

The Challenge of Greatness

Edward Fiske of *The New York Times* made an altogether astonishing claim about St. John's College. But first, let's be sure we know which school we mean. This is not the university in New York City, nor the one in Collegeville, Minnesota. In fact, it's not *one* place at all, but two. Mr. Fiske's comment makes it clear why we've included them: "St. John's . . . is perhaps the most intellectual college in the entire country."

And St. John's really is an extraordinary place. Indeed, although we do recommend it, it's so remarkable that it cannot be for every student. (Imagine this: there are just two tests—in algebra during the sophomore year, and French during the senior year—and no grades—actually, grades are kept, just not revealed—yet a third of St. John's students drop out.)

A Collection of Books

What makes St. John's so different and challenging? Samuel Johnson observed: "I cannot see that lectures can do so much good as reading the books from which the lectures are taken." And again, Thomas Carlyle: "The true university of today is a collection of books." Both men would have appreciated St. John's. There are no lectures; there aren't even any professors (here they're called *tutors*). But, oh my, there are books. Nowhere—*nowhere* —do students read so much. The tutors are more like tour guides; their method is Socratic. It may seem odd to say it, but students at St. John's must truly want to be educated, and must be willing to undertake that process largely on their own initiative. It sounds great—until you have to do it.

Did we mention that some reading is required? The Great Books are read chronologically in each sequence of the curriculum (freshmen read the ancients, seniors arrive at the twentieth century). High school students who thought *Catcher in the Rye* was a tough read are advised to peruse the list of authors (see facing page) while seated in a comfortable chair.

Impressive, isn't it? Or is *scary* a better word? All those books, plus four years of math, two of ancient Greek and of French, three years of lab sciences, and one year of music. St. John's is the third-oldest college in the country (1696 was the founding date of the Annapolis campus; the Santa Fe site was opened in 1964), but its method of instruction was last popularly used in Athens circa 450 B.C.

The Socratic Tradition

The college itself describes the academic program as "liberal education in the most traditional and yet radical way," but it's radical only in the sense that what is old is new. The instruction at St. John's takes place in seminars, in tutorials (for languages and music), and in laboratories (for the sciences). Everybody takes everything, in Annapolis as in Santa Fe. (Indeed, students and faculty move freely between the two campuses. But if you consider transferring to St. John's remember: The *everybody/everything* rule means each student must do the "Program," as it's called, and credits from another school are meaningless.)

St. John's College
Annapolis Campus

Year Founded: 1696
Total Cost: $20,600
Total Enrollment: 408
Total Applicants: 303
  84% accepted
  42% of accepted enrolled
SAT Middle Range
  Averages: 560–670V/
  530–670M
Financial Aid:
  61% applied
  70% judged to have need
  100% of those judged
  were given aid
No ROTC Program Offered
Application Information:
  Mr. John Christensen
  Director of Admissions
  St. John's College
  Annapolis, MD 21404
  Telephone: (301) 263-2371
Application Deadlines:
  No early decision
  Regular decision: 3/1

	Literature	Philosophy/Theology	History/Social Science	Math/Natural Science	Music
Year 1	Homer, Aeschylus, Sophocles, Euripides, Aristophanes	Plato, Aristotle, Lucretius	Herodotus, Thucydides, Plutarch	Euclid, Nicomachus, Ptolemy, Lavoisier, Dalton, Archimedes, Torricelli, Pascal, and 16 others	Palestrina, Bach, Mozart, Beethoven, Schubert, Stravinsky, Haydn, Des Prés, Webern
Year 2	Virgil, Dante, Chaucer, Rabelais, Shakespeare, Donne, Marvell	Aristotle, Epictetus, Plotinus, M. Aurelius, the Bible, Augustine, Anselm, Aquinas, Luther, Montaigne, Bacon	Plutarch, Tacitus, Machiavelli	Ptolemy, Apollonius, Copernicus, Descartes, Pascal, Viète	
Year 3	Cervantes, Milton, Swift, Racine, Fielding, Melville, La Fontaine, Austen, La Rochefoucauld	Descartes, Pascal, Hobbes, Spinoza, Locke, Berkeley, Leibniz, Hume	Locke, Rousseau, Adam Smith, the Constitution, the Federalists, Tocqueville	Galileo, Kepler, Young, Euler, Mayer, S. Carnot, L. Carnot, Kelvin, Taylor, and 6 others	Mozart
Year 4	Molière, Goethe, Tolstoy, Dostoevsky, Baudelaire, Rimbaud, Valéry, Yeats, Kafka, Wallace Stevens, Twain, Joyce, Conrad, T. S. Eliot, Woolf, Flannery O'Connor	Hegel, Kierkegaard, Nietzsche, William James	Hegel, Marx, Documents of U.S. Political History, Tocqueville, Opinions of the Supreme Court, Frederick Douglass	Faraday, Lobachevski, Lorenz, Rutherford, Minkowski, Bernard, Davisson, de Broglie, Mendel, J. J. Thompson, Bohr, and 9 others	Wagner

167

Classes are blessedly small: the maximum size is twenty-one. We said there are no tests or grades. True, but there are individual oral exams, and lots of writing assignments. Freshmen, sophomores, and juniors submit essays inspired by the seminar discussions—twice a year in Santa Fe, once a year in Annapolis. And each student is evaluated twice a year, face-to-face, by his tutors.

Those seminars are led by a tutor, who by the way must be able to lead a seminar in *any* subject. (The students-to-faculty ratio is eight to one—an astonishing figure when you realize that all the tutors at St. John's are in the classroom.) The purpose of the seminar is to stimulate discussion of the books being read, usually at the clip of eighty pages for each class. Students must speak up—no slinking down in a chair in the back of a big lecture hall —and the seminars become a kind of crucible in which the student presents opinions, offers evidence in support, and defends his conclusions against the questions of his fellows, always using formal modes of address. It's looser than it sounds, though. Hands aren't raised, and a tutor (all tutors hold the same rank—no assistants or fulls) may offer an opinion (his primary role is to guide and define), but, like the students, he has to fend for himself against questions.

St. John's College
Santa Fe Campus

Year Founded: 1964
Total Cost: $20,650
Total Enrollment: 387
Total Applicants: 275
  83% accepted
  50% of accepted enrolled
SAT Middle Range
  Averages: 530–690V/
  520–690M
Financial Aid:
  61% applied
  75% judged to have need
  100% of those judged
    were given aid
No ROTC Program Offered
Application Information:
  Mr. Larry Clendenin
  Director of Admissions
  St. John's College
  Santa Fe, NM 87501
  Telephone: (800) 331-5232
Application Deadlines:
  No early decision
  Regular decision: 3/1

The St. John's Edge

There are some more traditional lectures—one each week on Friday evening. But these are given to the entire college by a tutor or a visiting speaker. Sometimes it's not talk, but music. In any case, St. John's is proud to point out that these are the only occasions when "students are lectured to."

The student body is not especially conservative —at least not in the political sense. But a certain "cultural" conservatism inevitably arises from the pursuit of the core curriculum. And both the Annapolis and Santa Fe campuses are certainly congenial environments for students who are politically conservative.

Some aspects of St. John's intellectual life do seem to go "over the top." Although intercollegiate athletics were banned in 1939, a crack in the abolition has recently emerged: Annapolis Johnnies annually tangle with the Naval Academy in . . . croquet. And Santa Fe Johnnies do compete against other schools in soccer and fencing.

St. John's is liable to sound like heaven or hell

depending on one's degree of diligence and independence. If it seems a paradise, you may wonder how to get in. Easy: learn to write. SATs are "optional," and grades "may be made irrelevant by what the candidate writes." What must be written is an application consisting of a "series of reflective essays."

St. John's graduates come away with a B.A. in liberal arts, and the ability to think. The latter, more than any diploma from even the most prestigious university, and more than any specific knowledge learned in four years, is what gives St. John's students an edge in life. St. John's students go to the best graduate schools and are welcomed by America's top corporations, which recognize young men and women able to identify and analyze problems, and create and implement solutions.   □

Saint John's/Saint Benedict

Collegeville, Minnesota

Partners in Excellence

Excuse a digression, but before we talk about Saint John's University and the College of Saint Benedict it may be edifying to take a moment's look at the University of Minnesota for a sense of contrast, if nothing else. Think of this as a brief Dantesque journey into academic hell.

Lynne Cheney, the erudite former chairman of the National Endowment for the Humanities, recounts that the humanities department at UM recently unveiled plans to scrap its traditional programs centered on Western civilization and substitute three new courses, with appropriately trendy titles: Discourse and Society, Text and Context, and Knowledge, Persuasion, and Power. Instead of reading Shakespeare, or Dante, or Milton, she noted, students will now study—and she quotes from the course description—"the ways that certain bodies of discourse come to cohere, to exercise persuasive power, and to be regarded as authoritative, while others are marginalized, ignored, or denigrated.

"Instead of reading George Eliot or T. S. Eliot and trying to understand what they have to say about love and failure," Cheney remarks, "students will study—and again, I quote—'hegemony and counter-hegemony.' " One proposed course, "Music as Discourse," which includes the study of music videos, attendance at a Heavy Metal concert, and the analysis of "songs sung at a worker's strike."

Unfortunately, Minnesota is hardly unique in its gadarene rush toward the cutting edge of academic trendiness and cultural boobyism. The flight from reason embodied in a curriculum that replaces Shakespeare with music videos is a symptom of a larger academic disease, and not merely a sign that the cold Minnesota climate has frozen the minds of UM's faculty.

Saint John's University/ College of Saint Benedict

Year Founded: 1857
Total Cost: $14,400
Total Enrollment: 3,599
Total Applicants: 1,641
  90% accepted
  59% of accepted enrolled
ACT Average: 23
Financial Aid:
  86% applied
  85% judged to have need
  100% of those judged
    were given aid
ROTC Program Offered
Application Information:
  Ms. Mary Milbert
  Saint John's University
  Collegeville, MN 56321
  Telephone: (612) 363-2196
Application Deadlines:
  No early decision
  Regular decision: rolling

Underlying Values

The contrast between the University of Minnesota and Saint John's University and the College of Saint Benedict helps dramatize the chasm between the new ideologies of academe and the values that underlie the traditional liberal arts. Saint John's and the College of Saint Benedict are far from perfect by our lights, but we think it is important to have some idea of just how bad a school can be to get some idea of how good others can be.

Like Saint Anselm in New Hampshire, Saint John's is run by the Benedictines and draws upon the principles of their order. Saint John's Abbey, in fact, is the largest Benedictine monastery in the world. "The monastic tradition," the school's mission statement declares, "embodies a fundamental respect for learning and the intellectual and spiritual quest for truth. . . . By this emphasis, Saint John's aims to foster free intellectual inquiry, clear thinking, speaking, and writing, and knowledge of human history and culture."

This clearly sets Saint John's apart from the kind of thing going on at the University of Minnesota, even though Saint John's would probably not be considered a politically conservative institution. Indeed, the faculty tends to be liberal, even though the student body remains eminently more sensible, and the balance appears conducive to a liberal education in the best sense.

Shared Experiences

Founded in 1857 by Benedictines who wanted a school to serve the needs of German Catholic immigrants, the school has a long tradition of academic excellence. More than half of its students ranked in the top third of their high school graduating classes, and on average scored in the 80th percentile in college entrance exams. Saint John's sister institution, the College of Saint Benedict, shares the same traditions, as well as the same core curriculum. (Although Saint John's is all-male and Saint Benedict all-female, the two schools are a mere four miles apart and are linked by a shuttle bus. Because all of the academic programs are shared, the two schools effectively comprise a coed institution.)

The curriculum is centered on the theme of "Exploring the Human Condition." Rather than considering the issues of "hegemony" and "counter-hegemony," the curriculum "emphasizes a common base of essential knowledge in an ethics-based environment." The program addresses three basic questions:

1. How did we, and others, get to this place in the world?
2. How can we think about our lives in this world and discover our roles in it?
3. How ought we, both personally and communally, respond to the world and its demands?

The schools' catalog notes that such questions "have helped men and women focus their spiritual and intellectual lives throughout history. . . . For today's students that search must begin with an examination of their cultural heritage."

The core curriculum is comprised of proficiency-based requirements (foreign language and mathematics), cross-disciplinary freshmen and senior symposia, distribution requirements, and so-called flagged courses. The first-year symposium is a two-semester course required of all freshmen. Classes are limited to sixteen students—equally divided between men and women—and deal with a wide range of subjects. They are all linked, however, by an emphasis on good writing and critical thinking. The professor serves as academic adviser to the students in his or her symposium.

The senior seminar, which serves as a capstone of a student's four years at Saint John's/Saint Benedict, gives "explicit and focused attention . . . to developing the ability to make good moral judgments on issues that affect our lives."

Other requirements include six credits in the fine arts; five courses in the humanities, including one course in Judeo-Christian heritage; and one intro-

> Do not say, the people must be educated, when, after all, you only mean amused, refreshed, soothed, put into good spirits and good humor, or kept from vicious excesses.
>
> —*John Henry Newman*

ductory course in theology. Students must also take two lower-division and one upper-division course in history, literature, philosophy, or theology.

After demonstrating mathematical proficiency, students must also complete one course in mathematics, two courses in the natural sciences (from a designated list of courses in astronomy, biology, chemistry, geology, and physics), and two courses in social sciences—one introductory course in economics, government, psychology, or sociology, and one upper-division course.

The final requirements are the "flagged courses" in five areas: writing (two courses), discussion (one course), global perspectives (one course), quantitative reasoning (one course), and "gender perspectives" (one course).

Buyer Beware

Okay, we know—we're bothered by that last requirement, too, "Gender perspectives" almost invariably translates into politicized, jargon-loaded courses in feminist ideology. Not even Dartmouth *requires* such courses—at least not yet. So this is a major strike against Saint John's. But we are willing to make allowances (albeit somewhat grudgingly) because of the curriculum's overall strength. There are, of course, some gaps, but it appears to give students the intellectual weapons to confront the sophistry of feminist studies. And this is more than we can say of most of the schools we have looked at—including most of the elite Ivy League schools.

But the "gender" requirement is also a reminder of how deeply the new ideologies have penetrated in higher education. It is also a cautionary note that despite its strengths, Saint John's can be a left-leaning institution in some ways. Its monks, for example, have been (Lord, forgive them) at the forefront of liturgical reform, and the school hosts the Institute for Ecumenical and Cultural Research, which has ties to the World Council of Churches.

But even these factors do not eclipse the overall excellence of the schools, nor the pervasive atmosphere of intellectual tolerance. The students tend to be conservative, and the Catholicism of the campus is a real (rather than merely formal) presence. (About a fourth of the schools' faculties are monastic priests, brothers, or sisters.) The pre-medical and pre-business programs are outstanding, and the English, medieval studies, theology, and music departments win widespread plaudits. Faculty interaction with students is exceptionally close; the strong emphasis on faculty advising is cited by students as one of the schools' distinctive strengths. ("In fact," says one college publication, "we value the process of academic advising so highly that annual awards are awarded to the top faculty advisors.")

One notable aspect of the Saint John's/Saint Benedict's programs is their January term, a chance for students to break away from the regular curriculum and study a subject in-depth, or to study abroad (the school offers numerous opportunities).

Great Conversations

Saint John's compensates for its relative physical isolation by its annual Forum, which brings in leading intellectual figures to engage in a series of debates on critical issues. The program also provides an unusual opportunity for faculty and students to debate one another. The Forum is patterned on the Cambridge Union Society of Great Britain; every year about a hundred students are selected for participation, including preparatory seminars conducted by faculty members from a field related to the issue being debated.

Other opportunities include a special major in the humanities and an honors program focused on the Great Books in which students are exposed to the basic texts of the sciences, arts, theology, and the humanities. The program includes a yearlong seminar in Great Books, Great Ideas that takes students through Plato, Aristotle, the Bible, Augustine, Montaigne, Shakespeare, Goethe, Brontë, Marx, Dostoevsky, Tolstoy, Freud, and Flannery O'Connor.

From among the programs for studying abroad, our attention was drawn to the school's Greco-Roman program, which "is particularly concerned with study of classical and contemporary art, literature, history, religion and philosophy in Athens and Rome." The courses are taught in English, are primarily on historical and archaeological sites or museums, and carry up to sixteen credits. In Athens, courses discuss various aspects of Greek civilization and trace the development of the Eastern Church through Byzantine iconography, while the program in Rome continues the same theme, offering courses in Roman art, history, and literature and a

173

theology course describing the development of the Western Church.

One final word: we know that Minnesota can't compete with southern California or Florida for climate, but we could hardly discuss Saint John's/ Saint Benedict without mentioning the beauty of their campuses. The Saint John's campus alone comprises 2,400 gorgeous acres, including several of Minnesota's thousand lakes, and a nature preserve. Said one student: "I chose Saint John's because when I visited, I liked the people, the atmosphere; and the campus is beautiful. You can focus on your studying in this environment."   □

Saint Mary's College of California

Moraga, California

Beauty on the Bay

The Christian Brothers were founded in 1680— during the reign of Louis XIV—and dedicated to "the Christian education of sons of poor and working class families." Three centuries later, the order continues to take that mission very seriously. Today, the Christian Brothers operate seven colleges and universities, including the order's crown jewel, Saint Mary's College.

Reflecting its traditions, Saint Mary's Catholicism is anything but an afterthought. It is buttressed, moreover, by an extraordinarily strong commitment to liberal education. Students who attend Saint Mary's will not find a curriculum formed by happenstance or faculty whim; they will be treated to a program of liberal learning that is both rigorous and exceptionally well thought out. In short, Saint Mary's is a classic example of a school committed to teaching students *how* to think rather than *what* to think.

Twenty-five Centuries of Thought

Since 1941, a Great Books curriculum has been at the heart of the educational program at Saint Mary's—a program that is at the center of the college's identity and its sense of community. All students must take four semesters' worth of Collegiate Seminars "covering over 25 centuries of Western thought and examining the works of great minds—poets, philosophers, scientists, and historians." In the seminar on "Greek Thought," Saint Mary's students read Homer, Aeschylus, Sophocles, Euripides, Thucydides, Aristophanes, Plato (a *lot* of Plato—*Euthyphro, Apology, Crito,* and *Meno*), Aristotle, Euclid, and Ptolemy. In the seminar on Roman, Early Christian, and Medieval Thought, students read and discuss Cicero, Lucretius, Virgil, Plutarch, Catullus, Horace, Ovid, Galen, Augustine, Aquinas, Dante, the Goliard Poets, Trouvere and Troubadour Poets, and Chaucer. In the seminar on Renaissance, Seventeenth and Eighteenth Century Thought, students read and discuss Machiavelli, Martin Luther, Cervantes, Shakespeare, Galileo, Descartes, Hobbes, Pascal, Racine, Swift, Sor Juana Ines de la Cruz, Voltaire, Rousseau, and the Declaration of Independence. The seminar on Nineteenth and Twentieth Century Thought introduces students to Adam Smith, Cardinal Newman, Darwin, Dickens, Kierkegaard, Marx, Tolstoy, Freud, Pius XI, Virginia Woolf, Kafka, and García Márquez.

In describing the Collegiate Seminars, the college reflects a well-thought-out understanding of liberal learning:

> In introducing students to the great writings that have shaped the thought and imagination of the Western World, the program aims to develop in students skills of analysis, critical thinking, interpretation and communication that will help them read and discuss significant works with increased understanding and enjoyment. More specifically, the program brings students into direct contact with the works of great minds—poets, philosophers, scientists, historians—to help them understand the ideas that shaped the present.

Because all professors are encouraged to teach a seminar, they are taught by faculty members from throughout the college—often in fields outside of their academic specialty. The seminars are kept quite small and meet around a table "so that each person can participate actively in the discussion." In the Socratic tradition, faculty members are encouraged to formulate questions about the reading "to challenge the students to develop, through the process of discussion, defensible interpretations of their own." In addition to the Collegiate Seminars, all students must complete general education requirements that include two courses in religious studies, two courses in the humanities, two in

Saint Mary's College of California

Year Founded: 1863
Total Cost: $18,775
Total Enrollment: 2,095
Total Applicants: 2,715
  71% accepted
SAT Middle Range
  Averages: 460–600V/
  500–590M
Financial Aid:
  60% applied
  51% judged to have need
  81% of those judged were
  given aid
ROTC Program Offered
Application Information:
  Mr. Michael Beseda
  Admissions Director
  Saint Mary's College of
  California
  P.O. Box 4800
  Moraga, CA 94575
  Telephone: (510) 631-4224
Application Deadlines:
  No early decision
  Regular decision: 3/1
  Early action: 11/30

mathematics and science, and two in social sciences. Students are also required to demonstrate their competence in written English. Saint Mary's operates on a four-one-four calendar, and all students are required to take a four-week winter-term class.

A Sound Wager

Students may either major in one of the school's degree programs or craft an individual or interdepartmental major of their own. Most intriguing is the college's alternative curriculum known as the Integral Program, a four-year college-within-a-college course of study devoted to the Great Books. "The Integral Program in Liberal Arts," the school explains, "is founded on the wager that it is still possible to appreciate and evaluate all the main kinds of human thinking." Students in the program take three tutorials—in mathematics, language, and laboratory—and a seminar in classic works of literature, philosophy, politics, economics, and theology. In the language tutorials, students study Greek for the first two years and advance "through the arts of grammar, logic, and rhetoric into the modern studies of linguistics, hermeneutics, and method." In mathematics, the tutorials begin with Euclid. "This example is significant because it illustrates the central difficulty in reviving liberal arts so that they are able to do for our era what earlier versions of them did for their respective times," the college explains. "Euclid is expressible in words, and presents a universe our imagination can enter. Thus his world is not wholly foreign to the world of literature, of history, and of ethics." Having studied Euclid, students are led on to "as high a point in its symbolic development as possible" so that they can "understand to some degree the outstanding intellectual developments of our time." By their fourth year students in the program are studying advanced calculus "and enough geometry to permit them to read, for example, some of Einstein's work."

Subjects covered in the laboratory tutorials range from optics, astronomy, and acoustics in the freshman year to classical mechanics, pneumatics, chemistry, and genetics as juniors. Meanwhile, students in the Integral Program have also been reading the Greek classics as freshmen; the Bible, Virgil, Lucretius, Rabelais, Machiavelli, Montaigne, Shakespeare, Aquinas, Anselm, Dante, and

> Men must be taught as if you taught them not, And things unknown proposed as things forgot.
>
> —*Alexander Pope*

Chaucer (among others) as sophomores; Cervantes, Descartes, John of the Cross, Milton, Spinoza, Pascal, Corneille, Racine, Molière, Hobbes, Swift, Locke, Berkeley, Fielding, Leibniz, Hume, Boswell, Kant, Diderot, Rousseau, Voltaire, Blake, and the *Federalist Papers* as juniors; and Goethe, Austen, Bernard, Hegel, Tolstoy, Nietzsche, William James, Freud, Proust, Joyce, and Heidegger as seniors. A student's performance is monitored closely by tutors and is discussed personally with the student once a semester in so-called Don Rags. The program's culmination is a "major essay on a serious topic" which seniors are required to defend in public. "A confident grasp of fundamental truths, a healthy skepticism toward passing dogma, and a reliance on reasoned deliberation should mark the graduate of the Integral Program," according to the school's catalog.

If this sounds familiar, it is. Saint Mary's has a long association with two other schools in this book—St. John's College of Annapolis and St. John's College of Santa Fe. As the college itself points out, however, its approach remains distinctive. "The College seeks to maintain its Roman Catholic character," the school's catalog declares, "striving to create an environment where Christian concerns occupy a central place in learning and community life, and where questions of faith and practice inform all aspects of the educational process."

Life by the Bay

Close student-faculty relationships are a hallmark of Saint Mary's. The college boasts that it has no classes of more than thirty students and students often work with professors one-on-one in tutorials. This sense of community extends beyond the classroom, and accounts for the active religious life among the student body. We're happy to report that students tend to be both socially and politically conservative. But they pursue their traditionalist education with notable zest.

Several years ago, the college's dean (and baseball historian), Paul Zingg, revived and coached students in a sixteenth-century game of "Rounders," which is based on the siege of a castle. He reports that "the Saint Mary's tallymen and -women defeated the Marin Cricket Club 32–21 in a two-inning game." Is this the birth of another Notre Dame–style sports factory?

The academic successes of Saint Mary's students speak for themselves. Its liberal arts graduates have become successful businessmen, artists, lawyers, judges, teachers, theologians, and curators. The college reports that since 1986 more than 90 percent of Saint Mary's medical school applicants have won admission to the school of their choice; the acceptance rate for dental schools has been 100 percent. Biology graduates have also had a 100 percent acceptance rate at the graduate level. Ninety-three percent of accounting graduates have accepted positions even before they graduate. Saint Mary's business program is so well regarded that the school reports that most accounting majors have received four offers by Christmas of their senior year. This record of excellence extends to every area of the school's program. In 1992, every Saint Mary's student taking the licensing exam for registered nurses passed.

Having detailed all this, it is probably superfluous to point out that Saint Mary's 420-acre campus in the Bay Area's Moraga Valley is one of the nation's most beautiful, surrounded as it is by rolling, green hills. The view is breathtaking, on-campus housing is safe and comfortable, and the environment at Saint Mary's is often likened to a country club. Students who tire of this are within close proximity to San Francisco and the other attractions of northern California, which we need not enumerate. The more adventurous have the option of participating in study-abroad programs with Catholic institutions in Rome, France, and England.

Why anyone would want to leave, however, is quite beyond us.   □

St. Mary's
St. Mary's City, Maryland

A School Set Apart

It is no coincidence that most of the schools on our recommended list are private institutions. Rare is the public university that has been able to withstand the combined pressures of politicization (in the name of "diversity"), the clumsy intrusion of government controls, and the irresponsibility of its legislative overseers.

But St. Mary's College of Maryland is an exception. With all of the trappings of a small liberal arts college, St. Mary's is one of Maryland's finest schools. It is also a public institution, a fact reflected in its price tag and in its student body, which includes students from lower-income families. Perhaps most exceptional of all, St. Mary's has not succumbed to the politics of "diversity" by watering down its liberal arts curriculum to accommodate its students or its "public" mission.

This is all the more striking when we reflect that St. Mary's has been a four-year college for just over two decades. (Although in existence since 1840, it granted its first baccalaureate degree in 1971). Its success in the last two decades has been striking, a reflection of what can be accomplished if a school builds upon a sound basis of academic integrity and liberal education. Its students consistently receive among the highest SAT scores in the state. And one survey ranked St. Mary's as the top regional liberal arts college in the Northeast.

The Spirit of Toleration

St. Mary's appears acutely conscious of its distinctiveness as a school "set apart." "Unlike the other state colleges and universities," a college publication remarks, "St. Mary's offers an undergraduate liberal arts education and small-college experience of the sort more commonly found at fine private colleges." It does so with high academic standards, small classes, a challenging and highly structured curriculum, "a sense of community, and a spirit of care and intellectual quest." The National Endowment for the Humanities also recognized St. Mary's as a national leader in the movement to return sanity to the liberal arts curriculum when it gave the school a $171,000 grant. Only seven other colleges nationwide received similar curriculum grants. St. Mary's faculty members used the money to design their own anthology of readings in Western civilization. "Embracing great works from the Bible to Rousseau, from Plato to Freud, the new book underpins the history requirement and provides a context for course work in literature and philosophy as well as in the history of art, music and theater," the college says.

Located on the horseshoe bend of the St. Mary's

St. Mary's College of Maryland

Year Founded: 1840
Total Cost:
  Residents: $8,180
  Nonresidents: $10,280
Total Enrollment: 1,510
Total Applicants: 1,685
  45% accepted
  19% of accepted enrolled
SAT Middle Range
  Averages: 1110–1260
Financial Aid:
  37% applied
  67% judged to have need
  93% of those judged were
    given aid
No ROTC Program Offered
Application Information:
  Mr. Richard Edgar
  Director of Admissions
  St. Mary's College of
    Maryland
  St. Mary's City, MD 20686
  Telephone: (800) 492-7181
Application Deadlines:
  Early decision: 12/15
  Regular decision: 1/15

River, the campus sits on land that was first settled in 1634 by colonists who arrived on the *Ark* and *Dove*. St. Mary's City is the third oldest continuously inhabited English settlement in the New World after Jamestown and Plymouth. Until 1692 St. Mary's City actually served as the capital of Maryland. After the capital moved to Annapolis, the settlement languished, all but disappearing. But by then, St. Mary's City had already secured its place in history. The Act of Toleration—envisioning tolerance between Catholics and Protestants—adopted by Maryland's colonists in 1649 made it the birthplace of religious freedom in the New World. That tradition is still reflected in the college's goals, which not only include a broad understanding of the liberal arts, critical thinking, and clear expression, but also encourage students to enter "into that spirit of toleration, which is the special legacy of the early settlers of St. Mary's City."

> Teaching is an instinctual art, mindful of potential, craving of realizations, a pausing, seamless process.
>
> —*A. Bartlett Giamatti*

Categories of Learning

St. Mary's College divides its general education core into four main categories: Abilities and Competencies, The Western Heritage, The Sciences in the Modern World, and Integration and Analysis.

In the first, Abilities and Competencies, students are required to take introductory English composition and mathematics courses. While other schools might end their emphasis on writing and quantification skills with those courses, St. Mary's has much tougher requirements. Before graduating, students must also complete two courses designated as having a substantial writing component, and another two courses with a substantial quantitative or mathematics component. Students must also take at least two hours in either art, music, theater, or in an introductory foreign language.

Under the rubric of Western Heritage, St. Mary's students must take two history courses, The Western Legacy I and The Western Legacy II, an introductory course in the history of art, theater, or music, and a survey course in English or classical and biblical literature. (The final requirement can also be fulfilled with an intermediate course in French, German, or Spanish.)

Requirements in the sciences and social sciences are also extensive. Students must take one course in physical science (from a relatively short list of designated courses), an introductory course in biology, and an introductory course in psychology or sociology/anthropology. Students must also choose either Economics 101 (Introduction to Economics), or Political Science 101 (American Politics).

Finally, in either the junior or senior year, students must take a course titled Philosophical Inquiry, which "entails careful reading and analysis of the writings of major philosophers of Western civilization." As seniors, St. Mary's students must also complete a senior seminar that "will discuss a theme from the student's major field in an interdisciplinary context . . . to integrate the components of the total education received at the College."

Although we could wish for tougher foreign language requirements, the St. Mary's curriculum ensures that graduates of the college will have been exposed to the history, art, thought, sciences, and literature of the West. In that respect, it ranks among the finest and most well conceived programs we encountered—in fact, far better than what passes for a curriculum at many of the elite liberal arts colleges with which St. Mary's is often compared.

Growing into the World

Although it had a late start, St. Mary's has worked hard to catch up with the more established four-year colleges in the region, and is in the process of completing a major expansion of its campus facilities, including doubling the size of its library, constructing a new science building, and generally upgrading the entire campus under a master plan design that seeks to preserve St. Mary's traditional beauty, while enhancing its "tidewater village" character.

Also promising for this upstart college is the leading role it has taken—far ahead of its Maryland counterparts—in offering students access to computers. It has also managed to put together an impressive program of foreign study, including its special program at the Centre for Medieval and Renaissance Studies in Oxford, England. The program, affiliated with Keble College, offers courses in literature, history, archaeology, art history, politics, philosophy, law, music, drama, the history of science, and religious studies. Other programs include four weeks of study at the Institut Catholique in Paris, which includes a reception by the mayor of Paris, an evening at the Comédie Française, and excursions into the French countryside, including

181

a sojourn in the wine country of Burgundy. Ooh-
la-la.   □

Saint Olaf
Northfield, Minnesota

The Elegant Vikings

We'll put our reservations about Saint Olaf on
the table first: Despite the conservative orientation of its student body, the administration and
faculty at Saint Olaf have been zealously pushing
for more "diversity" and "multiculturalism" in the
curriculum. The result is a relatively robust special
studies program in American Racial and Multicultural Studies that insists that students "be aware
of current social problems that result from the historical dominance of Americans of European origin
in a society increasingly multicultural in nature." If
you detect a note of politically correct sermonizing
there, you're not alone. We detect a similar tendency in such recent courses as American Minorities and Inequality and From Wounded Knee to
Red Power.

Even more members of the faculty are involved
with Saint Olaf's women's studies program, which
boasts of having "added substantially to the map of
reality" and features such courses as Gender Issues
in Cross-Cultural Perspectives, The Goddess, and
Ecofeminism: Ecology and Feminist Issues Con-
verge. A trend toward "relevance" has also contrib-
uted to making such courses as Human Sexuality
and Ballroom Dancing popular choices on the campus.

"Forward! Forward!"

We suspect that some of this fustian about diversity is a reaction to the fact that Saint Olaf is in
reality about as diverse as a Viking raid. Saint Olaf
students are heavily Norwegian and the predomi-
nant look on campus is blond and blue-eyed (97
percent white, 60 percent from Minnesota). Its
curriculum is also heavily weighted toward the traditional liberal arts. Some elements at Saint Olaf
don't want that taken the wrong way. Too bad.

The fact is that the radical elements of the faculty have a long way to go to enroll Saint Olaf in the ranks of the academic gulag. The school was founded in 1874 by Norwegian Lutherans, and its seal continues to proclaim, *"Fram! Fram! Kistmenn, Krossmenn"*—"Forward! Forward! Men of Christ! Men of the Cross." The college still requires three religion courses, and voluntary chapel services are held each weekday morning. Classes are small, and professors *teach*. Compared with the experience at the region's impersonal megaversities, Saint Olaf's students are considered "pampered." The school's strongest departments continue to be the humanities and the sciences.

It takes more than a few program in "multiculturalism" to efface that sort of tradition. As the trustees reaffirmed in 1987, Saint Olaf "stimulates students' critical thinking and heightens their moral sensitivity; it encourages them to be seekers of truth, leading lives of unselfish service to others; and it challenges them to be responsible and knowledgeable citizens of the world." Nor will Saint Olaf ever be confused with Dartmouth. Despite student protests, the administration held firm in banning the on-campus sale of condoms. (An unusually decisive move, considering how many leading universities have taken to handing out free safe-sex kits—condoms and all—to undergraduates when they register.)

The Great Conversation

What is genuinely radical, however, is Saint Olaf's return to the classics. In his memoirs, John Buchan, Lord Tweedsmuir, wrote:

Indeed, I cannot imagine a more precious viaticum than the classics of Greece and Rome, or a happier fate than that one's youth should be intertwined with their world of clear mellow lights, gracious images, and fruitful thoughts.

Lately those gracious images and fruitful thoughts have to a large extent given way to the cramped stylings and barren cant of academic scholarship. So it is remarkable that we should find something like Saint Olaf's Paracollege, designed along the lines of the tutorial system of the great British universities. Every year 120 or so students also participate in the five-course Great Conversation Program, in which students meet in small

Saint Olaf College

Year Founded: 1874
Total Cost: $16,250
Total Enrollment: 3,015
Total Applicants: 2,205
  69% accepted
  47% of accepted enrolled
SAT Middle Range
  Averages: 460–590V/
  510–650M
Financial Aid:
  65% applied
  81% judged to have need
  100% of those judged
    were given aid
No ROTC Program Offered
Application Information:
  Mr. John Ruohoniemi
  Director of Admissions
  Saint Olaf College
  Northfield, MN 55057
  Telephone: (507) 646-3025
Application Deadlines:
  Early decision: 11/15
  Regular decision: 2/15

classes to read and discuss the Great Books. The program is self-consciously conservative, drawing its title from Robert Maynard Hutchins's vigorous defense of a curriculum based upon the classics. So intense is the Great Conversation that students in the program live together in a dorm so they can continue the conversation outside of class hours.

In their first year, students study The Tradition Beginning: The Greeks and Hebrews. Readings include Homer, Thucydides, Sophocles, Plato, Aristotle, and the Old Testament, while discussions focus on the contrast between "the Hebrew notion of one God and the believer" and "Greek polytheism and the hero," as well as between "the Hebrew ideal of a religious covenant and historical destiny" and "Greek notions of civic community and earthly life." This semester is followed by an interim course in the Romans and early Christianity, with discussions of Stoicism, Epicureanism, and the teachings of Christ. Readings include St. Paul, Cicero, Horace, Virgil, and Epictetus. The first year concludes with The Medieval Synthesis, which traces the expansion of Christianity and the synthesis of the Judeo-Christian and Greco-Roman in the Middle Ages. The course explores "the development of a unified world view as expressed in religious devotions, philosophy, literature and art, and represented in the religious and political arrangements of monasticism and feudalism in Church and Empire." Readings include St. Augustine, St. Benedict, St. Thomas Aquinas, Dante, and Chaucer, as well as writings on Gothic art and architecture and medieval drama.

In the second year, the conversation continues with The Tradition Renewed: New Forces of Secularization during the first semester, and The Tradition Challenged: Dissenters and Defenders in the second semester. Students read and discuss Thomas More, Machiavelli, Luther, Shakespeare, Descartes, Locke, Hobbes, Voltaire, Rousseau, Jefferson, Goethe, Darwin, Marx, Freud, Dostoevsky, Nietzsche, Wollstonecraft, and the Romantics. "Each course," the catalog explains, "is designed to emphasize the interrelationship of Western tradition."

This brings us back to the reason we have some faith in Saint Olaf. We suspect that students who are exposed to the masterworks and best thoughts of the West will easily be able to recognize the intellectual distinction between the study of such giants and small-beer courses like "Norwegian Women

> A society that thinks the choice between the ways of living is just a choice between equally eligible "lifestyles" turns universities into academic cafeterias offering junk food for the mind.
>
> —*George F. Will*

Writers: Feminist Perspectives." Keep the Mickey Mouse courses out of the core, and let the market make its own judgment.

More Core

Outside of the Paracollege, Saint Olaf's core curriculum requires courses in English composition, religion, foreign language, physical education, and a "cross cultural component" to "increase awareness of cultural differences, facilitate cross cultural relations, and stimulate a search of explanations of cultural diversity." In addition, students are required to take one course each in history, literature, and philosophy, two courses in the fine arts, two courses in the behavioral sciences, and two courses in the natural sciences.

Although attending school in Northfield, Minnesota, may strike some as a form of internal exile, the school's fine arts department provides an impressive array of on-campus diversion and entertainment. The school also affords ample opportunity for respite from the Minnesota winters through its study-abroad programs. More than half of Saint Olaf's students take advantage of the chance to study in warmer, foreign climes.

For a conservative student, the decision to attend Saint Olaf means recognizing once again the need to be a guerrilla student, cutting through the thicket of academese jargon and the rhetoric of "diversity" to obtain a quality education. Our guess is that the effort is a lot easier at St. Olaf than at most places. □

Saint Vincent

Latrobe, Pennsylvania

Keepers of the Flame

It was in Monte Cassino, South of Rome. A barbarian invasion threatened the culture of an important civilization. Classical works of art and literature were being deliberately burned. But before much of it could be destroyed, Benedictine monks hid it away. Their courage and foresight helped do far more than preserve a culture. They laid the foundation for European civilization.

—From *The Secrets of St. Vincent*

In the last decade of the millennium, it's easy for us to identify with those early Benedictines. As Peter Shaw wrote in *The War Against the Intellect*, we too "are in an exceedingly bad period for the humanities: a period of anti-humanism that deserves to be called a Dark Age of the Humanities."

"In the dark ages of Europe after the Roman Empire," writes Professor Shaw, "the danger to the humanities had to do with the destruction and neglect of the great texts. In our own dark age, the texts are suffering from the wrong kind of attention. They are being subjected to a system of interpretation that is extinguishing their spirit quite as effectively as if they were again literally under assault by Vandals and Goths."

Ideals of the West

In a sense, this entire book is devoted to the recovery and preservation of the traditions under attack from an academic culture overrun by moral confusion and ideological nihilism. But, let's face it, the Benedictines have been at this a lot longer than we have.

Founded in 1846, Saint Vincent is the nation's oldest Benedictine college. More than a century and a half later, it continues to provide a solid, morals-centered liberal education. (It went coeducational in 1983.) Hardly the best-known Catholic school in the country, Saint Vincent is nevertheless one of the standouts. It ranks among the top 6 or 7 percent of all colleges nationally in the percentage of its students who go on to earn Ph.D.s—and second among Catholic colleges and universities. Its library was also judged to be among the top 5 percent of the more than six hundred liberal arts colleges—and the best among Catholic colleges—by the U.S. Department of Education.

More important than these ratings, however, is the school's commitment to liberal learning. Faced with widespread confusion and doubt over the ends of higher education, Saint Vincent clearly defines itself as Catholic, Benedictine, and liberal, by which it means that "it chooses to answer these questions in the spirit of the liberal arts tradition which, for over 2,000 years, has been the educational ideal of the Western world. The college believes that the life of learning is a value in itself, independently of being a prime instrument of national purpose' [as U.C. Berkeley's Clark Kerr put it in 1963] because learning opens the gate to 'the service and comprehension of life itself' [Alfred North Whitehead]." Says the college: "*Non scholae sed vitae discitur* should read in contemporary transposition: Learning is not a school exercise, nor the first rung on the corporate ladder, but entrance to a richer life."

Following in the Benedictine tradition, the atmosphere at Saint Vincent reflects an exceptionally close contact between faculty and students. Classes are small and professors are explicitly encouraged to "take the students' personal achievement to heart."

A Catholic Core

The Saint Vincent curriculum is built upon a core that requires all students to take three courses in history, including at least two survey courses in European, American, English, or Asian history. Students must also take three courses in philosophy: Ancient and Medieval Philosophy, Modern Philosophy, and Contemporary Philosophy. An introductory English course, Language and Rhetoric, is also required of all students, plus two additional literature courses, which are not specified. The core also requires three courses in religious studies, beginning with a course in Exploring Religious Meaning; two courses at the intermediate

Saint Vincent College

Year Founded: 1846
Total Cost: $13,298
Total Enrollment: 1,091
Total Applicants: 902
  83% accepted
  46% of accepted enrolled
SAT Middle Range
  Averages:
  400–510V/420–550M
Financial Aid:
  90% applied
  94% judged to have need
  100% of those judged
    were given aid
ROTC Program Offered
Application Information:
  Rev. Earl J. Henry,
    O.S.B.
  Dean of Admission and
    Financial Aid
  Saint Vincent College
  Latrobe, PA 15650
  Telephone: (412) 537-4540
Application Deadlines:
  No early decision
  Regular decision: rolling

or advanced level in a foreign language; four courses in the social sciences, with no more than two courses in any one discipline; eight credits in the natural sciences; and a course in mathematics.

While some of the faculty members at Saint Vincent may be liberals, the dominant mood on campus appears to be apolitical and open-minded. The McKenna Foundation, for example, has sponsored an economics lecture series that has brought to campus Nobel laureate James Buchanan, Murray Weidenbaum, and Walter Williams. Although the seminary has a Peace and Justice committee, the college's "Threshold on the Twenty-first Century Lecture Series" featured cold-warrior Jeane Kirkpatrick (who has not always found herself welcome on less tolerant campuses). Saint Vincent's openness to the sort of conservative ideas derided as politically incorrect on other campuses means that whatever the political leanings of the faculty, conservative students will find at the college a congenial environment that will challenge and stimulate their intellectual development rather than try to "cure" them of ideas unacceptable to the political Zeitgeist. (A little—albeit lame—political correctness sneaks into Saint Vincent's p.r., to wit: ". . . divine mystery in creation extends beyond people to material creation and is expressed in CARE OF THE ENVIRONMENT. The medieval monks taught Europe how to farm as well as how to read and write. Thus, the monks were environmentalists long before it became fashionable." Well, we don't think agricultural techniques in the *Christian* Middle Ages quite precisely equate with the *pagan* notions of today's Greens.)

> Science's latest attempts to grasp the human situation—cultural relativism, historicism, the fact-value distinction—are the suicide of science.
>
> —*Allan Bloom*

A Future for the Past

Located near Pittsburgh in an area known as the Laurel Highlands, Saint Vincent is surrounded by some of the most beautiful countryside in the eastern United States. It is, moreover, one of the safest areas in the country, often ranked as among the most crime-free areas in the nation. Nor, despite its monastic roots, is Saint Vincent cut off from the world at large. Although Saint Vincent is hardly an athletic powerhouse, the Pittsburgh Steelers have held their summer camp on the campus since 1967. Arnold Palmer lives just across the street. And for those interested in the arts, Saint Vincent's Summer Theater has been rated one of the best in Pennsylvania.

But it is Saint Vincent's academic quality that has drawn national attention. In 1989, it was one of only sixteen colleges and universities chosen by the National Endowment for the Humanities to receive a $270,000 challenge grant that, with matching funds, provide more than $1 million for faculty development, classroom renovations, and upgrading of the library. The school recently completed a $10 million fund-raising campaign.

All of which tells us that although the barbarians may be roaming freely through the wilds of the Ivy League, having sacked the elite citadels of learning, the Benedictines are still keeping the light of civilization burning—as they did fourteen centuries ago at Monte Cassino.

This time, though, they are doing it in Pennsylvania.   □

Southwestern
Georgetown, Texas

The Intellectual Whole

In a recent restatement of its institutional mission, the trustees of Southwestern University wisely noted that the school's most important assets "are qualitative, not quantitative." Although it insists on calling its phys ed department the "Department of Kinesiology"—usually a sign of academic status envy—Southwestern does not as a rule attempt to mimic the values or style of its huge neighbor in Austin. Instead, Southwestern is striving to become the finest liberal arts college in the region, committed to teaching, academic quality, and what John Wesley called the union of "knowledge and piety."

In a reasonably forceful statement (these things are usually the quintessence of intellectual mush) the trustees also reaffirmed Southwestern's institutional identity as a school "committed to a broad-based, value-centered education," and its commitment to a liberal arts curriculum that "forms a coherent, intellectual whole." By value-centered, the trustees declared, "we mean that we want our students to understand that knowledge is not value-free. Facts and information do not exist in isolation. . . ."

In part, that reflects Southwestern's Methodist roots, which stretch back to 1840, when Southwestern became Texas's first university a mere four years after the fall of the Alamo. Although Southwestern is still affiliated with the United Methodist Church, the ties are more or less informal. Not so the tradition of academic excellence. Southwestern students published the first literary magazine in Texas history, and three of the first five Rhodes Scholars from the state were from Southwestern. That tradition remains strong.

Southwestern University

Year Founded: 1840
Total Cost: $14,557
Total Enrollment: 1,204
Total Applicants: 1,214
  69% accepted
  38% of accepted enrolled
SAT Middle Range
  Averages: 1010–1220
Financial Aid:
  78% applied
  63% judged to have need
  100% of those judged
    were given aid
No ROTC Program Offered
Application Information:
  Mr. John W. Lind
  Vice President for
    Enrollment
    Management
  Southwestern University
  Georgetown, TX 78626
  Telephone: (800) 252-
    3166
Application Deadlines:
  Early decision: 11/1
  Regular decision: 2/15

The General Education Program

All Southwestern students must complete an extensive general education program that begins with the freshman symposium. Each symposium, devoted to a single, different subject every year, is specifically intended to provide a common intellectual experience and to develop "competence in analytical and critical thinking, writing, and speaking." In the fall of 1991, for example, the symposium focused on "Europe Rediscovered: 1492–1992." Other so-called Foundation Courses (which must be taken in the freshman year) include a course in English composition and one in mathematics.

The second major area of the general education program is known as Perspectives on Knowledge. Students must choose from a designated list of introductory courses and select one course from each of the following categories (but no more than two in any one department): American and Western Cultural Heritage, Other Cultures and Civilizations, The Religious Perspective, Values Analysis, The Natural World (two courses), Aesthetic Experience (two courses), and Social Analysis (two courses). Because the options for fulfilling these requirements are limited to broadly based courses, there are few easy ways to circumvent the requirements, and students should receive a fairly good introduction to the major disciplines of the liberal arts. (There are no "gut" courses on the list.)

The final area of general education includes courses that provide advanced competencies. Students must demonstrate "computer competence" by taking courses that provide computer literacy. (Lest this sound too narrow, the list of courses approved for this requirement includes not merely accounting and science courses, but also offerings in history, English, and even the classics.) It is perhaps worth noting that Southwestern has a state-of-the-art computer network, one of the finest in the country for a school its size. Other requirements include "continued writing experience" and a special "capstone" project or course in a student's senior year "in which students are expected to bring together and apply what they have learned." The requirement can be satisfied by a comprehensive written examination. Southwestern students are also required to take two semester hours of physical education courses.

Staying Awake

Southwestern's greatest strength is its teaching. Classes are small and faculty members are quite accessible, often letting students work closely with them on their various projects. One Southwestern tradition involves having faculty members cook and serve late-night breakfasts to students who are pulling all-nighters before final exams. Only thirty miles from the state's capital, the college offers its government students the opportunity for on-site study through the Texas Politics Internship (though we think they should have to read Robert Caro first). Study-abroad programs include a London semester, a semester or year's study in Grenoble, France, exchanges with the Universität Osnabruck in Germany, as well as summer study programs in France, Austria, Greece, England, Mexico, Spain, and Asia.

The vast majority—86 percent—of Southwestern's students come from Texas, but that mix may change as Southwestern is discovered by applicants from across the country. Although the number of students is holding steady at 1,200, the number of applicants has more than doubled in the last decade, a change that has allowed the school an increased selectivity. More than 50 percent of the entering students graduated in the top 10 percent of their high school classes, and had average combined SAT scores that topped 1110.

Southwestern's prospects for continued improvement are good. In part, that is the result of having an endowment of more than $125 million—one of the highest per-students endowments in the nation. Southwestern also ranks among the top 15 percent of institutions of its type in voluntary support. Now for the caveats.

> It is the supreme art of the teacher to awaken joy in creative expression and knowledge.
>
> —*Albert Einstein*

Troubled Dreams

Despite its strongly tradition-based curriculum, Southwestern has a robust feminist contingent in its faculty, reflected in the fact that the university not only has a women's studies program (not unusual) but actually offers a *major* in women's studies (not a good sign at all). Moreover, there are indications the feminists have a certain amount of clout within the institution beyond their actual numbers. In recent years they have managed to stage a coup of sorts by inducing the Freshman Symposium to devote time to "gender questions and public life" and "insiders and outsiders in the areas of race, class, and age."

The real danger—and we won't try to conceal our anxiety on this point—is that in a school of Southwestern's size it might be difficult to avoid an active contingent of academic feminists intent on what one theorist calls the "reconstruction of reality." Even the trustees seem to have been infected to a certain extent with the new politics, adopting what amounts to a racial quota for the student body —5 percent black and 15 percent Hispanic—and setting as a goal that the faculty and staff reflect a proper "diversity of gender, race, and culture."

However, we trust that sanity will prevail. By and large, Southwestern's students are from conservative backgrounds, the trustees seem, on the whole, quite reasonable, and the faculty—generally—has a reputation for academic integrity. Together they constitute a potent bulwark against the worst ravages of gender politics. This is one fight we think can be won. And given Southwestern's traditions it is surely one that is well worth winning. □

Stetson University
De Land, Florida

Tradition in the Sun

A few years ago the *Insider's Guide to the Colleges* began its profile of Stetson by writing: "Rumor has it there's a Young Democrats club at Stetson University. If there is, it hasn't been heard from very much lately. On the other hand, everyone knows there's a Young Republicans club here: Stetson has a decidedly conservative flavor." But that's not why Stetson wins our approval. Although its conservatism hardly counts against it, Stetson's solid curriculum and record of quality teaching are what distinguishes the school for our purposes.

Academically, Stetson now ranks as one of the ten top schools in the Southeast, and is especially well known for its business program, music school, and Russian studies department. Students are enthusiastic about the quality of Stetson's faculty, which is said to be unusually accessible to undergraduates. Teaching is taken seriously at Stetson, a priority that shows up both in the classroom and in the involvement of professors in campus activities. This comes up again and again in discussions with students and faculty alike; students are just as likely to bring up the close relationship of students and faculty as they are to mention Stetson's gorgeous campus, which is high praise indeed.

The Business of the Liberal Arts

Even so, Stetson is not often thought of as a liberal arts school. Best known for its business school—which enrolls half the university's students—Stetson has a notable pre-professional feel about it. Nonetheless, Stetson seems to take liberal education more seriously than many of the better-known liberal arts colleges in the country. Requirements for the bachelor of arts degree include a freshman English sequence; a religion course on The Judeo-Christian Heritage; an additional course in either religion or philosophy; a mathematics course; ten credits in a foreign language; two courses in the humanities, including one in a nonverbal art; a senior research project in the major; twelve credits in the natural sciences from three different departments; twelve credits in the social sciences from three different departments, including one course in history or a foreign culture; and two one-hour physical education classes.

While this is unlikely to be mistaken for a Great Books curriculum, it reflects a commitment to provide coherence to the undergraduate experience. That emphasis on making sure that Stetson students actually learn something pervades the campus.

Stetson is justly famous for its school of business administration, which recently moved into a new 55,000-square-foot facility. Although a lot of

Stetson University

Year Founded: 1883
Total Cost: $16,440
Total Enrollment: 2,104
Total Applicants: 1,630
  82% accepted
  38% of accepted enrolled
SAT Middle Range
  Averages: 920–1120
Financial Aid:
  62% applied
  87% judged to have need
  99% of those judged were given aid
ROTC Program Offered
Application Information:
  Ms. Linda Glover
  Dean of Admissions
  Stetson University
  Campus Box 8378
  De Land, FL 32720-3771
  Telephone: (800) 688-0101
Application Deadlines:
  Early action: 12/1
  Early decision: 11/15
  Regular decision: 3/1

Nature without
learning is blind,
learning apart from
nature is fractional,
and practice in the
absence of both is
aimless.

—*Plutarch*

schools give lip service to providing students with a "hands-on" education, Stetson puts its money where its mouth is—literally. Students in the finance program are allowed to manage a portfolio worth more than $1 million, which they use to generate the income to pay for scholarships, to pay visiting professors, and to underwrite library purchases. Stetson points with particular—and, we think, justifiable—pride to the fact that graduates of its accounting department have one of the highest success rates on the CPA exam of any school in the country. (Stetson now ranks third nationally in the percentage of students passing the exam.) Although a small school, Stetson prides itself on its international focus, including a high-quality Russian studies program. News broadcasts from Russia, as well as cultural television programs, are beamed via satellite to Stetson's library. The school also has a visiting professor from Moscow State University on its faculty, and students are eligible to participate in an exchange program with good ol' MSU. The school also has study programs in Madrid, Freiburg, Dijon, and Nottingham. In conjunction with American University, Stetson's political science department also offers a fall semester in Washington, D.C., where students can study the nation's capital, both in the classroom and through internships in government offices. An especially notable special program is the Charles E. Merrill Program of American Studies, which stresses an understanding of "our country's values, philosophy, and culture."

Stetson also offers a four-week winter term, where students can earn credit either with off-campus activities or through intensive on-campus study. Stetson generally designates a theme for each year's "interim" activities.

A True Community

Stetson takes its Baptist affiliation seriously. Its motto remains "For God and Truth," which seems to us an excellent starting point for any institution of higher learning. Chapel services are held every Wednesday morning, although attendance is said to be somewhat uneven. Alcohol is banned from campus and visitation at the school's dorms is strictly limited. Visits by the opposite sex are barred after 12:30 A.M. on weekdays and 2:00 A.M. on weekends, and students caught breaking the rules three times face expulsion. Stetson students are notoriously clean-cut and well-dressed, and the Catholic and Baptist ministries are among the most visible and active groups on campus.

We recognize that the attractions of Stetson are not merely academic. Located on a 117-acre campus in central Florida, Stetson is about twenty-five miles from Daytona Beach and thirty-five miles from Orlando. The appeal of a campus in that climate—especially one lined with oak and palm trees—would be obvious enough. But Stetson appears to exude a genuinely friendly atmosphere of community that is increasingly rare in higher education. And then there is the student body. Although we do not recommend schools solely on the basis of the conservatism of the student body, Stetson is a welcome change from much of academia. Compared to many of its better-known counterparts, Stetson is a monument to tolerance, diversity, and good sense. □

Thomas Aquinas

Santa Paula, California

New Lights

It is 7 p.m. at Thomas Aquinas College and Machiavelli holds sway in a moonlit classroom, just as he did 450 years ago in the intrigue-filled court of a Florentine prince. In this room, however, there are no critical anthologies, no lectures, no teachers. There is only Machiavelli's essay, *The Prince*, a tutor, and 14 students, grappling with good and evil . . .

So began a 1988 article in the *Los Angeles Times* describing Thomas Aquinas College. The school's philosophy is classically simple. "We read only the greatest minds and the greatest works in every discipline," the college's dean explains. That means that instead of reading the latest monograph on "Existential Meaning in Plato," the students actually read Plato; instead of "Gender, Class, and Meaning in the Middle Ages," the students read Dante.

Thomas Aquinas College

Year Founded: 1971
Total Cost: $16,940
Total Enrollment: 203
Total Applicants: 135
  57% accepted
  50% of accepted enrolled
SAT Middle Range
  Averages: 1010–1270
Financial Aid:
  81% applied
  80% judged to have need
  100% of those judged
    were given aid
No ROTC Program Offered
Application Information:
  Mr. Thomas Susanka, Jr.
  Director of Admissions
  Thomas Aquinas College
  Santa Paula, CA 93060
  Telephone: (800) 634-9797
Application Deadlines:
  No early decision
  Regular decision: rolling

Thomas Aquinas takes its Catholicism and its patron's philosophy of education seriously. "Thomas Aquinas," a college publication says, "is devoted to scholarship in the Catholic tradition. . . . Rather than compromise the tradition, Thomas Aquinas College meets the secular challenge to Christian wisdom by offering an education that is carefully grounded in the fundamentals of that wisdom and thorough in the development of its parts. Reading the greatest works in this tradition and examining them closely; working in small seminars, tutorials, and laboratories; aiming at the intellectual life instead of activism; believing that education is not an experiment and that teaching without a claim to the truth is both empty and arrogant; giving the entire effort of the faculty to teaching; these things make Thomas Aquinas College unique."

The school's ringing restatement of the creed of liberal learning has proved successful: applications have risen sharply and Thomas Aquinas has been acknowledged as one of the finest schools in the country by *The Wall Street Journal.* Despite its tiny size (it has only about two hundred students) and its relative youth (it was founded in 1971), law school deans describe its graduates as "sensational, top-drawer."

Classical Roots

There is no mistaking the traditionalism of campus life at Aquinas. Students address one another as Mr. and Miss in the classroom, adhere to a dress code, eschew drugs, and follow a strict moral code. The L.A. *Times* noted that when someone found a $10 bill on campus, he tacked it up on the wall of the cafeteria where it went untouched for two weeks, "a mute testament to the school's traditions and values." (Eventually, the money was placed in the chapel donation box.)

True to its medievalist roots, the curriculum is self-consciously modeled on the trivium (grammar, rhetoric, and logic) and quadrivium (arithmetic, geometry, astronomy, and music). Students are introduced to the trivium through a two-year-long language tutorial and a year-long logic tutorial. The quadrivium is covered by a four-year-long mathematics tutorial (students are required to pass an exam demonstrating proficiency in algebra by the end of their sophomore year) and a one-year music tutorial. Students also take a three-year philosophy tutorial, a four-year theology tutorial, and four years of laboratory study, in addition to four years of seminars in various subjects.

The reading lists are impressive, clearly owing much to the Great Books curriculum formulated by John Erskine at Columbia in the early years of this century. A sweeping tour of the greatest and most influential works of Western civilization, it is surely one of the most rigorous curricula of any school in the country—St. John's College included. And, like St. John's, it is not for the faint of heart. In their first year, for example, students read the ancient Greeks: Homer's *Iliad* and *Odyssey;* Plato's *Ion, Republic,* and *Symposium;* Aeschylus' *Agamemnon, Choephoroe,* and *Eumenides;* Sophocles' *Oedipus Rex, Oedipus at Colonus,* and *Antigone;* the *Histories* of Herodotus; Aristotle's *Poetics* and *Rhetoric;* Plutarch's *Lives;* and works by Euripides, Thucydides, and Aristophanes. In the language tutorial students are assigned Latin: An Introductory Course Based on Ancient Authors, and Aids to the Study and Composition of Language. In the mathematics tutorial they read Euclid; in the laboratory the reading list includes Aristotle *(Parts of Animals),* Fabre *(Souvenirs Entomologiques),* Tinbergen *(Evolution of Gull Behavior),* and works by Von Frisch, Galen, Harvey, Schwann, and Linnaeus. In the philosophy tutorial students read and discuss more Plato, as well as Porphyry and Aristotle. The theology tutorial consists of readings from the Bible. And all this is for freshmen! It provides a good taste of what lies ahead: at Thomas Aquinas, the pace does not slacken, nor are there "gut" courses in the "Theory of Rock 'n' Roll" to distract students.

In the second year, students move on to ancient Rome and the Renaissance: they read Virgil, Lucretius, Cicero, Tacitus, Epictetus, St. Augustine, Boethius, Dante, Chaucer, Spenser, and St. Thomas Aquinas in the seminar. In the language tutorial the study of Latin continues, including Thomas of Erfurt's *Grammatica Speculativa,* selections from Horace, and more Virgil. Readings in the mathematics tutorial include Apollonius, Ptolemy, Copernicus, Plato, and Kepler; and in the laboratory, students read Aristotle, Aquinas, Lavoisier, Avogadro, Couper, Gay-Lussac, Dalton, and Cannizzaro. The philosophy tutorial includes readings from the pre-Socratic philosophers, Aristotle, and Aquinas. The sophomore reading list in the theology tutorial includes St. Augustine, St. Athanasius, St. Anselm, and St. John Damascene.

The true University of these days is a collection of books.

—*Thomas Carlyle*

197

The third-year seminar requires students to read Cervantes, Aquinas, Machiavelli, Bacon, Shakespeare, Montaigne, Descartes, Pascal, Hobbes, Locke, Berkeley, Hume, Swift, Milton, Gibbon, Corneille, Racine, Rousseau, Spinoza, Hamilton, Madison, John Jay, Adam Smith, De Tocqueville, the Lincoln-Douglas debates, and Comte. In their music tutorial they study Boethius, Aristotle, Plato, and Mozart; in the mathematics tutorial they read Viète, Descartes, Archimedes, Griffin, and Frege; in the laboratory course they read Galileo and Newton; in the philosophy tutorial they study (once again) Aristotle; and in the theology tutorial they read, of course, Aquinas.

In their senior year the reading list brings students to the very edge of the modern era, but retains its classical roots. Students read and discuss Tolstoy, Leibniz, Kant, Goethe, Hegel, Feuerbach, Malthus, Marx, Engels, Darwin, Mendel, Nietzsche, Twain, Austen, James, Freud, Jung, Newman, Melville, Kierkegaard, Dostoevsky, Keynes, Eliot, St. Pius X, Leo XIII, Pius XI, Pius XII, and—completing the circle—Plato. In mathematics: Taylor, Dedekind, Lobachevski, and Einstein; in the Laboratory, students are introduced to modern physics; while in Philosophy and Theology they continue their reading of Aristotle and Aquinas.

Reading and Writing

Students at Thomas Aquinas are expected to write often and well. Freshmen in need of extra help participate in a writing preceptorial. Moreover, all students must write a senior thesis, which is considered an integral part of the curriculum. The thesis provides both an opportunity and a challenge, since it demands considerable independence of thought on the student's part. In effect, the student is expected to join in what the University of Chicago's Robert Maynard Hutchins called the "Great Conversation" of Western civilization. "[The student] frames a question of the sort that the authors in the program themselves frame," the college explains, "and, under the direction of a tutor, refines, explores, and answers that question. The student's answer need not be ultimate, but must not be superficial or simply the repetition of authority."

As an example of the close interaction between faculty and students, all students meet twice a year with all of their tutors in what is known as the "Don Rags" to discuss their work. The close contact with faculty members is consistent with Thomas Aquinas's distinctive culture. This it traces to the Latin source of the word "college," which suggests a "sending together on a mission." Says a college publication:

> This implies something to be accomplished, and the need of working with one another to do it. Basically, the association is between teacher and students; all other college relationships refer to this one. . . . The community of teachers and students, being unified by a common objective, should be organic. The parts, like the organs of the body, cooperate in the work of the whole. The College is deliberately small so that the individual is not lost, and his needs are not ignored.

If the campus itself is far from luxurious (new construction *is* adding to its amenities), Thomas Aquinas has succeeded in making itself an active intellectual center. A regular Friday lecture series brings in noted scholars from around the country on a regular basis to speak on subjects ranging from "Newman's Idea of a University" and "C. S. Lewis: A Literary Approach," to "Restoring the Constitution" (by *National Review*'s Joe Sobran). (This scholarly quality is nicely introduced in the school's 1991–93 bulletin, which concludes with two fine essays about the liberal arts written by two Thomas Aquinas tutors.)

In 1982, Mother Teresa delivered the school's commencement address. Her advice to Thomas Aquinas's graduates: "You should be a new light." The school seems to have taken her encouragement to heart. □

Thomas More

Merrimack, New Hampshire

Up-and-Coming

Since we announced the forthcoming publication of the first edition of this book in the July 23, 1989, issue of *National Review*, hardly a day passed when the postman failed to bring at least one letter

The Thomas More College of Liberal Arts

Year Founded: 1978
Total Cost: $10,400
Total Enrollment: 76
Total Applicants: 27
  74% accepted
  51% of accepted enrolled
SAT Averages: 528V/530M
Financial Aid:
  76% applied
  76% judged to have need
  76% of those judged were
    given aid
No ROTC Program Offered
Application Information:
  Mr. Peter I. O'Connor
  Director of Admissions
  The Thomas More
    College of Liberal Arts
  6 Manchester Street
  Merrimack, NH 03054
  Telephone: (603) 880-8308
Application Deadlines:
  Early action: 12/15
  Regular decision: rolling

recommending new England's Thomas More College. At first glance, it seemed to us not a viable candidate: it has a faculty of just half a dozen souls; its facilities for teaching science are quite limited; it lacks an extensive library (Thomas More students often use the library at nearby Saint Anselm College). Besides, does this guide really need *another* Catholic college? But the more we read the many testimonials (solicited for our edification by Thomas More's president, Peter Sampo), the more we came to believe we would be remiss in excluding it from our list.

One notable letter came from no less an authority on quality education than Russell Kirk, author of the classic *The Conservative Mind.* Dr. Kirk called the college "strong in historical and humane-letters studies. . . . *All* members of the staff at tiny Thomas More are good and reliable; and the costs . . . are surprisingly modest for this age." You know he means it, because he plans to enroll his youngest daughter there.

Other letters—some from parents, some from graduates of Thomas More—spoke eloquently of its commitment to the West. The Great Books program, one student's parents wrote, "offers students a solid foundation in the major works of the Western Tradition. . . . [and] helps the student discover that there is no conflict between right reason and true faith." A graduate testified to the impact of her years at TM: "The school promotes responsibility, respect, and a foundation for growth as a human being."

Formidable in the Humanities

We'll cut to the chase: it's a wonderful place. But is Thomas More College of the Liberal Arts sufficiently developed to warrant recommendation? Founded only in 1978, the campus consists of four buildings and a faculty of seven professors, four of whom have Ph.D.s. The college catalog courageously admits that:

> One of the problems of small schools is that they can afford to have only a small number of full-time faculty on the payroll. This may mean that the range of subjects or disciplines presented to the student, correctly limited on principle, is further narrowed because of economic limitations.

A visiting-professors program eases the crunch somewhat. And we asked one of those distinguished visitors, physicist Donald A. Cowan, former president of the University of Dallas, to give us his impressions of Thomas More, which he and his wife, Dr. Louise Cowan, have played an active role in advising.

> The requirements for math and science at TM are quite usual [six hours of each]. . . . The results, too, are usual: scores on the [Graduate Record Exam] are pretty much as they are elsewhere, reflecting more the entering SATs than the subsequent education. . . .
> [*National Review*'s] disappointment with the math and science stems no doubt from the failure of [those] courses to match the genius of the humanities offerings (in which primary texts are read in literature, philosophy, theology, and politics, with history as an organizing stratagem). . . . [N]owhere else is there quite so formidable an approach to the humanities. . . . And the students *do* read documents in the history of science and mathematics along with the other primary texts.

Fair enough. Perhaps pre-med students or young men and women looking forward to careers at NASA should choose another school, but our interest in the humanities is so strong, we'll set aside for the moment our concerns about math and science (and the laboratory facilities needed to study them). Let's understand what Thomas More itself intends to do.

Three Major Fields

For a school dedicated neither to the discipline of the New Science nor to the profligacy of the New Age (far from it), TM's catalog can still wax with the neo-mysticism of contemporary physics: "The curriculum reflects the many layers of reality that exist simultaneously in every action completed in a single moment of time, while it acknowledges the mysterious chains of causality between events which are visible only partly at any given time." In other words: We believe in God, and in the interconnection of the liberal arts. Although, again, we are speaking primarily of the trivium; after the first two years of prescribed study students must concentrate in just one of three areas: political science, philosophy, or literature.

The core reminds us, as any Great Books program inevitably must, of the sequence at St. John's (Annapolis/Santa Fe). Students attack the litera-

> We need education in the obvious more than investigation of the obscure.
>
> —*Oliver Wendell Holmes II*

ture chronologically, reading the ancients as
freshmen, and coming to the authors of our own
time in the senior year. A writing seminar is taken
each semester. Latin and Greek are studied in the
first years, as are math and physics. No electives
are taken until the junior year, and then—in two
years—only seven; which is all the elective courses
offered in each of the three areas of concentration.
It is, well, rigid. But, again, this is what a core of
studies must be when taken as far as TM and St.
John's take it—and at St. John's there are no electives.

The core is completed by two-semester sequences of theology and the fine arts in the junior
and senior years, respectively. The second section
of the fine arts, The Art and Architecture of Rome,
fits nicely with an aspect of the program similar to
the one at the University of Dallas: a semester
spent studying in Rome.

Passionate Supporters

It *may* be important to mention that Thomas
More is currently not accredited; which we state in
the conditional, because the reason apparently has
to do with the school's lack of a medical facility (it
also lacks a gym, and so offers students the facilities of a Merrimack health club across the street),
and because we understand that TM students have
had no difficulty gaining admission to postgraduate
programs at the best universities.

Size should probably not be considered a criterion of academic excellence, so do not hold it against
Thomas More that it is, in Russell Kirk's word,
tiny. But size does make for some charmingly
unique characteristics: President Peter Sampo is
also a professor; Virginia Arbery, who teaches politics, was formerly the admissions dean; her husband, Glenn, is assistant professor of literature and
director of student life. We don't know if other faculty cook in the cafeteria, or shovel snow from the
sidewalks—if there are sidewalks. Actually, the
students themselves perform various of the school's
maintenance functions. Witness the commentary
we received from one of Thomas More's first graduates:

> [We] confront[ed] nature at a primary level: clearing
> out the old dung beneath the barn to make room for
> the cafeteria, raking leaves which refilled the
> ground like a spilling dam, and shoveling snow as
> late as Easter. . . .

Deep fellowship is the fruit of a faith bound in a common enterprise. And our enterprise at this point wasn't merely intellectual, but overflows from the classroom and seeps into the world at large.

In all the hundreds of letters *National Review* received from around the country about scores of different schools, none equaled in eloquence or passion the ones from the friends of Thomas More. □

Transylvania
Lexington, Kentucky

Bluegrass Thoroughbred

Fortunately, the folks at Transylvania University have a sense of humor, though we suspect it gets a bit strained from having to explain that, *no*, Transylvania's classes do not always meet at night, that students do not have to wear garlic around their necks, and that, in fact, the university has less to do with Count Dracula than with Daniel Boone.

As any classics major surely knows, Transylvania means "across the woods" in Latin, and the name derives from the wooded frontier first settled by pioneers whose chief guide was Daniel Boone. The first institution of higher learning west of the Alleghenies, Transylvania was founded in 1780. Early supporters included George Washington, Thomas Jefferson, John Adams, and Aaron Burr. Henry Clay actually taught in its law school and served on its board of curators. Over the years, alumni have included Jefferson Davis, two U.S. vice presidents, fifty senators, and thirty-six governors.

No Cinderella Story

Most important of all, Transylvania's traditions continue to be reflected in its sense of institutional mission and its curriculum. The administration is unusually clear in declaring that the university's *raison d'être* is its commitment to teaching. In defining Transylvania's priorities, the dean of the college delivers a backhanded indictment of much of what passes for a university education in the 1990s.

"We have no impersonal figures lecturing to hundreds of beginning students, no cold images on a television screen, no struggling and indifferent graduate assistants, no professors who begrudge their time away from the research laboratory or library, no instructors who vanish, Cinderella-like, at the end of their lectures," says Dean Asa A. Humphries, Jr. "But we do have able and concerned professionals who have committed their lives to the challenge of undergraduate teaching."

We suspect that it may not be as uniformly wonderful as the good dean suggests, and we've heard tell of a few Cinderellas on the faculty, as well as the usual recidivist left-wing academics, but the overall culture of Transylvania seems squarely focused on the classroom, and on providing students with a solid liberal education. That is even true in the sciences and pre-med areas—notorious wastelands at many universities.

Says one pre-med student at "Transy": "Large schools tend to have a lot of teaching assistants, particularly in the math and science curriculum. Here there aren't any assistants; the professors are here to teach. They're very accessible. . . . There's no hassle about tracking them down here. They're either in class or in their offices."

Transy's commitment to teaching is evidenced by the Bingham Awards for Excellence in Teaching, a salary-enhancement program for the best faculty.

Transylvania University

Year Founded: 1780
Total Cost: $14,140
Total Enrollment: 975
Total Applicants: 821
  94% accepted
  36% of accepted enrolled
SAT Middle Range
  Averages: 1030–1250
Financial Aid:
  50% applied
  43% judged to have need
  97% of those judged were given aid
ROTC Program Offered
Application Information:
  Ms. Patricia Bain
  Director of Admissions
  Transylvania University
  Lexington, KY 40508
  Telephone: (800) 872-6798
Application Deadlines:
  Early decision: 11/1
  Regular decision: 3/15

A Truly Common Core

Freshmen at Transylvania must take a two-course sequence in Images of Human Nature and Images of Civilization as part of the school's freshman studies program. The sequences are designed to improve skills in research, writing, and thinking. They do so by introducing students "to basic questions that have engaged influential writers in Western civilization." Says the former director of the freshman studies program: "Our reading selections are chosen to expose students not just to good writing, but to outstanding examples of critical thinking on important topics. It's a matter of ingraining that clear thinking precedes clear writing. When students learn to think carefully, they become better skilled at articulating their ideas."

At some schools, required freshman courses are often mob scenes taught more or less by rote, but Transylvania students often cite the freshman courses as among the highlights of the college experience. They also embody the difference between hyper pre-professionalism and the values of liberal education. One college publication quotes a pre-med student (who happens to be active in College Republicans) as saying that she had planned to concentrate strictly on science, but changed her mind after taking the freshman studies class. "It reminded me," she said, "how much I love English, and it made me realize that literature would be an inspiration and an outlet for me all my life. I think my literature courses will humanize my career by helping me see the whole person I'm treating."

Other required courses focus on honing academic skills the students will need in their collegiate careers. Students must take a course in the development of Western civilization—either up to the seventeenth century or from the seventeenth century to the present. Students must also take two courses from two different fields in the humanities; two courses from two fields in the fine arts; two courses from two fields in the natural sciences; two courses in mathematics, computer science, logic, or linguistics; three courses in three different fields in the social sciences; two courses in modern foreign languages; several courses in physical education; and one course in a non-Western civilization. Each requirement can only be satisfied by specially designated courses, and most are general introductory courses. At least in that respect, the narrow range of acceptable courses distinguishes Transylvania's curriculum from distribution requirements that are merely Chinese menus, and often include every course in the catalog. Thus the Transy core is a truly *common core*.

An Old Kentucky Home

Transylvania remains affiliated with the Christian Church (Disciples of Christ). This association is reflected in part by its approach to its *in loco parentis* responsibilities. Eighty per cent of the students live on campus, and residence halls are locked at midnight on weeknights and at 2 A.M. on Friday and Saturday. Visitation by members of the opposite sex is permitted only during specified hours.

No discussion of Transylvania would be complete without commenting on its location: in the heart of Kentucky's bluegrass region, yet also within three blocks of downtown Lexington. The campus is known for being tight-knit and offering a wide

> Education makes a people easy to lead, but difficult to drive; easy to govern, but impossible to enslave.
>
> *—Lord Brougham*

range of activities for students, from forensics to field hockey to men's and women's swimming teams. In addition, Transylvania offers off-campus study programs in France, England, Mexico, and Washington, D.C., as well as a special European study program that explores the "cultural heritage of the West." Students with a bent for public service can also take advantage of Kentucky legislative internships.

If this sounds a trifle too boosterish, don't take our word for it. Graduate and professional schools have come to recognize the quality of Transylvania students. In 1989, for example, nearly 93 percent of Transy students who applied to medical school were accepted. □

Trinity

San Antonio, Texas

Understanding Fundamentals

As in the case with the St. John's schools, there are several Trinitys—eight, to be exact. The one we recommend is in beautiful San Antonio, Texas—arguably America's most gorgeous big city. Trinity University has a reputation as a yuppie school, and it's not an entirely unjust description. But it also has a liberal arts core curriculum that suggests the University of Dallas to the north, except it is more self-consciously secular, slightly less traditional, and more "vocational." We hear Trinity's most popular sport is tennis.

A $288 million endowment—per student, the fifteenth highest in the country—has made Trinity hungry to expand, but in a era when a debasement of standards has tended to accompany growth, Trinity has actually raised its requirements, upgraded its faculty, and resisted pedagogic extremes. During the last decade Trinity's SAT averages rose steadily from 1070 to 1200, a respectable mark for any school. Teaching is the number one priority among the school's professors, and although there are some graduate students earning degrees at Trinity, there are no TAs. Dr. Ed Roy, Trinity's vice president of academic affairs, is particularly proud of the faculty's efforts to include undergraduate students in their research. Dr. Roy, himself a geologist, said sophomores, juniors, and seniors work closely with their teachers on projects entailing library research and even field work. (In this, Trinity echoes Claremont-McKenna.)

Rebuilding the Core

The core at Trinity, called the Common Curriculum, was initiated during the 1980s to give the general education requirements a more traditional focus. According to Dr. Roy, ethical issues and value judgments are included in the Common Curriculum, and its purpose is to "set [the students] up for this type of continued learning we would expect from all Trinity graduates." Unlike most cores, however, many of Trinity's common requirements are avoidable. Placement test scores or high school work may excuse the student from taking a number of courses.

The Common Curriculum begins with a first-year seminar consisting of shared goals, requirements, and grading priorities that emphasize reading, writing, and class discussion. The themes, which in the past were common for all, now vary depending on a professor's preference, and include such topics as progress, love and death, and freedom and responsibility. Small groups of no more than fourteen students meet with a faculty member and an upperclass student mentor acting as peer counselor. Like freshman tutorials and small discussion groups at other schools, Trinity's seminars force students to sink or swim, learning in the process how to discuss and debate ideas. The seminar remains the favorite aspect of the Common Curriculum among most of the students.

All students must take English 302, the Writing Workshop; achieve "intermediate" competence in a foreign language; and have mathematical skills equivalent to three years of solid "college prep," including pre-calculus or trigonometry. In the spirit of postgraduate realities, students must have "hands on" knowledge of computers. Oh, and there is the lifetime sports and/or fitness requirement. Tennis, anyone?

You can see how the yuppie charge may have come about. Lifetime fitness? What would G. K. Chesterton have made of that? Well, we move on to more substantial ground—to the "Seven Fundamental Understandings." In a way, the Trinity approach gets more to the heart of the matter than the distribution requirements at many other col-

Trinity University

Year Founded: 1869
Total Cost: $13,736
Total Enrollment: 2,538
Total Applicants: 2,141
  75% accepted
  36% of accepted enrolled
SAT Averages: 582V/623M
Financial Aid:
  74% applied
  62% judged have need
  100% of those judged
    were given aid
ROTC Program Offered
Application Information:
  Ms. Sara M. Krause
  Director of Admissions
  Trinity University
  San Antonio, TX 78212
  Telephone: (800)
    TRINITY
Application Deadlines:
  Early decision: 11/15
  Regular decision: 2/1

The direction in which education starts a man will determine his future life.

—Plato

leges, because it does not simply dictate courses and readings, but requires *understanding*. There is also an emphasis on the relationships (what Robert Maynard Hutchins called "connections") among the various areas of knowledge. "We wanted to see integration among disciplines," said Dr. Roy. Among the Seven Understandings are three-course requirements in the Intellectual Heritage of Western Culture, the World through Science and the Human Social Context, and one-course requirements in Aesthetic Experience/Artistic Creativity, Other Cultures, the Role of Values, and the Nature of Knowing. A Common Curriculum Committee reviews each course proposed for the Seven Understandings. There are courses in history, philosophy, science (natural and theoretical), psychology, the fine arts, and business and/or government. Frankly, we've seen better selections of required courses, but given Trinity's other qualities, it works just fine.

One of Trinity's virtues is its concern about the students' ability to express themselves, both orally and on paper. The freshman seminar and the Writing Workshop exemplify the concern. And, in fact, *all* "Understandings" courses must meet not only the criteria set by the Common Curriculum Committee, but those regarding the oral and written exercises in each.

After the Core

Along with the traditional major areas of study, Trinity offers popular interdisciplinary minors in areas such as cognitive studies and environmental studies, as well as an international studies major. Many students enjoy the latter because it allows them to pursue combined interests in business, international politics, culture, and language.

The departments of business administration and economics claim the most majors, but Trinity also graduates a large number of aspiring attorneys. Immediately upon graduation 40 percent of the total class will enter graduate school, 30 percent will begin a job, and 30 percent will float. After five years, though, 80 percent will have received some type of postgraduate degree. In recent years there has been a noticeable increase in the number of graduates who pursue doctorates, probably a reflection of the rise in SAT scores.

As for general trends in higher education, Dr. Roy sees the 1980s as a decade of returning to the core, and the 1990s as the decade of bringing faculty back into the classroom. At Trinity, of course, they're already there. Let's hope he's right about the rest of America's colleges.

At the end of our profile of Trinity in the first edition of this book, we observed that this Texas jewel has not only evaded the debilitating "virus" of political correctness and curricular debasement, but has actually grown stronger, and "seems prepared to grow stronger still." We hope this is true. We think it is, and so were understandably perplexed when we received a letter informing us that Trinity has a very PC policy regarding the use of "inclusive language." Indeed, we flat missed it first time around. Adopted by the faculty in 1986 (and integrated into faculty and student handbooks), the policy encourages, but does not mandate, the use of the familiar—and ugly—neologisms (such as "he/she"), and even touts such horrors (in chapel no less) as "Godself," which is used, we're informed, as a . . . reflexive pronoun? A Trinity official tried to assure us that the inclusive-language guidelines are just one part of Trinity's antiharassment code which "intends to promote social equality . . . but not to regard as harassment" most of what we'd all consider protected by the First Amendment. And the nonspecific use of the masculine pronoun in term papers does not affect a student's grade.

We're not reassured . . . except by the knowledge that Trinity students have the intelligence and the character not to abuse the language, not even to soothe the fragile egos of a few faculty radicals. □

Union

Schenectady, New York

The Big One

There was a time, in the early nineteenth century, when Union College was ranked with Harvard, Yale, and Princeton as one of the "Big Four." Its alumni include President Chester Arthur (Class of 1848), FDR's father, Winston Churchill's grandfather, fifteen U.S. senators, ninety-one congressmen, thirteen governors, seven cabinet secretaries, and one hundred college presidents. Union traces its origins to 1779, when a

handful of prescient New Yorkers recognized that Burgoyne's defeat at Saratoga presaged the birth of a new nation that would require its own institutions of higher learning. Sixteen years later, in 1795, Union became the first college chartered by the regents of the state of New York. One of the first nondenominational colleges in the nation, the college derived its name from the union of the various religious denominations and nationalities in the new country. In 1845, Union became the first liberal arts college in the nation to offer an engineering program (it is still one of only a handful).

But Union's real attraction is less its history than its current academic program. Four of its faculty members are former Guggenheim fellows, while classes in astronomy and astrophysics are taught by Ralph Alpher, who helped develop the "Big Bang" theory. Its own alumni include a Nobel laureate (Baruch Blumberg, winner of the Prize for Physiology in 1976). In recent years Union students have won eight Watson fellowships, one Truman scholarship, one Rhodes scholarship, one Fulbright-Hays fellowship, and two NCAA fellowships, among other honors. More than 40 percent of Union's students participate in Union-run terms abroad.

Union College

Year Founded: 1795
Total Cost: $19,643
Total Enrollment: 2,036
Total Applicants: 2,941
  49% accepted
  34% of accepted enrolled
ACT Average: 28
Financial Aid:
  43% applied
  80–90% judged to have
    need
  100% of those judged
    were given aid
ROTC Program Offered
Application Information:
  Mr. Kenneth A. Nourse
  Dean of Admissions and
    Financial Aid
  Union College
  Schenectady, NY 12308
  Telephone: (518) 370-6112
Application Deadlines:
  No early decision
  Regular decision: 2/1

Culture of the West

Adding to that record of academic excellence, Union recently introduced a new core curriculum focusing on Western history and culture.

The core is a clear reaction to what Union's dean of faculty calls "the formless cafeteria-style general education requirements that came to dominate many colleges in the 1970s. . . ." He described those curricula, which had little focus or rationale beyond making life easy for the faculty itself, as "a retreat from responsibility on the part of faculty and administrators." Under Union's old "liberal learning" core, almost anything went. Said one professor: "When you put every course into one of half a dozen categories, you get no sense of the college saying what's important. Everything's important, because everything got a liberal learning category."

"Kids don't have a sense of where they've come from," another faculty member says. "There was no sense [under the old plan] of Western civilization, its glories and its follies, its blessings and its burdens." Some professors are disappointed that the school did not adopt a single, common Western civilization course for all students. And Union's dean of faculty somewhat churlishly attacked the National Endowment for the Humanities' proposed core curriculum as "superficial, rigid, and impractical."

Even so, Union's compromise is still a far stronger curriculum than we found at many other schools. Union faculty members, for example, frankly admit the new program is Eurocentric. Union does not ignore foreign cultures, but it notes (quite rightly, we think) that students "need a context in which to put their ideas"— which means a grounding in the thought and history of the West.

The Sequence of Study

All students begin their education with a freshman preceptorial, which is focused on reading great works, such as Euripides' *Medea*, Plato's *Crito* and *Apology*, Genesis, Exodus, and the Gospel of Matthew, Machiavelli's *The Prince*, as well as readings from Charles Darwin, Emily Brontë, Virginia Woolf, Karl Marx, Sigmund Freud, and Richard Wright. Afterward, students must choose their history sequence: either ancient history, History of Greece and History of Rome; European history, History of Europe I and II; or American history, History of the United States to the Civil War and History of the United States Since the Civil War.

In the core's first year, 20 percent of Union's freshmen opted for the ancient history sequence, and 40 percent each for the American and European sequences. The history sequences are followed by two additional required courses in the literature, philosophy, religion, art, or intellectual life of the area chosen. Students can fulfill this requirement by taking either two courses in literature (one of which must be a survey course) or one course in literature and one course in civilization (one of which must be a survey course). They must also take an introductory course in the social sciences, either Introduction to Cultural Anthropology, Introduction to Economics, Introduction to Politics, Contemporary American Politics, A First Course in Psychology, Introduction to Sociology, or Social Problems and Social Policy. Students round out their requirements by taking a course in mathematics and two courses in basic or applied science. A course in a foreign language is encouraged.

Beginning with the class of 1994, Union will also

We must recover the element of quality in our traditional pursuit of equality. We must not, in opening our schools to everyone, confuse the idea that all should have equal chance with the notion that all have equal endowments.

—Adlai E. Stevenson

require students to earn a certain number of writing credits through the courses they take.

Signs of the Times

Union's faculty tends to be quite accessible and its classes small. Full professors can be found teaching freshman classes—an unheard-of heresy at many large research universities. If we have one major concern, it is the note of university-wannabe we detect in Union's heavy and growing emphasis on research, especially its involvement in "undergraduate research." Union is so enthusiastic about this sort of thing that it has hosted the National Conference on Undergraduate Research. Unfortunately, despite the attractive rhetoric about getting students involved in their professor's work, undergraduate research often means that the faculty can just pretend the undergraduate students are really graduate students, whom they would rather be teaching anyway. Union's strength and its attraction, however, are its commitment to undergraduates and the traditions of a liberal arts college. It would be a shame to lose that.

In the meantime, Union deserves a close look from students in search of a sound curriculum and top-notch teaching.   □

University of the South
Sewanee, Tennessee

Dressed for Success

For those of us who are traditionalists in the matter of higher education, a visit to a modern campus is often a distressing occasion, although it is often hard to pick out what is worst—the classes in "Phallic Imagery in Elizabethan Poetry," the slumlike ambience of a campus green covered with anti-apartheid shanties, the illiteracy of the student body and faculty alike, or the apparently mandatory slovenliness of the undergraduate wardrobe, which often appears scrupulously modeled on the latest in bag-lady chic.

Oxford Volunteers

So we were pleasantly surprised when we ventured onto the Sewanee campus. Reflecting the historical and educational ties to Oxford University, the professors at Sewanee still teach classes clad in academic gowns—also worn by honor students. Undergraduates follow a similarly traditional, although voluntary, dress code that requires men to wear a coat and tie to class and women to wear skirts or dresses.

The Oxford connection runs deep. The British played a major role in rebuilding the school after the Civil War, and both Oxford and Cambridge universities donated books to help start Sewanee's first library.

Perhaps most important of all, Sewanee still reflects the Oxonian tradition of commitment to liberal learning, with close contact between faculty and students. Over the past several generations, Sewanee has produced no fewer than twenty-two Rhodes Scholars. On a per capita basis, that places Sewanee in the top five institutions nationally. Sewanee also offers a very popular six-week study program at St. John's College, Oxford.

All of this is essential to the culture of Sewanee. "The University of the South," commented the British historian Arnold Toynbee on a visit to the campus, "fruitfully combines the best features of both the English and the American educational systems."

We agree, so we won't make any attempt to conceal our enthusiasm for a school we regard as one of the finest and most remarkable institutions in the country.

Faculty and Student Togetherness

Very few classes at Sewanee have more than thirty students; the vast majority have fewer than twenty. The close interaction between students and faculty members begins at freshman orientation, where students are introduced to their faculty adviser and his or her family, together with an upperclassman. In most cases, the freshmen will actually join the faculty member's family for a picnic supper or even dinner at the professor's home. In other words, an incoming freshman at Sewanee will have more give-and-take with a faculty member on his or her "first" day than some students at schools like Harvard or the University of Wisconsin have in

University of the South

Year Founded: 1857
Total Cost: $17,760
Total Enrollment: 1,123
Total Applicants: 1,419
  66% accepted
  36% of accepted enrolled
SAT Average: 1146
Financial Aid:
  72% applied
  86% judged to have need
  86% of those judged were
    given aid
No ROTC Program Offered
Application Information:
  Mr. Robert Hedrick
  Director of Admissions
  University of the South
  Sewanee, TN 37375
  Telephone: (615) 598-1238
Application Deadlines:
  Early decision: 11/15
  Regular decision: 2/1

four years. Nor is this a one-shot deal. Almost all faculty members live on campus and are reported to be readily available to students outside of class. Student-faculty dialogues are held weekly, while a popular Thursday-morning coffee hour in the Bishop's Common provides another opportunity for informal discussions.

Sewanee is perhaps best known for its outstanding English department—English is still the school's most popular major—and for publishing the nationally respected *Sewanee Review*. Tennessee Williams thought enough of the school to leave his estate to the university after his death. The departments of history and biology also are highly touted.

Sewanee was originally founded by the Episcopal Church and retains its affiliation, as well as its conservative style. "While non-sectarian in its teaching and recruiting of students and faculty," the university explains, "the College honors its Christian heritage and finds that faith and reason enrich each other." Although the rhetoric of higher education often falls short of the reality, that does not appear to be the case at Sewanee, which *The New York Times*'s Edward Fiske calls "a conservative's paradise and an activist's nightmare. . . ."

> It is the great end of education to raise ourselves above the vulgar.
>
> —*Richard Steele*

Wisdom by Design

Sewanee's commitment to the liberal arts is reflected in its rigorous and well-designed curriculum, encompassing fifteen required general education courses and a demanding foreign language requirement. Following the Roman philosopher Seneca's admonition that "no man ever became wise by chance," all students are required to take a survey course in the history of Western civilization and a nonsectarian introductory course in religion. Students are required to take three courses in language and literature, including an upper-division foreign language course, and English composition courses. Other requirements include three courses in mathematics and the natural sciences; four introductory courses in the social sciences; two courses in philosophy and religion; two courses in physical education; and one course in fine arts, music, or theater arts.

Sewanee's students also have the opportunity of studying abroad as part of a program that includes eight centers of the Institute for European Studies, the Cambridge semester or year, international studies in Oxford, Sewanee-in-Oxford at Hertford College, the British studies program at St. John's in Oxford, as well as programs for study in Japan. Sewanee also hosts the annual Sewanee Medieval Colloquium, which attracts scholars from Europe, Canada, and the United States. (It also hosts something called the "Sewanee Conference on Women," but we'll let that pass.)

An Elegant Domain

The administration at Sewanee has declined to drop its *in loco parentis* obligations. When Tennessee raised the drinking age to twenty-one, the university cracked down on undergraduate drinking, which remains a campus pastime. Sewanee students have a conservative attitude toward sex, consistent with the school's genteel traditions. Visitation hours are reportedly strictly enforced in the dorms. The school also encourages active volunteer involvement by students; many Sewanee undergraduates serve with the Sewanee Volunteer Fire Department, the emergency medical service, or as Big Brothers/Sisters. Other activities are managed by the Christian Social Relations Board and the Community Service Council. Despite the gowns, Sewanee's formality is not stifling. Classes are sometimes held outside and are occasionally attended by one or more campus dogs—another Sewanee tradition. Sewanee students typically know the dogs' names, as well as those of their fellow students.

Sewanee's campus has a special attraction for those who enjoy the out-of-doors and want to take advantage of the 10,000-acre campus—known as the "Domain." As *Southern Living* magazine noted: "You can hike trails, explore caves, view wildflowers, watch birds, climb rocks, picnic, and bike long distances without leaving the property."

But it is the neo-Gothic cloisters, towers, and spires that give Sewanee its character, best captured by the All Saints' Chapel. Modeled after the Chapel of St. Mary the Virgin at Oxford, it is the embodiment of high-church Episcopalianism with its marble floors, solid oak pews, and extraordinary stained-glass windows. Alongside the more traditional images, the stained-glass windows also memorialize many of Sewanee's teachers, deans, and benefactors, including one professor's old Volkswagen, a fighter jet squadron, and another professor illustrating the theory of relativity.

"It's all part of the institution's effort to accept the paradoxes of its past and to acknowledge the balancing act of its educational mission," the school's historian told *Southern Living*.

While most Sewanee students are from the South, the vast majority are from out of state, representing thirty-nine states and twelve foreign countries. Reflecting the quality and ambition of the student body, 63 percent of Sewanee graduates go on to graduate or professional schools. Their acceptance rate for medical schools tops 90 percent, while the school says that Sewanee graduates have an almost perfect acceptance rate for law and business schools.   □

Wabash

Crawfordsville, Indiana

Of Sound Mind and Body

This book is not a guide to *conservative* liberal arts colleges. If it were, though, Indiana's Wabash College might qualify as the best in America. By almost all accounts it is a conservative place (*"traditionalist"* is probably a better word). But it is also one of the nation's best smaller schools, and by almost any measure, from academics to athletics. Because Wabash has a $155 million endowment (the joke around campus is "Wallies are well endowed"), it accepts no federal aid, and so preserves its complete independence. Its continued resistance to coeducation gives testimony to that.

The all-male character of Wabash gives it some of the feeling of an ancient university, or so one imagines, and the general attitude is one of confident optimism. "You'll play to win at Wabash, no matter what you're doing, because working hard and playing hard are what the Wabash tradition is all about," reads a college pamphlet. Monday through Friday the campus mood is serious and studious, and when Wallies aren't hitting the books they're on the playing fields, participating in either varsity sports or one of many intramural activities. The school competes in ten Division III intercollegiate sports, including baseball, basketball, cross-country running, football, golf, sailing, soccer, swimming and diving, tennis, track and field, and wrestling; and an incredible 90 percent of the students involve themselves in the intramurals.

Come the weekend, the frat houses begin to rumble. More than two-thirds of Wabash men go Greek. Because of Crawfordsville's rural locale, all students are allowed on-campus automobiles, and the "road trip" was practically invented at Wabash. The campuses (and the women) of DePauw, Purdue, Butler, Indiana University, and Indiana State are all within two hours' drive; Notre Dame and Chicago are two or three hours away.

Uncharacteristically Exciting

The curriculum at Wabash is made up of a core —a required freshman tutorial and a two-course sophomore requirement entitled Cultures and Traditions; a language studies (English and foreign) requirement; a series of distribution requirements (twelve courses in all, covering the range of the humanities and sciences); a major area of concentration; and either a minor or an interdisciplinary area concentration. Here's another plus: each senior is required to pass both a written and an oral comprehensive exam in his major field of study before he can graduate.

Wabash freshmen begin their education in tutorials "designed to insure the first-year student's participation in small group discussions that will challenge him intellectually and suggest the kind of quality of experience characteristic of the liberal arts." The tutorials, which are collaborative teaching efforts made by members of (usually) fifteen of the eighteen different departments, are not Mickey Mouse, get-to-know-your-college courses, and comprise some surprising subjects. In a recent academic year you could choose from such diverse offerings as Human Genetics and the Human Genome Project (analyzing what's known about mapping and sequencing all 6 billion pairs of the genome), and Mind, Metaphysics, and Materialism (about "the struggles of scientists to reclaim the view that humans are different and somehow better than the rest of the animal kingdom . . ."). These and other notable courses (such as Fundamentalism in the Twentieth Century and Protest and Revolution) are meant to put the freshman into the academic fire—listening and discussing, researching and writing. The fascinating topics bring an untypical excitement to the orientation process.

The excitement continues with the sophomore

Wabash College

Year Founded: 1832
Total Cost: $13,270
Total Enrollment: 800
Total Applicants: 751
 72% accepted
 41% of accepted enrolled
SAT Middle Range Averages:
 460–580V/540–650M
Financial Aid:
 80% applied
 75% judged to have need
 100% of those judged
 were given aid
No ROTC Program Offered
Application Information:
 Mr. Greg Birk
 Director of Admissions
 Wabash College
 Crawfordsville, IN 47933
 Telephone: (800) 345-5385
Application Deadlines:
 No early decision
 Regular decision: 3/1

requirement—the two-term, six-module Cultures and Traditions—which also draws professors from most departments. The program's goals, as stated in the course guide, are:

> a. To widen our horizons by studying the arts, philosophies, religions, sciences, and social theories created by several cultures.
> b. To obtain a deeper knowledge of the arts and acts that constitute our historical tradition.
> c. To encounter through the great creative works of past ages the timeless conflicts of the human experience.
> d. To strive toward self-knowledge by examining and perhaps modifying our own values and beliefs.
> e. To participate in an intellectual experience shared by all students and a large part of the faculty.

The modules include topics such as the Hebrews, Fifth Century B.C. Athens, the Renaissance, the Reformation, Classical China, Turn of the Century Vienna, African-Americans, and Women's Issues. Each year a minimum of one new module is introduced to the six-lesson line-up, enabling the program to renew itself constantly. Both the freshman tutorial and Cultures and Traditions are shared learning which, as always, spurs intellectual discussion and strengthens communal bonds.

Indeed, to hold that objectivity is a myth is tantamount to denying the distinction between fiction and history, guilt and innocence in relation to the admitted evidence.

—*Sidney Hook*

Wabash Winners

The prevailing Wabash optimism endures, and the alumni success record is apt proof. First of all, more than 75 percent of the students who enter Wabash actually graduate from Wabash—a retention rate well above that of most schools, even some included in this guide. The school attributes the high figures to the students' character: "Wabash men have the sheer willpower it takes to survive—and to succeed."

And with little of the usual worry over the applicability of liberal learning in the "real world," once out the Wabash men continue to prove themselves, whether in graduate school, a professional field, or the corporate world. Seventy-five percent of all graduates go on to pursue some type of advanced degree, and the school has a higher percentage of graduates with Ph.D.s than Harvard or Yale. As is evidenced by the aforementioned endowment, many graduates strive for and achieve great financial success. On a per capita basis the endowment makes Wabash one of the wealthiest schools in the nation.

Such success is bound to be the result of Wabash's traditional approach to education (as an environment both academically and athletically rigorous), as well as adherence to such principles as healthy competition, hard work, and determination. □

Washington and Lee

Lexington, Virginia

A Speaking Tradition

Two of Washington and Lee's most cherished traditions testify to its historical antecedents. The first is honor—"No one attends the University," one publication says, "without becoming aware of new dimensions of honor and integrity." The second is the speaking tradition. When students or faculty meet or pass anyone on the campus, they acknowledge their colleagues, or even strangers, in a ritual of civility that is truly the mark of a conservative institution.

Located at the southern end of Virginia's Shenandoah Valley, Washington and Lee has a history that spans the history of the nation itself. In 1796, when Liberty Hall Academy—as it was then known—was facing financial collapse, George Washington came through with a $50,000 donation that saved the school. In 1865, faced with the southern tradition in ruins, the school was once again rescued, this time by Robert E. Lee, who became its president and began the long building process that was to make Washington and Lee one of the nation's outstanding liberal arts colleges. In 1972, the front campus was designated a National Historic Landmark, only the third college campus in the country so named.

A Teaching College

Often regarded as a shrine of the fallen South, Washington and Lee remains overwhelmingly conservative, although that tradition has been challenged in recent years. Even so, it has maintained a sense of fierce independence, reflected in its commitment to teaching and the liberal arts. "Its steady purpose," a university publication proclaims, "is to be one of the nation's great 'teaching' colleges. Research is encouraged as a part of the learning and teaching process, not as a substitute for it or as a way of determining promotion or tenure of its faculty." The professors, moreover, routinely give out not only their office numbers but also their home phone numbers to their students. Most classes are small, seldom above fifty students. (At some research universities a mass class might have as many as 1,200 students and a fifty-student class would be considered positively intimate.) Many of W&L's classes have fewer than ten students.

Washington and Lee University

Year Founded: 1749
Total Cost: $16,735
Total Enrollment: 1,610
Total Applicants: 3,433
  28% accepted
  43% of accepted enrolled
SAT Middle Range
  Averages: 1170–1350
Financial Aid:
  40% applied
  27% judged to have need
  90% of those judged were
    given aid
No ROTC Program Offered
Application Information:
  Mr. William Hartog
  Dean of Admissions and
    Financial Aid
  Washington and Lee
    University
  Lexington, VA 24450
  Telephone: (703) 463-8710
Application Deadlines:
  Early decision: 12/1
  Regular decision: 1/15

Washington and Lee is a university because it has a law school, a School of Commerce, Economics and Politics, as well as an entity named The College. But, except in law, no graduate degrees are awarded. All students in the School of Commerce, Economics and Politics must have completed their first two years in The College. Furthermore, students in either of the undergraduate schools may take courses in the other. There are only about 1,600 undergraduates altogether, making Washington and Lee, despite its "university" status, really a small college, the law school aside.

The W&L Curriculum

The curriculum, while not as structured as it might be, is still quite traditional, including requirements in English composition; foreign languages, literature (six credits), fine arts, history, philosophy, and religion (twelve credits), laboratory science, and mathematics (ten credits), and social sciences (nine credits). These general studies requirements account for between forty and fifty-six of the one hundred twenty-one total credits needed to graduate. Unfortunately, many alternatives can satisfy these requirements, including some that enable students to take easy ways out. It would be possible to graduate with no courses in history or philosophy, and no economics or political science, while a student could satisfy the literature requirement with a course in modern novels. That most Washington and Lee students do better than that is to their credit and attests to the attraction substantial courses have both for good teachers and for students. W&L has so far avoided the trendy and politically tendentious courses that have subverted education at so many other colleges and universities.

W&L's strongest departments include English, history, and the commerce school, which consists of departments of political science, economics, business administration, and accounting. But its overwhelming asset is the overall culture of the institution.

Says one student, "Washington and Lee is probably the least politicized college in the country at this point." Alumni include novelist Tom Wolfe, evangelist Pat Robertson, and retired Supreme Court Justice Lewis Powell.

Although the school in 1985 went coed, the change has had little effect on the institution, because most of the new students come from families with the same conservative moral and social standards as the traditional W&L students. There are a few courses on women in the art, English, and history departments, but there is still, mercifully, no mention of women's studies per se.

Caution Ahead

But despite all that, W&L is not immune to pressures felt throughout academia. That liberal faculty members and administrators have made inroads—albeit modest ones thus far—into such a conservative school is testimony to the power of the academic Left. The administration has been metastasizing at a fair rate, including a new associate dean of students with special responsibility for "minority and international affairs," with all of the usual consequences.

Worse, the administration has imposed a vaguely worded ban on racial, religious, or sexual harassment on campus that could be applied to speech deemed "intimidating," "hostile," or "offensive." Ignoring the school's normal honor system, it then created a confidential review committee to enforce the speech limits. The latter initially included no white males (by far the largest group on campus)—a telling sign of academia's new race/gender political tests. (The school's president, somewhat nervous about a federal court ruling that tossed out Michigan's gag rule, has said that the policy should be reexamined.) The English department's 1990 spring seminars also showed signs of being "updated," as the *Washington and Lee Spectator* noted, to include "black American Women Writers

> It is better to be Socrates, dissatisfied, than a pig satisfied.
>
> —*J. S. Mill*

of the 20th Century," as well as relatively obscure academic poets. These are still relatively isolated outcroppings, but many of W&L's finest professors are nearing retirement age, and liberal faculty members have openly exulted at the opportunity to change the demographic mix of the faculty in the name of "diversity."

For all that, Washington and Lee remains for the present the fine institution it always has been. The student body remains conservative and open-minded, the faculty liberal but serious about its scholarship and teaching, and the curriculum loosely defined but of exceptionally high quality. □

Wheaton

Wheaton, Illinois

The Use of Sunday

Students who choose to attend Wheaton College are in good company—C. S. Lewis, G. K. Chesterton, Dorothy Sayers, J. R. R. Tolkien, George MacDonald, Owen Barfield, and Charles Williams. Well, not exactly in the flesh, of course. Wheaton's Marion E. Wade Center, however, holds special collections of the papers, memorabilia, and books of those seven champions of Christendom, and is therefore both a research center and a shrine of sorts. As the alma mater of Billy Graham, Wheaton is also home to the Billy Graham Center, a major training center for worldwide evangelism.

As the powerhouse of evangelical colleges, Wheaton is sometimes dubbed the "Evangelical Harvard," but the reference to Harvard is a cruel slander—at Wheaton classes are small, the professors actually teach, and the curriculum is informed with solid and well-articulated values. From its founding in 1860, Wheaton's history has been one of unusual stability and continuity, reflected in its commitment to "provide a liberal arts education that acquaints students with the organized fields of learning in the context of a Christian view of nature, of humanity, and of culture through the study of both biblical and general education."

They Are Gentlemen

How well does Wheaton live up to that goal? Wheaton ranks twelfth among private four-year colleges whose graduates go on to earn Ph.D.s, and its science programs are ranked among the top fifty in the nation. Its graduates are eagerly sought by graduate and professional schools—85 percent of those who apply to law or medical schools are accepted. Wheaton remains one of the most selective (albeit self-selective) schools of its kind in the nation. Nearly 60 percent of its entering freshmen were in the top 10 percent of their high school classes. One accrediting report noted: "Wheaton students are intelligent, interested, ready and able to talk about their education, their Christian commitment, their goals, themselves."

"When you play football against Wheaton," one observer notes, "they hit just as hard, fight just as hard. But they don't [swear] every other word, and when you ask for the ball they give it to you. They are all very polite. They are gentlemen."

Wheaton has also been consistently cited in other guides as one of academia's best bargains—a quality education for a reasonably modest tab.

Wheaton has also become something of a magnet for the powerful. Of the five U.S. presidents since the end of the sixties, four—Nixon, Ford, Reagan, and Bush—have visited the Wheaton campus, and then–vice president Bush delivered the 1985 commencement address.

But, we are quick to note, Wheaton is not for everyone. Students are expected to sign a pledge saying they will abstain from "alcohol, tobacco, gambling, illegal drugs, occult practices, and most forms of social dancing, and to practice thoughtful Christian choices in matters of entertainment, associations, and the use of Sunday." All students must live on campus unless they live with their parents or spouse, or have obtained special permission from the college. Religion classes are required, and there is a strong sectarian streak to the school, including belief in biblical inerrancy. (Even so, the student body includes representatives of forty-five different denominations.) We point this out because, for some students (including some Christians), these doctrinal matters may affect the decision to attend. But for many students interested in a conservative Christian education, Wheaton offers an outstanding opportunity.

Wheaton College

Year Founded: 1860
Total Cost: $14,250
Total Enrollment; 2,606
Total Applicants: 1,387
  68% accepted
  58% of accepted enrolled
SAT Middle Range
  Averages:
  1080–1260
Financial Aid:
  57% applied
  89% judged to have need
  94% of those judged were
    given aid
ROTC Program Offered
Application Information:
  Mr. Daniel Crabtree
  Director of Admissions
  Wheaton College
  Wheaton, IL 60187
  Telephone: (800) 222-2419
Application Deadlines:
  Early decision: 12/1
  Regular decision: 2/15

Wheaton's Extensive Program

General education requirements are extensive. Students are required to take eight hours of a foreign language, two hours of mathematics, four hours of writing, two hours of speech, fourteen hours of Bible and theology classes, and two hours in "other cultures." In addition they must complete thirty-nine hours of "area" requirements, including two hours in music and art; six hours in world history (History of Civilization is recommended); six hours of literature (Literature of the Western World is strongly recommended); eight hours of natural science, including at least one course in biology or geology, and one course in chemistry, physics, or astronomy. Students are also required to take four hours in philosophy (Issues and World Views in Philosophy is recommended); eight hours of introductory courses in the social sciences; and three hours of physical education.

Despite its small size, Wheaton offers majors in more than thirty fields, plus eight in its conservatory of music. It also offers an innovative liberal arts/nursing program or liberal arts/engineering double degree. Moreover, Wheaton runs its own overseas study program, including an eight-week summer interdisciplinary study of the people and culture of East Asia; a Wheaton-in-England summer program in English literature at St. Anne's College at Oxford University; summer courses in French language, literature, and civilization in France (including visits to Paris, the Loire Valley, Provence, and Normandy); programs in the German language, literature, and civilization in Germany (including visits to Cologne, Stuttgart, Amsterdam, Aachen, Bonn, Heidelberg, Ludwigsburg, the Black Forest, and the Swiss Alps); a study program in the Holy Land in cooperation with the Institute of Holy Land Studies in Jerusalem; and a program in Spanish language and civilization in Madrid. Wheaton also offers a Wheaton-in-Washington program, sponsored by its political science department, combining on-campus study at Wheaton with "briefings with leaders and learning about job opportunities on Capitol Hill, with interest groups, and government agencies." Wheaton also offers cooperative programs in social science at American and Drew Universities, a European seminar conducted by Gordon College, and a Latin American studies program of the Christian College Coalition in Washington, D.C. In the field of music,

Never regard study as duty, but as the enviable opportunity to learn to know the liberating influence of beauty in the realm of the spirit for your own personal joy and to the profit of the community to which your later work belongs.

—Albert Einstein

the school offers students a Wheaton-in-Aspen program in which regular course work is supplemented
by the resources of the Aspen Music Festival. And
finally, Wheaton operates the Black Hills Science
Station in South Dakota and an educational center
at Honey Rock Camp in northern Wisconsin, which
the school uses for leadership training.   □

Whitman

Walla Walla, Washington

Pacific Powerhouse

O ne of the basic decisions a student choosing a
college must make is whether to attend a big-
name multiversity or a smaller liberal arts college.
The difference is more than merely size.

The choice could hardly be more sharply drawn
than between schools like Whitman College in col-
orfully named Walla Walla, and the University of
Washington in Seattle. UW has more than 25,000
undergraduates, while Whitman has a student body
of 1,200. The real distinctions, however, show up
most dramatically in the classroom priorities of
each institution. As at many large state universities, much of the teaching at UW is done not by
professors at all but by teaching assistants—some
of them with only the shakiest grasp of English;
some introductory classes at UW have topped 1,000
students. In the scramble of too many students
chasing too few professors willing to teach undergraduates, courses are often difficult for UW students to get into—even in their majors. That may
be one reason why only 42 percent of UW freshmen
get their bachelor's degree, even after five years.
That contrasts sharply with Whitman's 77 percent
graduation rate.

None of this should come as much of a surprise,
since the resources and priorities of UW—like most
large institutions—are radically skewed not toward
teaching undergraduates but toward research, specifically activities that can lure westward a larger
chunk of the federal government's research cash.

No Teaching Assistants

Whitman, on the other hand, typifies everything UW and the multiversities as a whole lack. It is known not only for its commitment to a traditional liberal education, but for its concern for students, the close interaction between faculty and undergraduates, and its outstanding educational quality.

So strong is Whitman's commitment to teaching that the faculty actually rejected a proposal to cut teaching loads from six courses a year to five courses. Despite the obvious benefits for the profs, such a cut would have meant larger and fewer classes for the students. In the end the faculty decided that such a move would undermine Whitman's educational mission. Needless to say, we know of very few faculties who have resisted the siren call that has turned the movement from teaching into a stampede throughout higher education. (They did approve a generous sabbatical policy for themselves.)

Because of such commitments, Whitman is unchallenged as the Pacific Northwest's premier liberal arts college. What makes the school particularly attractive is Whitman's solid conservatism, both in its student body and in its curriculum. One recent sociology major has griped that "the term 'conservative liberal arts institution' fits Whitman much better than 'liberal arts.' " We guess it is too much to expect that a sociology major have the slightest clue what the "liberal arts" actually are, but we take his grumbling as a very good sign indeed. "For some reason," a faculty member says, "we have managed to survive most of the counterculture, so far." Could that reason be common sense?

Despite a vocal liberal contingent among both the student body and faculty, and a new administration that frequently expresses its desire to bring more "diversity" to Whitman, the college's "luck" will probably hold.

Teachers Teaching the Classics

Founded in 1859, Whitman has prided itself on its independence. In the early years of the century it successfully weathered a brief attempt to turn the college into a full-scale German-style university. Instead, the challenge to its core values resulted in a remarkable revival of the spirit of

---

Whitman College

Year Founded: 1859
Total Cost: $19,810
Total Enrollment: 1,205
Total Applicants: 1,278
  80% accepted
  31% of accepted enrolled
SAT Averages: 550V/590M
Financial Aid:
  63% applied
  59% judged to have need
  100% of those judged
    were given aid
No ROTC Program Offered
Application Information:
  Ms. Madeleine R. Eagon
  Director of Admissions
  Whitman College
  Walla Walla, WA 99362-
    2085
  Telephone: (509) 527-5176
Application Deadlines:
  Early decision: 12/1
  Regular decision: 2/15

comprehensive and liberal learning at Whitman. The school's philosophy can probably best be described by turning again to the University of Chicago's Robert Maynard Hutchins, who insisted that the liberal arts "are not merely indispensable; they are unavoidable."

> Nobody can decide for himself whether he is going to be a human being. The only question open to him is whether he will be an ignorant, undeveloped one or one who has sought to reach the highest point he is capable of attaining. The question, in short, is whether he will be a poor liberal artist or a good one.

That sense of the primacy of liberal learning permeates Whitman's curriculum. The college's freshman core requires students to take two four-credit courses in one of three options: Great Works, Classical Greece, or Origins of Modernism. The program draws on faculty from the school's departments of religion, history, philosophy, English, classics, sociology, politics, physics, and astronomy. Despite their different focuses, the three courses ensure that Whitman students will graduate with a broad introduction to the major streams of Western thought. And none of the classes has more than twenty students.

Great Beginnings

The Great Works program, the catalog explains, is "not a survey but an investigation into how certain central human concerns have been formulated and how these formulations have evolved in Western thought." The first semester's reading might, for example, include Homer's *Odyssey*, Plato's *Republic*, Aristotle's *Ethics*, Sophocles' *Oedipus Rex*, Lucretius' *On the Nature of Things*, selections from the Bible and Dante's *Inferno*. In the second semester students read Bacon, Descartes, Machiavelli, Marx, Shakespeare, Rousseau, Freud, and Conrad.

In Classical Greece, the students focus on fifth-century B.C. Athens, but also study "the major components of Greek culture: mythology and religion, language and literature, theater, art, and architecture, political and economic theory, and philosophy." The first semester's reading includes Homer's *Iliad*, Herodotus' *Histories;* selected poems of Pindar; Aeschylus' *Oresteia* and the development of the Greek theater; the growth of the

Disinterested intellectual curiosity is the lifeblood of real civilization.

—*G. M. Trevelyan*

Athenian empire; and the arts and architecture of Periclean Athens. In the second semester students study the decline of Athens, reading Thucydides' *Peloponnesian War*, plays by Sophocles, Euripides, and Aristophanes, and selected dialogues of Plato.

The third sequence, Origins of Modernism, studies the period of revolutionary change in Western civilization from 1848 to the outbreak of World War I. The course examines the influence of writers like Darwin, Freud, and Marx in transforming ideas about social, economic, and scientific theory. Writers studied include Dickens, Dostoevsky, Baudelaire, Hardy, Tolstoy, Nietzsche, Freud, Conrad, Ibsen, Chekhov, Shaw, Lawrence, and Kafka.

Having completed the freshman core, students must complete a minimum of six credits in six of seven areas: the fine arts, history and literature, language and linguistics, physical science and mathematics, philosophy and religion, descriptive science, and social science. Whitman students round out the requirements with a senior colloquium, a twelve-person seminar on a contemporary issue taught by two faculty members. Recent topics have included the Vietnam War and "Vanishing Forests." Seniors are also required to take a comprehensive exam in their major, a Whitman requirement since 1913.

Walla Walla and Beyond

Although Walla Walla may seem a bit off the beaten track, it is a notably livable community, with a reasonably low cost of living. Whitman students describe their sense of community, and the atmosphere on campus seems unusually friendly. It is also active. More than three-quarters of Whitman's students take part in one or more athletic activities, and 25 percent are on a varsity team. More than 60 percent study a musical instrument or sing in a chorus. A majority of Whitman students even try their hand at acting during their undergraduate careers, in one of the twelve plays the dramatic arts department puts on every year. A fifth of the students volunteer some of their time to community service, while about a third of the junior class elect to study abroad. Whitman's study-abroad program includes affiliations with the Council on Internation Educational Exchange, the Institute of European Studies, the University of Manchester, St. Andrews University, the University of Exeter, and Japanese universities. Whitman also offers combined program in engineering with Cal Tech, Columbia, and Duke, and a law program in conjunction with Columbia. And it offers a business administration program with the University of Chicago.

How successful is a Whitman education? In one recent year 94 percent of Whitman graduates who applied were accepted in their first-choice graduate or professional school. Twice in recent years, 100 percent of Whitman's applicants won acceptance into medical school. And on the LSAT, Whitman students also consistently outscore students from every other college and university—public or private—in the Pacific Northwest. Its record is powerful evidence of the continued vitality of the traditional liberal arts. □

William and Mary
Williamsburg, Virginia

America's Alma Mater

Although William and Mary is technically the second oldest college in the United States, there is considerable merit in its claim to be the "alma mater of a nation." Chartered by King William III and Queen Mary II of England in 1693, the school is a reminder of the power of ideas, and the role of higher education, in human history.

Undergraduates still study in the Sir Christopher Wren Building (built in 1695) and walk to classes on pathways worn down by three centuries of their predecessors, who include Thomas Jefferson, James Monroe, John Tyler, and John Marshall—all products of William and Mary's classical curriculum.

It was at William and Mary that George Wythe established the first chair of law in the United States, and numbered among his pupils the author of the Declaration of Independence. It was also William and Mary that gave George Washington his first and last appointments to public office. In 1749, the faculty named him surveyor in Culpeper County. And at the end of his life, he served as William and Mary's first American chancellor. William and Mary was also the birthplace of Phi Beta

Kappa, founded there in 1776; and it originated the collegiate honor system in higher education.

It is not an accident of history that the erudition of the Founding Fathers should owe so much to a single institution. The authors of the *Federalist Papers* and the Constitution were steeped in the Judeo-Christian heritage and were products of the classical curriculum. At William and Mary, they discussed Aristotle, Cicero, and Tacitus, and perhaps debated among themselves the works of John Locke. At the early college, ideas were considered of the utmost importance, and it was understood that they had the gravest consequences.

College of William and Mary

Year Founded: 1693
Total Cost:
  Residents: $7,142
  Nonresidents: $12,992
Total Enrollment: 7,542
Total Applicants: 9,478
  27% accepted
  50% of accepted enrolled
SAT Averages: 590V/634M
Financial Aid:
  48% applied
  51% judged to have need
  100% of those judged
    were given aid
ROTC Program Offered
Application Information:
  Dr. Jean A. Scott
  Dean of Admissions
  College of William and
    Mary
  Williamsburg, VA 23185
  Telephone: (804) 221-3999
Application Deadlines:
  Early decision: 11/1
  Regular decision: 12/15,
    1/15

The Best "Liberal" Principles

Despite some troubling changes in recent years, that sense of tradition still suffuses William and Mary, making it a school no conservative could help but love. Its current chancellor is former chief justice Warren Burger, and it has one of the largest and most active conservative student bodies in the country, including particularly robust chapters of the Young Republicans and Young Americans for Freedom. William and Mary remains the most selective public university in the country.

But its strength continues to be its allegiance to the principles of liberal education and the quality of its faculty. Thomas Jefferson, a member of the class of 1762, once remarked that it "was my great good fortune, and what probably fixed the destinies of my life," that he had a professor of the quality of Dr. William Small, whom he described as "a man profound in most of the useful branches of science, with a happy talent of communications, correct and gentlemanly manners, and an enlarged and liberal mind." Today, all classes continue to be taught by professors who are accessible, responsive, and almost uniformly praised for their quality. They may not all live up to the standards of the esteemed Dr. Small, but one conservative we know sent his daughter to William and Mary and actually went out to dinner—at various times—with eight of his daughter's professors, all of whom he found to be gentlemen and scholars.

The curriculum requires students to demonstrate proficiency in a foreign language, physical education, and writing, and to take eleven courses distributed among the humanities, social sciences, and sciences. Of these, the writing requirement is the most impressive. All students who have a combined

SAT (verbal) and English Composition Achievement score under 1300 (or who scored less than a 4 or 5 on the English Advanced Placement Test) must take a course in writing, normally in their first year. (High enough scores will excuse a student from the writing course.) And more: each department or school in which a student may "concentrate" (i.e., major) must establish a concentration writing requirement in which its majors are provided a "series of opportunities to practice their writing, especially as commented upon by an instructor." This normally occurs during the junior and senior years. In our experience, it is rare for a college or university to follow through in this way—by demanding continued attention to writing and by insisting that individual departments attend to their majors' general educational needs. Such tenacity is a sign of a serious educational purpose.

Students must take nine credits in each of the three areas, with at least six of those credits coming from a two-course introductory sequence in a single department (the third three-credit course must come from a different department). Students choose these classes from among basic courses designated by each department as "area" courses. A student must also take at least two higher-level courses, designated as "sequence" courses, in one of the departments in which he has completed two area courses. Less complicated in practice than its description might lead you to believe, this requirement ensures some depth and coherence in a student's education in at least two fields of study not closely related to his major field. The sequence requirement is another sign of educational seriousness, a thoughtful addition to the usual sort of distribution requirements.

The Fruits of Tradition

William and Mary's curriculum is not the most comprehensive we've ever seen, and it potentially leaves rather large gaps, but the college compensates somewhat for the paucity of its requirements by its humanistic approach to the various subjects.

One professor of philosophy, for example, is quoted in a college publication as saying: "The study of the great humanists is an enriching experience in itself; it enlarges our awareness of the subtlety and richness of human thought, and makes us conversant in our appreciation of our cultural heritage." If that sounds like the usual thing a phi-

> To be well informed, one must read quickly a great number of merely instructive books. To be cultivated, one must read slowly and with a lingering appreciation the comparatively few books that have been written by men who lived, thought and felt with style.
>
> —*Thomas Huxley*

losophy professor would say, you obviously haven't been hanging around philosophy departments recently.

You can often tell a good deal about a school's culture by the kind of speakers it invites to campus. In the early 1980s, William and Mary defied the Zeitgeist not only by declining to invite one of the usual radical standbys, but by reinforcing its royalist roots: it chose Prince Charles to address its convocation as the college's first honorary member. Other signs of William and Mary's traditionalism include its resistance to the grade inflation that has swept over much of the rest of academia; William and Mary faculty members are notoriously tough graders. But that has proved no disadvantage to students who want to go on for graduate degrees. More than 80 percent of W & M graduates with grade point averages of 3.2 or above who apply to medical school are accepted; 85 percent who apply are accepted by at least one law school.

There are, of course, problems. Although predominately a liberal arts college, William and Mary has a strong university-like component of research and of graduate and professional training. This combination has worked well, to date. The administration, however, seems to be leading the institution toward becoming a full-fledged university, and many of those whom William and Mary has so well educated are worried—and with good cause. They fear that a first-rate *college* may be lost in a vain effort to become a first-rate *university*. It is rumored that in decisions on faculty hiring and retention those who publish often but teach less well are being given preference over outstanding teachers who publish little. Money, in the form of grants, is being used to promote research. Already, faculty are teaching less, with the result that some classes are too large and popular classes are hard to get into. As yet, however, these new tendencies have not been taken too far.

Nor has "diversity," the other threat, yet become the reigning mantra on the campus, although its proponents are heard frequently enough to signal that William and Mary will not be immune to the pressures felt by virtually every other school in the country. (One correspondent told us that W & M is a place of "intellectual confusions and sexual revolutions . . . where the chairman of [an] honors group was also a [homosexual activist] . . . and where a religion teacher penalized any student who did not use 'inclusive language' in speaking or writing.")

There is currently little racial tension on campus, but a marked separation exists between black and white students. This separation is promoted in part by the administration's emphasis on affirmative action. (One black dean is alleged to have said that blacks and whites have distinct cultures that cannot be mixed, and black freshmen have their own orientation program.)

There is also an outspoken liberal faction on campus, and as older members of the faculty retire the shift toward the trendier approaches to the humanities may become more pronounced.

But having said all that, we have more than a little confidence in William and Mary's traditions and in its ability to withstand even the worst batterings of the Left. In the end, the academic pygmies are no match for the traditions of Thomas Jefferson and John Marshall.   □

Wofford

Spartanburg, South Carolina

A Sense of Place

Among its many other strengths, Wofford College surely offers the most unusual foreign study program of any school in the country. Every year one student—a junior or senior—is, in effect, given an American Express card and sent on a nearly yearlong tour of the world, all expenses paid. The only requirement is that the student choose an itinerary that will take him to developing countries in five different language areas of the world and that he be prepared to report on his travels to his fellow students on his return. One recent Presidential International Scholar (as the lucky student is designated) visited Central and South America, Asia, Africa, Eastern Europe, and Russia. "The purpose is to take the best brains and put them out there to see what the world is really like," says the South Carolina businessman who endowed the program, but who has remained anonymous. Equally unusual, students do not apply for the program—they are simply chosen.

The Presidential International Scholar program reflects the creativity and imagination to be found at Wofford, one of the finest liberal arts schools in the South. The college's willingness to innovate is all the more striking for its solid conservatism and its pride in being what it calls a "classical college." It has eschewed trendy politics and academic deconstruction while preserving a solid, traditional liberal arts program. Its Latin motto, *Intaminatis Fulget Honoribus*, means "Untarnished, she shines with honor," a fitting watchword for a school so loyal to its classical roots.

Wofford College

Year Founded: 1854
Total Cost: $12,965
Total Enrollment: 1,127
Total Applicants: 1,227
  79% accepted
  29% of accepted enrolled
SAT Middle Range
  Averages: 950–1160
Financial Aid:
  74% applied
  66% judged to have need
  99% of those judged were
    given aid
ROTC Program Offered
Application Information:
  Mr. Charles H. Gray
  Director of Admissions
  Wofford College
  Spartanburg, SC 29303-
    3840
  Telephone: (803) 585-4821
Application Deadlines:
  Early action: 12/1
  Regular decision: 2/1

A Search for Truth and Freedom

At Wofford's founding in 1854 all entering students were required to have studied English, Latin, Greek, and prosody; ancient and modern geography; arithmetic, algebra, and geometry; and to have read four books of Caesar, six books of Vergil's *Aeneid*, and six books of Xenophon's *Anabasis—just to gain admission*. Remarks a Wofford publication: "Obviously, the subject matter taught at the college has changed over the last 130 years, but the basic philosophy of a Wofford education has not."

Wofford is affiliated with the United Methodist Church, and its statement of purpose declares:

> [Wofford's] chief concern is the development of an intellectual, spiritual, and aesthetic atmosphere in which serious and inquiring minds of students and faculty alike will be challenged to a common search for truth and freedom, wherever that search may lead, and in which each person may become aware of his or her own individual worth while aspiring to high standards of learning and morality.

As an expression of that commitment, teaching is taken very seriously at Wofford. Senior faculty teach all introductory courses, and classes are seldom larger than twenty students. And the humanities seminar, taken by all freshmen, is seldom larger than sixteen to eighteen students. The seminar emphasizes "reading and discussion on value questions and issues, as well as English composition skills and the writing of essays."

The Wofford Way

Having completed the seminar, Wofford students must also fulfill a rigorous set of general education requirements: two courses in English literature, including a seminar in Literature and Composition involving "an in-depth study of some topic in literature," and a literature survey course; and four courses in history, philosophy, and religion, including at least one course in each department. In history, only Modern Western Civilization to 1815 and Modern Western Civilization since 1815 can be taken to satisfy the requirement. The philosophy requirement is usually satisfied with one of the following: Introduction to Philosophy, Reasoning and Critical Thinking, or Philosophy and Contemporary Issues. The religion requirement can be satisfied by taking The Old Testament, The New Testament, or The Christian Faith.

Other requirements include three or four credits in art, music, or theater; two courses in a foreign language (or by demonstrating proficiency); eight credits in a natural science; one course in mathematics; and two credits in physical education.

Wofford's curriculum is both comprehensive and well designed. No Wofford student graduates without studying the great monuments of Western culture, history, literature, philosophy, and science in an atmosphere where first principles are more than a mere afterthought. There are no junk courses at Wofford that we could see, and we would certainly match its course of study with that of any school in the Ivy League.

True education makes for inequality; the inequality of individuality, the inequality of success, the glorious inequality of talent, of genius.

—*Felix E. Schelling*

The Old Main Plaque

Wofford operates on a four-one-four academic calendar, which includes a one month interim session in January during which students are encouraged to "explore the new and untried, and in so doing to run risks that could not be justified in the semesters." In order to graduate, students generally must have participated in at least four interim projects during the winter term.

In addition to its extraordinary Presidential International Scholar program, Wofford students have the opportunity to study in Austria, France, Switzerland, Italy, Great Britain, Ireland, Germany, Spain, the Soviet Union, Singapore, Japan, Australia, Costa Rica, and the Dominican Republic. It also has joint programs with Columbia University and Georgia Tech offering a two-degree, five-year curriculum in engineering and the liberal arts; and a cooperative program with Emory University for students pursuing a degree in nursing.

Wofford's success has won wide recognition. One 1987 survey of college presidents ranked Wofford as having the most outstanding humanities program from among 161 southern liberal arts colleges. Five Wofford graduates have been Rhodes Scholars, and in the last decade Wofford students have won four Truman Scholarships, four Rotary International Fellowships, and a Fulbright teaching fellowship. Forty of its graduates have become college presidents.

But its strength remains in its traditions. The original college bell still rings out to celebrate victories and to mark major events; students still rub a misspelled word on a plaque in the Old Main building, a ritual that generations of undergraduates have believed will guarantee them accuracy in their examinations. Students and alumni alike also describe the almost ineffable sense of community—a "southern sense of place," or even a "Wofford Way" —that gives Wofford its character and that seems to place an indelible mark on its graduates.

One member of the class of 1970, John Burbage, once wrote: "As I was leaving, I stood before the twin towers of Old Main, that magnificent classroom building in the heart of the 130-year-old campus, where, as an uneasy freshman, I had come face-to-face with growing up. The return to that spot renewed my strength, not as a young student away from home for the first time, but as a husband, a father, and a mortal man who prays a lot and still wonders what lies ahead. And isn't that what a college is supposed to do?"

We think so. ☐

PART II

The Academic Gulag

The Academic Gulag

Being an Opinionated Survey of Brand-Name Schools (or Why There Ought to Be a Collegiate Truth-in-Packaging Law)

Introduction

Practically the first thing some critics note—and deplore—about *The National Review College Guide* is what they perceive to be the book's "omissions." Many of the nation's best-known and most renowned institutions of higher learning are nowhere to be found among our profiles of America's top liberal arts schools. Quite frankly, those schools are not omitted by accident or caprice; they simply do not measure up to our criteria. But having heard the complaint so often, we've decided to add the following profiles of a few of those prestigious schools—by way of making clear why, for instance, Brigham Young is in and Brown is out. Too many of these famous schools represent the antithesis of the values we celebrate.

They have been consigned to the Gulag for reasons that should be obvious: they do a poor job of teaching undergraduates (or they ignore them altogether); they have eviscerated or abandoned their graduation requirements and academic standards; or they have succumbed to attempts to impose an ideological orthodoxy on the intellectual life of the university. Some are guilty on all three counts. Our list is not thorough. We make no effort to list *all* the brand-name schools that have turned over the classroom to teaching assistants who can't speak English. We don't attempt to *comprehensively* chronicle the number of schools that have allowed curricula to be transformed by intellectual fads. And we present no *complete* accounting of the schools that have lately been running roughshod over the rights of students and faculty considered politically incorrect.

It is in regard of this last matter that many of the schools described below fall short. Whether in the form of draconian gag rules, politicized curriculums, or the imposition of an ideological orthodoxy onto campus life, PC represents an assault on the fundamental values of liberal education. One Princeton professor bragged to *The New York Times,* "I teach in the Ivy League in order to have direct access to the minds of the children of the upper class." A faculty member at Duke university wrote in a respected academic publication that it is not enough to teach students to think critically, because that will not necessarily bring them to "radical visions of the world." Instead, he wrote, "the teacher must recognize that he or she must influence (perhaps manipulate is the more accurate word) students' values through charisma or power."

During her term as National Endowment for the Humanities chairman, Lynne Cheney remarked: "These views of teaching—and the ethic they imply—are a sharp departure from the way faculty members have traditionally viewed their responsibilities in the classroom. . . . It used to be thought that they [students], like professors, should have academic freedom. They did not come to the college or university to be indoctrinated in the views of their professors. They came to learn about a variety of views on a host of subjects, to explore and challenge a wealth of ideas on how to live and what to value."

Unfortunately, the virus attacking such values has spread widely throughout higher education—and the eminence of an institution provides no immunity to infection. On the contrary, as our "Academic Gulag" makes clear, many of the worst depredations against the liberal arts and academic freedom occur beneath the cover of prestige.

We hasten to point out, however, that the dozen schools in our gulag are not necessarily the worst sinners. And many fine teachers and departments can be found at these schools. But if they are not the worst, these schools all present the several academic heresies writ large. Whether it is the gigantism of Berkeley, the trendy politics of Duke, the stifling orthodoxy of Smith, or the bogus core curriculum of Harvard, each in some way represents the deplorable state of higher education in America today. Other guides may list them as among the nation's best schools, but here they are strictly back-of-the-book.

The Gulag

Amherst College
Amherst, Massachusetts

A few years ago another publication—*U.S. News & World Report*—named Amherst the best liberal arts college in the country. In raising it to such eminence the magazine cited the high test scores of its students, the school's exclusivity, and its overall academic reputation. And if that were all there is to higher education, we would surely be joining in a chorus of praise. But Amherst does not make the cut in our book. Why not?

Well, listen to what one Amherst student told us. "While the media has shown Amherst as an idyllic place where dialogue is open and fair," Robert Witwer wrote, "some students have found the opposite to be true." Mr. Witwer is more than a casual observer. As the editor of the *Amherst Spectator*, a conservative newspaper on campus, he was on the front lines of the struggle against political correctness. So we take him seriously when he paints the following picture: "In a school that pursues diversity to such an extreme that 55 percent of Black applicants are accepted (compared to 17 percent of the Caucasian applicants), there is tolerance for about everything but a conservative opinion." Although campus conservatives are nowhere near as visible or rambunctious as, say, staffers of the *Dartmouth Review*, Mr. Witwer writes, they "are forced to weather anonymous threats and arbitrary labels whenever they choose to dissent from the reigning liberal hegemony."

Like many elite colleges, Amherst has all but done away with both its religious affiliation and its curricular requirements. One can easily sail through four years at Amherst utterly unacquainted with the classics of Western (and, for that matter, non-Western) thought. This void is filled with trendier offerings. The 1992–93 catalog, for example, continues to list Amherst's justly famous sociology course, Sport and Society, which is described thusly:

> A cross cultural study of sport in its social context. Topics will include the philosophy of play, games, contest, and sport; the evolution of modern sport in industrial society; Marxist and neo-Marxist interpretations of sport; economic, legal, racial, and sexual aspects of sport; social mobility and sport; sport in literature and film.

Frankly, one almost expects that sort of thing in the social sciences, but at Amherst the humanities have been similarly affected. "The English Department," Mr. Witwer writes, "is being gutted by classes such as 'Creating a Self: Black Women's Testimonies, Memoirs, and Autobiographies'; 'Queer Fiction: Some Texts from the Turn of the Century'; 'Topics in Film Study'; and 'Issues of Gender in African Literature.' (These four courses compromise the junior seminar required of all English majors.) There are literally dozens of courses focusing on race, class, or gender—all at the expense of substantial classes in English literature.

"It is a running joke at Amherst," he adds, "that English majors couldn't get a 'great books' curriculum even if they wanted it."

In this way as in others, Amherst has come a long way from its roots. Founded as a Congregationalist offshoot from Williams College, Amherst went coeducational in 1976 and in 1984 abolished its fraternity system. Administrators tend to be timid and compliant whenever the Left makes its usual demands. Even so, some things remain intact. Classes remain small, and the quality of teaching is still quite high. (The science departments are said to be especially good.) But Amherst's intimacy can become claustrophobic in classes where professors insist upon pushing "gender politics" or other ideological fads.

Political correctness at Amherst is both noisy and petty—an especially nasty combination. Several years ago, Amherst banned Coca-Cola from campus (because of the company's ties to South Africa), as well as CIA recruiters (presumably because of their ties to the United States). Despite such moral breast-beating, Amherst has a notably ambivalent attitude toward apartheid. While condemning the foreign brand in uncompromising terms, the college enthusiastically practices its own form of separatism, encouraging every sort of racial and ethnic enclave, including separate housing for minorities. While railing against racism, sexism, and homophobia, Amherst College funds have been used to bring to campus such notorious bigots as Kwame Ture (once known as Stokely Carmichael, who famously 241 remarked: "The only good Zionist is a dead Zionist") and Brother Abdullah Yasin Muhammad, whose speech was titled "People of a Lesser God: The Making of the Caucasian Race." A poster for Mr. Muhammad's speech asked: "Is it true that whites evolved from blacks? Did the Hon. Elijah Muhammed teach racism when he referred to whites as a 'race of devils'?"

Given the climate of opinion at Amherst, it's unlikely either question is being debated openly or honestly.

The University of California at Berkeley
Berkeley, California

Two episodes in 1992 won national attention for the University of California at Berkeley. First, of course, there was "Naked Guy," a student who tested the limits of Berkeley's tolerance by walking around campus clothed only in a backpack. The second was the strike by teaching assistants—the graduate students who actually do most of the teaching at Berkeley. The first story reminded us that Berkeley is still, well . . . Berkeley; while both reminded us of the tale of the Emperor's New Clothes. Although the administration bravely tried to put the best face on it, the strike rather nakedly exposed Berkeley's attitude toward undergraduate education. So reliant had Berkeley become on TAs that when they went on strike, three-quarters of the university's classes were left without *professors*. Berkeley insists that it is a world-class institution, but it turned out to be academically starkers.

The strike made it impossible to gloss over the fact that Berkeley had turned over the bulk of its undergraduate program to this academic lumpenproletariat, while its high-priced faculty churned out more unread, unreadable, and irrelevant "research." Worse yet, many of those TAs are unable to communicate in understandable English, a glaring indication of institutional contempt for undergraduate teaching. For years, Berkeley has bragged about its eminent faculty and, in literature distributed to undergraduates, touted its Nobel laureates. But as Martin Anderson noted in *Imposters in the Temple:* "The reality of teaching [at Berkeley] is very different than described in university advertising. If this were a business, or a profession such as law, would we stand for such false and deceptive advertising? Wouldn't we call it fraud?"

Well, *we* would call it "bait-and-switch" at least. Of course, Berkeley is hardly alone in its abandonment of undergraduate teaching. Throughout American universities, more and more classes are being turned over to student faux-professors. Seven years ago the American College Association declared:

> The teaching assistantship is now a device for exploiting graduate students in order to relieve senior faculty from teaching undergraduates. The tradition in higher education is to award the degree and then turn the students loose to become teachers without training in teaching or, equally as ridiculous, to send the students off without degrees, with unfinished research and incomplete dissertations hanging over their heads while they wrestle with the responsibilities of learning how to teach.

The result, the ACA concluded, was that "as an initiation rite, the teaching assistantship is almost invariably a disaster: it says to the initiate that teaching is so unimportant, we are going to let you do it." While Berkeley administrators routinely minimize their reliance on TAs, as Mr. Anderson told *The Wall Street Journal*, Berkeley's strike "ripped away the mask and pretense. . . . Now it's out in the open at Berkeley," he said. "People see the extent to which students are being used as fake professors. The simple solution is to call in the professors and say, 'the fun's over, start teaching.' That's. what the taxpayers of California pay them to do."

We certainly agree. But we expect TAs will continue to shoulder most of Berkeley's teaching burden. Nor is there any reason to expect that Berkeley will ever wean itself from its reliance on huge, impersonal classes (1,000 or more students is not unusual), or that students will ever be able to graduate in something reasonably approximating four years. That said, it is perhaps anticlimactic to report our other reasons for sentencing Berkeley to our *Gulag*, which include a politicized curriculum, a politically correct "sensitivity" code, and a meretricious admissions quota that until recently discriminated against Asian-Americans and other not officially victimized groups. Graduate education here may still be world-class; but for undergrads, Berkeley is an educational Bhopal.

Brown University
Providence, Rhode Island

About the best thing we can say about Brown is that it plays an indispensable role in academia. Ask a college administrator about political correctness, watered-down curricula, trendy post-structuralism, bans on free speech, and overall nuttiness at *his* school and he's likely to say, "Well, *we're* certainly not as bad as *Brown*." And he's right. Few schools have gone quite so far in embracing ideological purity or dismantling the liberal arts as has Brown, the designated bad boy of academia. Here is a school that has dropped all distribution requirements for graduation, eliminated any grades below C, and refused to record failures. The school is also so redolent with political correctness that it inspired student cartoonist Jeff Shesol to create the comic strip character "Politically Correct Person." (PC Person refers to little girls as "pre-women," and objects to a fraternity's planned "Water Party" as offensive to the "Artesian Community").

At Brown, however, satire is constantly being overtaken by reality. In 1990, the school banned ethnic theme parties (such as a "South of the Border" party) because they might be construed as insensitive. In the wake of the decision, Brown sophomore Karen Hirschfield called the ban "the most recent symptom of the festering disease of paranoid pluralism which seems to infect Brown, seething and boiling underneath the surface of our PC campus." Miss Hirschfield added:

> When I want to explain the atmosphere of Brown to friends at home, I tell them about how a Brown woman condemned a short story written by a Brown alum as racist, sexist and chauvinistic, without having actually read the book. She read a review of it, and decided that it should be banned from the bookstore, and that the author should not be allowed to speak at Brown. . . . Like the Puritans who shunned drinking, dancing and gaming so as not to offend the higher sensibilities of God, we too suppress freedoms (such as free speech) so as not to offend.

243

Ambivalent about the liberal arts, Brown seems to specialize in grievance. All entering minority students are assigned to the school's Third World Transition Program (a rather bogus name for a program designed for, among others, black students from New Jersey). In describing the program, journalist Pete Hamill noted: "It is race-driven; it assumes that non-whites are indeed different from other Americans, mere bundles of pathologies, permanent residents in the society of victims, and therefore require special help." As if such programs don't get the message across, Brown has also hired sensitivity "experts" and consultants such as Donald Kao, who openly acknowledges that his goal is to convince his clients that America is a racist society in which "privileged" whites have established arbitrary norms of acceptable behavior. "If you are feeling comfortable or normal," he insists, "then you are probably oppressing someone, whether that person is a woman or a gay or whatever. We probably won't rid our society of racism until everyone strives to be abnormal."

Perhaps that explains the academic culture at Brown. One of the most distinctive aspects of Brown is its curriculum—or rather, it's noncurriculum. Introduced in the late 1960s, it abolished all course requirements. As we noted, it banned giving grades below C. "But," as Mr. Sykes wrote in *Profscam*, "that hardly mattered because Brown students could take any number of courses pass/fail. And if by chance they did fail, that also did not really matter. Under the new dispensation, failures were not recorded on transcripts. ('I regard recording failures for the external world both superfluous and intimidating, or punishing,' a Brown dean explained.)"

In recent years Brown has become notorious for courses such as Introduction to Cinematic Coding and Narrativity, better known among students as "Clap for Credit." The course list continues to be filled with such delicacies as "When You Wish Upon a Star" ("How are Hollywood's stars produced in our culture? . . . We will read texts ranging from popular magazines, through movie reviews, to more academic studies . . ."); "Female Dicks" ("Readings include feminist theory . . ."); "Cryptic Signifiers: Dramatic Cross-Dressing" ("This seminar examines the fascination with transvestism in Western drama . . ."); "Sluts, Sin, and Sexuality: Seduction in American Literature"; and "Sexual and Textual Relations in the Middle Ages and Early Renaissance." Brown is the sort of school that Jimmy Carter, Jane Fonda, Geraldine Ferraro, and Claus von Bülow chose for their children.

We suspect our readers will know better.

Dartmouth College
Hanover, New Hampshire

In 1988, Angela Davis was selected to be the keynote speaker at Dartmouth College's celebration of fifteen years of coeducation. The unreconstructed Leninist was introduced by a Dartmouth dean as "an example of how one committed black woman has chosen to make a difference."

That's the way it goes at Dartmouth. Over the years, Dartmouth's administrators have been so eager to accommodate the merest whims of radicals on campus that (to echo Dorothy Parker's comment in a different context) if they were all laid end to end . . . we wouldn't be surprised. (If they were, they would no doubt do it in the safe₊ possible manner. Dartmouth has zealously distributed both condoms and rubber dams to its undergraduates.) The product of this flight from principle is a schizophrenic campus. While most of the students are moderate and reasonable, the faculty and administration are left-leaning and unusually intolerant, even by the standards of academic political correctness. We hasten to say that it is still possible to get a good education at Dartmouth—its history, English, Romance languages, and political science departments are justifiably well regarded—but it is increasingly difficult.

Lacking a semblance of a core curriculum, it is quite possible to graduate from Dartmouth without having read a word of Shakespeare or encountered a single question of Socrates. While Dartmouth requires no Western civilization courses, it *does* insist students study a non-Western culture. The good news is that none of this goes unchallenged. The *Dartmouth Review* remains a feisty and indomitable (and, we admit, occasionally sophomoric) voice on campus. We think its effectiveness is measured in part by the fervid (and often bizarre) attempts by the administration to gag it.

Another positive element is the presence on campus of the Ernest Martin Hopkins Institute, founded by concerned alumni to monitor college issues and to counter the usual propaganda from the school's bureaucracy. But radical feminism and "multiculturalism" remain in the ascendancy at Dartmouth, and conservatives who choose to brave Hanover's climate risk their intellectual health, their reputations, and their academic futures.

We need not rehash the entire sorry saga of Dartmouth versus the *Review* here, or the numerous episodes in which the administration's hypocrisy brought national infamy to Hanover. In their attempts to discredit and silence the conservative paper, Dartmouth's administrators have shown a remarkable willingness to ruin the reputations of their own students and run roughshod over the principle of due process. In the most recent episode, the college sought to exploit an anti-Semitic quotation inserted in the *Review*'s masthead. Ignoring evidence that the quotation had been maliciously inserted without the knowledge of the paper's editors, president James Freedman led a campus rally against "hate." Not content with attacking the integrity of the student editors, Freedman also attacked the paper's conservative supporters. "It is very unusual," Dartmouth English professor (and *National Review* senior editor) Jeffrey Hart remarked, "to experience an educational 'leadership' that lies so shamelessly." Hart, who knows the administration of president James Freedman firsthand, wrote in the journal *Heterodoxy:* "I believe that I have encountered only three people in my experience whom I would consider evil, and I do not use the word lightly. By evil I mean cold, arrogant, cynical, egotistical, and brutal. Those three are Gore Vidal, Roy Cohn . . . and Dartmouth's James Freedman."

Now, don't get us wrong. The malediction against Mr. Freedman does not extend to the entire school. Indeed, we have a lot of affection for the college and for the doughty conservatives who continue to fight for its honor. But Dartmouth is a symbol of what happens when colleges believe both too much and too little. Credulous in its embrace of the fashionable neo-orthodoxies of the day, Dartmouth has too little faith in the traditions of liberal learning, academic freedom, and tolerance. It is a deadly and tragic combination.

Duke University
Durham, North Carolina

Duke is a case study in what happens when a university has too many dollars but too little sense. Since the mid-1980s, Duke has been using its newfound wealth to transform itself into a bastion of trendy politics, literary deconstruction, and academic Marxism. It is certainly not alone in trying to buy its way to prestige, or in politicizing itself to win academic acceptance. But Duke yields to no one in its zeal. Duke's English department has hired so many avant-garde lit crits for such astronomical salaries that one wag calls Duke's English profs "the richest Marxists in America." Under the leadership of outgoing department chairman Stanley Fish, Duke stocked itself with professors who teach *King Lear* as an economic critique of seventeenth-century British capitalism and who declare that the "supreme mission of Marxist pedagogy" is the creation of "a Marxist intelligentsia for the struggle of the future. . . ." What does any of this have to do with studying English *literature?* Marxist professor Frederic Jameson explains that the role of the politically correct English teacher is not to teach Shakespeare or Milton or any of the other dead white guys, but to vandalize "pleasing, exciting and 'beautiful stories,' " which are really instruments for "promoting acquiescence to, and even identification with, the relations of domination and subordination peculiar to the late-capitalist social order. . . . Nothing can be more satisfying for a Marxist teacher than to 'break' this fascination for students. . . ." Eloquent, no? Sinister? Yes.

Unfortunately, the politicization of Duke colors nearly every aspect of campus life. When the president spoke to incoming freshmen a few years back, he didn't warn them about the dangers of cultural illiteracy, but about "homophobia." Although the new president may be more tolerant than her predecessor, Duke has not been amused in the past by dissent from the official ideology. The editor of one student magazine was fired when the publication ran a humorous piece on the school's food service program that Duke's powers-that-be deemed "racist." The corrosive atmosphere of intolerance at Duke was highlighted by the attempts of Stanley Fish to intimidate faculty members who had joined the school's chapter of the National Association of Scholars. Professor Fish denounced the NAS as "racist, sexist, and homophobic." But then he went further, writing a confidential memo to the school's provost urging the university to, in effect, blackball all NAS members from university committees that dealt with hiring, tenure, and curriculum. All this obviously comes as quite a shock to students and parents who have not kept up with the remaking of Duke in the image of the academic Left. Many students come to Duke still under the impression that it is a relatively conservative school. "I chose Duke under the belief that it would not be as bad as the Ivies," one student told us. "I don't know what it is like at an Ivy school, but it's a lot less comfortable here than I thought it would be."

One result of such misunderstandings is that the student body at Duke is far more conservative than the faculty, a point underlined by the success of the conservative *Duke Review.* There are other hopeful signs. Despite Fish's heavy-handed neo-McCarthyism, Duke's NAS chapter is flourishing with the support of principled liberals such as political scientist James David

Barber.

From the point of view of conservatives, the English and philosophy departments tend to be the worst, although history is also considered thoroughly infiltrated. Economics is considered more sound, while political science tends to be a mixed bag. "There is pressure among students not to take a conservative stand," one poli sci major told us.

> I've had a couple of bad experiences with TAs. There are certain views which are orthodox, and that's pretty well established. . . . There are a few conservatives, but they are very silent. I think they are forced into that submissive role because they are outnumbered. The conservative is an outsider looking in. Students are forced into a role where they feel that rather than say "I am a conservative," they will say nothing at all.

The push for academic glory has also meant that the emphasis in some departments at Duke has shifted decisively from teaching to research. Teaching assistants are increasingly taking the place of regular faculty members in fields such as math and the sciences. Nor are the high-priced "stars" particularly eager to soil their hands with Duke undergraduates. "For some reason," one student said, "they are rude and very impersonal. I tried to get in touch with one of the new profs and it was just impossible. It must be a new work ethic with them."

Harvard College
Cambridge, Massachusetts

College rankings may come and go, but Harvard remains pretty much alone at the top of the ziggurat. There is no way to minimize the impact of Harvard either on the nation's intellectual life or on academia itself. More's the pity. Despite its enormous prestige, Harvard simply does not live up to our standards of either quality teaching or curricular coherence.

In the preface, we noted some of the shortcomings of Harvard's core curriculum. Highly touted as an antidote to the decline of liberal education, the core has proven to be a notable and embarrassing bust. Former U.S. Education Secretary William Bennett quite aptly termed it "Core Lite." "There is an extraordinary gap between the rhetoric and reality of American higher education," he said. He was describing the Harvard core when he complained that "not only do students now tend to lack a knowledge of their own tradition, they often have no standpoint from which to appreciate any other tradition, or even to *have* a sense of tradition." Commented the student-run Harvard course guide (*The Confidential Guide*):

> He's right . . . because the core is not designed to teach any select body of knowledge, but to introduce presumably eager undergraduates to different "modes of inquiry." . . . Thus after four years you will hopefully [*sic*] be able to flip a mental switch and think like a historian or an economist or a scientist. And you better be able to, because the core won't give you a coherent picture about Western history, scientific advances or philosophical thought.

In other words, students can complete the core, and subsequently graduate from Harvard, utterly ignorant of the great literature of the Renaissance, the Middle Ages, or the Enlightenment; without having read the works of Shakespeare; or with little or no knowledge of American history. 247

As it turns out, not only are many of the courses in the core notorious "guts" —ridiculously easy and undemanding courses—but much of the teaching has been turned over to . . . you guessed it . . . teaching assistants, who are called teaching "fellows" at Harvard (many of whom seem to be thrown into the classroom at the last minute with little preparation). In 1992, Harvard relied on approximately eight hundred such "fellows" to teach classes. Perhaps it is the augustness of Harvard's reputation that allows the school to get away with charging more than $20,000 for students to take classes from other students.

Harvard's introductory economics class generally has more than 1,000 students. Since most of the teaching takes place in small sections, the teaching fellows play a crucial role. Said the student guide: "Most range from completely disorganized graduate students who are juggling two courses at both the law and business schools to Third World radicals . . . [and] to tidy economics Ph.D. candidates who are working on a dissertation comparing the consumer indifference curves for strawberry French yogurt and Hawaiian-grown alfalfa sprouts." Unfortunately, that reflects the not-so-subtle attitude of Harvard toward the nasty business of teaching undergraduates. At Harvard, the academic stars stay firmly fixed in the firmament, far from the tumult of actual education. Harvard's defenders are quick to say that this does not really matter, because at Harvard the students educate one another. They really don't have much choice. While Harvard boasts some genuinely outstanding lecturers, it also has a habit of denying tenure to award-winning teachers who were unwise enough to pay too much attention to the classroom. Too many senior professors make no effort to conceal their disdain for undergraduate teaching. As a result, they seldom teach and when they do, they often do it badly. When some of the better and more popular professors do deign to lecture, they often appear before classes so large as to preclude any meaningful interaction with students. In some classes the students sit so far from the rostrum that the student guide warns students to "pack a telescope." Indeed, Harvard seems to subscribe to an Academic Trickle-Down Theory, under which all of the great wisdom and scholarship of its faculty will somehow make its way down to the undergraduates, with little or no effort on the college's part. For some students it may be enough to simply breathe the same air as these eminent scholars, but it's not our idea of what a college should be.

While Harvard does not rank as one of the worst abusers of political correctness (but then schools like Duke skew the curve badly), the politics of race and gender often turn ugly and intolerant. In *Illiberal Education*, Dinesh D'Souza describes politically correct attacks on such respected scholars as Stephan Thernstrom and Ian Macneil that raise serious questions about Harvard's genuine commitment to the diversity . . . of ideas. But even here there is something to be said in Harvard's defense. Although they are confronted with the usual array of errant nonsense, most Harvard students are bright—and self-important—enough to avoid being cowed by PC blather.

Having said all this, we recognize that many prospective students frankly couldn't care less about the quality of the undergraduate experience at Harvard—just as long as they can get their hands on the coveted Harvard degree. That attitude is precisely what Harvard's hierarchs are counting on. It explains why they have been able to get away with constantly eroding the quality of their curriculum, and why they have succeeded in charging more and more for less and less.

The University of Michigan
Ann Arbor, Michigan

Graduate student Wesley Wynne proved that it is possible for a student to take on a megaversity and win. Identified only as "John Doe," Wynne successfully brought suit in federal court to have the University of Michigan's draconian ban on "racist," "sexist," and "homophobic" speech declared unconstitutional. Michigan's sweeping gag rule was aimed at wiping out every conceivable slur. Students were warned that they could be suspended or expelled for *any* act "verbal or physical, that stigmatizes or victimizes an individual on the basis of race, ethnicity, religion, sex, sexual orientation, creed, national origin, ancestry, age, marital status, handicap, or Vietnam-era veteran status." Because the policy was so broad—and vague—it raised the obvious question of how it would be enforced. How would students know exactly what words or gestures would actually stigmatize someone on the basis of, say, their "Vietnam-era status" or their "ancestry"? Most important of all, what sort of proof would be needed? The university's answer was direct: None. If it was one student's word against another, the accused was presumed . . . guilty. "Experience at the university," a publication explained, "has been that people *almost never make false complaints about discrimination*" [emphasis added]. Michigan's policy did more than simply invert normal standards that require accusers to shoulder the burden of proof. The ban was so sweeping that students faced discipline for suggesting that women were not as qualified as men in any given field; one student was actually brought up on charges of discriminatory harassment for suggesting that he could develop a "counseling plan for helping gays become straight." Another possible violation of the rule, students were told, would be if students gave a party at a residence hall but failed to invite someone because they thought she was a lesbian. Reflecting the politicized agenda of the speech ban, university officials never consulted the several First Amendment experts in Michigan's own law school. As the federal judge ruled in tossing out the gag rule, "I have a hunch they didn't want to ask the questions because they didn't want to hear the answers."

All of this tells us that something has gone terribly wrong in Ann Arbor. There are other troubling signs that an atmosphere of political intolerance is affecting what is happening in the classrooms. One of the school's top professors of sociology, Reynolds Farley, announced some time back that he would no longer teach a class in race relations. He had been harassed by radical militants who deemed him insufficiently politically correct in his handling of the issue. "Given the climate at Michigan," Professor Farley said afterward, "I could be hassled for anything I do or don't say in that class. I decided to drop the course. It certainly isn't worth it." One student told *The New York Times:* "Things have gotten to the point where students can't say anything about racism on campus without being called a racist." An indication of Michigan's eagerness to appease militants on campus was its capitulation to demands from the Black Action Movement in the spring of 1987, including the decision to hand over $35,000 a year in university funds to the Black Student Union, a payment described by the *Michigan* 249

Review as an "ill-earned bribe." The story of the money highlights the double standard in American higher education today. While Michigan had sought to ban "racist," "sexist," and "homophobic" speech, the BSU has used Michigan's money to bring in viciously anti-Semitic and racist speakers such as Abdul Alim Muhammad and Steven Cokely. ("There is only one devil walking on this earth, and he has been identified by God as the Caucasian white man," according to Mr. Muhammad. Mr. Cokely describes Jews as "violent people," and offers the insight that "the Jew hopes to one day reign forever.") The administration's indulgence of left-wing theatrics extends to anti-apartheid shanties on campus. "They have raised awareness of very important issues," president James Duderstadt opined, endorsing their continued presence. In 1990 the faculty approved a mandatory "diversity" course focusing on issues arising from "racial or ethnic intolerance."

This is all unfortunate, because the University of Michigan has long been one of the top universities in the country—its faculty is generally outstanding and many of its programs are of high quality. Michigan's honors program continues to focus on the Great Books. But it is also a multiversity whose main priority, unfortunately, is not teaching undergraduates. Classes can be quite large, and students can expect to spend quite a lot of time with teaching assistants. This is not a new development, but it appears to be getting worse.

Over the last decade Michigan's bureaucracy has metastasized at rates that would draw a sigh of envy from the Pentagon itself. In the decade ending in 1988, the University of Michigan's faculty grew by 7.1 percent, but during the same period its bureaucracy grew by 40 percent. What accounts for the disparity? Reported the *Ann Arbor News:* "UM officials point to a major increase in research funding as one of the reasons for growth in budget and salaried employees. . . ." Students in search of small classes, close relations with faculty, and a tolerant intellectual environment should approach Michigan with great caution.

The University of Pennsylvania
Philadelphia, Pennsylvania

If one stumbles into Penn's course on the The British Novel, taught by Professor Lennard Davis, one will learn, among other things, that Joseph Conrad's Kurtz and Marlowe were involved in a "homoerotic relationship"; that Frankenstein's monster represented Mary Shelley's "repressed female sexuality"; and that there is no such thing as "great literature." By the course's end, we can readily imagine that nauseated students will agree. As Penn graduate Debra Cermele recounts, Professor Davis's class is devoted to saving students from the "oppression of the imperialized discourse."

> Instead of analyzing the quality of the English classics as works of art, the class investigated the ways gender, class, and sexuality influenced political power within these novels. Rather than being a critical and comparative examination of the ideas that shaped Western thinking, Professor Davis's lectures were sessions for him to preach politics and sociology to a captive audience.

Of course, this goes on in a lot of literature classrooms these days, and one postmodern English professor does not automatically consign a school to our Gulag. But unfortunately, this tale reflects a deeper malaise at Penn, a school which has become a staple of critiques of political correctness in higher education. Perhaps the most notorious incident was recounted by Penn professor Alan Kors, one of the school's finest and most principled faculty members. As Kors tells it, an undergraduate member of Penn's "diversity education" committee wrote a memo expressing her "deep regard for the individual and my desire to protect the freedoms of all members of society." In response, a university administrator fired back a memo with the phrase circled and the word "individual" underlined. "This is a 'RED FLAG' phrase today, which is considered by many to be RACIST. Arguments that champion the individual over the group ultimately privilege the 'individuals' belonging to the largest or dominant group." In the second incident, lecturer Murray Dolfman became a literal outcast for comments he made during a class on constitutional law. During the fateful class, Professor Dolfman was discussing personal service contracts and the fact that such contracts could not be used to force someone to work against his will. This prohibition on involuntary servitude is found in the Constitution, he told the students. Then he asked: "Where in the Constitution?" No one answered. For Professor Dolfman this was an opportunity to make the issue of freedom personal for his students. "We will lose our freedoms if we don't know where they are," he frequently told his classes. He recounted how Jews reminded themselves of their liberation from bondage by celebrating Passover every year. And then he said: "We have ex-slaves in this class, who should know about—and celebrate—the Thirteenth Amendment." What followed was a tableau of academic witch-hunting. Students filed charges accusing Professor Dolfman of racism; university committees were convened to investigate. His class was disrupted and a rally was held to demand his dismissal. One of the leaders of the rally was Houston Baker, who held the title of Albert M. Greenfield Professor of Human Relations and was director of the Center for the Study of Black Literature and Culture. (Professor Baker is justly famous in his own right for saying that choosing between authors like Virginia Woolf and Pearl Buck is "no different than choosing between a hoagy and a pizza." He once told a *New York Times* reporter that "I am one whose career is dedicated to the day when we have a disappearance of those [literary] standards.") At a vigil and rally at the home of Penn's president, Professor Baker intoned: "We are in the forefront because some asshole decided that his classroom is going to be turned into a cesspool. . . ." The Black Student League denounced Dolfman as a racist, and a law professor at Penn declared "Dolfman must go."

As columnist and author Nat Hentoff later noted, "University president Sheldon Hackney did not defend academic freedom, free inquiry, common sense, or Murray Dolfman." Professor Dolfman was sentenced to attend a "sensitivity and racial awareness" re-education program, and was stripped of his teaching job for a year. He tried to awaken President's Hackney's conscience when he told him: "If a part-time professor can be punished on this kind of charge, a tenured professor can eventually be booted out, then a dean, and then a president." But Hackney was obdurate in his spinelessness.

Since then, mandatory "diversity education" programs have been imposed on all freshmen, which have (not surprisingly) exacerbated already tense race relations. We doubt that this is what Benjamin Franklin had in mind when he founded Penn back in 1755.

All is not lost, however. There are still fine professors like Alan Kors; 251

Penn still has reasonably tough foreign language requirements and its psychology, economics, anthropology, and archaeology departments are well regarded. Another bright spot is the Wharton School of Business, one of the most renowned undergraduate business schools in the country. Its student body, understandably, is notably more conservative than the university in general. But if you must attend Penn, avoid English. And watch your tongue: the thought police are especially vigilant here.

Smith College
Northampton, Massachusetts

For the unwary, Smith College might seem just the sort of school that might show up in a guide to outstanding liberal arts colleges. Classes are small, contact between students and faculty is generous, and the school is very much a tight-knit community.

But Smith is also a very bizarre place. Let's put it this way: This is not a school for anyone who is not prepared to have every aspect of her life (speech, behavior, and even unconscious thought) micromanaged by the campus PC police. The reigning deity on campus is *diversity*. "Embracing diversity," the college has declared, "involves identifying and undoing conscious and unconscious expressions of racism that exist in American society. The clearest steps we are taking to overcome racism are to define, implement and enforce a civil rights policy and to adopt an aggressive affirmative action policy." Lest this seem too timid, Smith followed up this declaration with sweeping new definitions of the "specific manifestations of oppression" that apparently abounded on Smith's campus. "As groups of people begin the process of realizing that they are oppressed, and why, new words tend to be created to express the concepts that the existing language cannot," the college explained. Thus we discovered *ableism* (the "oppression of the differently abled by the temporarily abled"); *lookism* ("the construction of a standard for beauty/attractiveness"); *classism* (oppression of the working and other lower classes); and *heterosexism* (oppression of alternative sexual lifestyles). In itself this might be little more than comic relief. But there is nothing risible about the climate of intolerance on Smith's campus. Smith never ceases to give new meanings to the word "draconian." Historian Fred Siegel reports that students and faculty alike have been chilled by the climate of ideological conformity at Smith. "Through a combination of sensitivity training sessions and the ideological weight of a document issued by the college president called 'The Smith Design,'" Mr. Siegel writes, "the administration has made it clear that no criticism of racial quotas in admission and student life, no matter how thoughtful, will be taken seriously." One English professor on campus told Mr. Siegel that students are subtly intimidated: "They censor themselves in class out of a fear of both peer pressure and the possibility of sanctions." In this environment, extraordinary power has devolved upon the affirmative action officer, who apparently is permitted to act as a sort of ayatollah of ideological conformity. In one incident, a professor was required to defend herself for allegedly asking an insensitive question on an essay exam. The question was: "Is Islam useful in the modern world? Describe the role of Islam in the political development of two countries in the Middle East since World War II." When a student complained that the question was anti-Muslim, the affirmative action officer called the professor on the carpet and compelled her to justify herself. Objecting to such an egregious violation of her academic freedom, the faculty member appealed for support from her colleagues on the faculty—and was rebuffed. Smith's faculty voted sixty-two to forty to support the affirmative action officer's continuing right to monitor faculty behavior. After that vote, Mr. Siegel noted, "some now fear that course content could become a matter of political negotiation—and ultimately of raw power."

Given its abandonment of such basic principles of liberal education, it will come as no surprise to learn that Smith has no core curriculum. It has, however, been rapidly creating new offerings that reflect its passion for "diversity." Our favorite: "Psychology through the Eyes of Minority Women Psychologists."

Stanford University
Stanford, California

When it turned out that Stanford's administration had been diverting federal research money for yacht parties, wedding receptions, and lavish flower arrangements, the university's president was (at first) unapologetic. "I wouldn't be embarrassed about saying that every damn flower in this house ought to be an indirect cost against research," Donald Kennedy insisted. That reaction helps illustrate why Stanford has become an institutional poster child for academic arrogance, intellectual confusion, and ideological conformity. There is, of course, much to be said about Stanford's strengths. Even Mr. Kennedy made points with us when he called on Stanford to renew its emphasis on undergraduate teaching. (Like other big universities, Stanford has turned over a huge portion—40 percent in the humanities—of its teaching duties to teaching assistants.) But Kennedy was already on his way out as president when he made his remarks, and there is little reason to imagine that anything will change. And the damage done has been extensive.

We can start with the curriculum. It would have been bad enough had Stanford merely gutted its outstanding Western Civ program (Remember the student chants: "Hey, hey, ho, ho, Western Culture's got to go"?), and undermined academic freedom with a politically correct speech code. But academia, like nature, abhors a vacuum. Filling the gap left by the demotion of dead white males like Homer, Sophocles, and Dante, are courses such as Black Hair and History, which explores how black hair "has interacted with the black presence in this country—how it has played a role in the evolution of black society." Students in the course are treated to lectures on "The Rise of the Afro" and "Fade-O-Rama, Braiding and Dreadlocks," and classes are visited by local hairstylists. The syllabus includes the musical *Hair*, Willie Morrow's *400 Years without a Combo*, and Dylan Jones's *Haircuts*. Describing the course in an article in *The Wall Street Journal*, Stanford junior David Sacks quoted Professor Kennell Jackson as boasting: "I wouldn't have taught this class ten years ago." No kidding.

There was a time when Stanford was distinguished by its intellectual rigor and academic quality. In 1980 Stanford had created its Western Civilization program, a cluster of courses centered on fifteen Great Books. For many undergraduates Western Civ was the highlight of a Stanford educa- 253 tion. "A miracle has happened among Stanford undergraduates," one observer noted in the program's early years. "They do talk about Plato at dinner and about Shakespeare on the grass." That was a long time ago. As David Sacks noted, the course in black hair "represents the logical conclusion of the [university's] obsession with racial, gender, and class differences" that justified the replacement of Western Civ with the more politically correct Cultures, Ideas and Values.

The politicization of Stanford does not stop in the classroom. In the mid-1980s, the faculty blocked a proposal to locate the Reagan Library on the Stanford campus—an example of narrow-minded intolerance that belies the university's constant celebration of "diversity." This is not to suggest that it is not possible to get a more traditional liberal arts education at Stanford. You can, although it's not very easy anymore. In an article titled "Disillusioned Student Muses on Stanford," published in *Campus*, senior Michael Newman confessed that "coming to Stanford in the first place was a gargantuan error on my part." Relying on the usual college rankings and guides, "I naturally assumed that the best possible education would be found at whatever school ranked highest in *U.S. News and World Report*'s college survey." Indeed, Stanford remains outstanding in the hard sciences and engineering. But to his chagrin, Mr. Newman reported, "it humanities programs have imploded, dominated as they are now by 1960s-bred professors whose interest in culture stems almost entirely from their desire to undermine it." Mr. Newman noted that he stayed on at Stanford out of stubbornness. "My parents still need evidence that, no, they did not waste one hundred thousand dollars of their over-taxed financial resources on a Stanford education only to have me emerge less intellectually vigorous than I was upon matriculation." Hoping to graduate "a well-educated, well-read, right-thinking citizen," Newman had opted to major in English, which turned out to be the study of virtually everything *but* literature. "All too often," Newman wrote, "I've walked into a class on the first day of the term, full of enthusiasm and anticipation over the expected readings, only to be subjected to a lecture on racism, sexism, white male imperialism, or anything else except what the title of the course would imply." Even a student who gives wide berth to such courses as Theorizing the Body, Newman writes, "will still end up swallowing more Marx than an economics major, more Freud than a psychology major, and infinitely more Nietzche than those mired in our stultifying philosophy department. . . ." "Apparently, many English majors choose their professor because they love political science, but find the readings as boring as I do. These is simply no other way to explain how Marxism, radical feminism, and other relatively recent intellectual fads have suddenly sprouted on every piece of literature from the *Oresteia* to the latest Stephen King novel." We'll take a pass.

Wesleyan University
Storrs, Connecticut

In a cartoon that appeared in an academic periodical, a woman speaking on the phone turns to her husband who is standing nearby. "It's our daughter calling from Wesleyan," she says. "She would like to ask us a few questions about the '60s." Indeed, Wesleyan seems to take its nostalgia for the sixties quite seriously these days—complete with the cancellation of classes for politically motivated moratoria, the harassment of speakers, and even (a few years ago) the firebombing of the president's office. As part of its regression to the sixties, Wesleyan has also become the scene of a flourishing and highly publicized drug culture. "There is no real stigma attached to drugs, not at all," one student says. In the past, Wesleyan has even hosted well-attended marijuana "smoke-outs" in one of the school's dining halls.

Unfortunately, that is not the only cloud over Wesleyan. Traditionally, Wesleyan has been one of the finest liberal arts schools in the country. Classes tend to be small and taught by actual professors, and many of the humanities and science departments are well regarded. But Wesleyan has no core curriculum, no language requirements, and contents itself with vaguely "encouraging" students to take courses in science, math, the humanities, and the social sciences. Worse, however, is the illiberalism of Wesleyan's intellectual climate. Given the importance of being politically correct, conservative students can expect to be branded as fascists by the radical thought police on campus. In a tribute to their political forebears, radicals on campus even staged a ritual burning of copies of the conservative *Wesleyan Review*. (Just imagine the national outcry if conservative students had staged a burning of the works of, say, Angela Davis.) The book burning was of a piece, however, with Wesleyan's growing intellectual intolerance. When South African anti-apartheid activist Helen Suzman spoke on campus a couple of years ago, for example, she was derided and harassed by activists who deemed her insufficiently militant for their tastes. "It's a war up here," one conservative says. As a result, conservative students tend to keep a low profile. "People are very, very reluctant to say what they feel if it doesn't mesh with the prevailing ideology. There is a form of self-censorship in which people can't say what they really think because of fear of being labelled insensitive or even worse, racist, or sexist," one student told us. "I like to think that the university is founded on the principle that there is a rational and free exchange of ideas—and that does not happen at a school like this." Pressures on conservative women are said to be especially intense. "I really don't know if a conservative woman would have a place at this school," says one undergraduate. "If you shave your legs and under your arms, even that's considered a bit conservative around here." Another Wesleyan student recently told the *Los Angeles Times:* "The classroom used to be the one place where anything went. There used to be dialogue. If you said something ridiculous people would take you apart on the merits of your argument. Now, the accusations are things like 'That's typical white male thinking.' "

There is more than a little irony in all of this, inasmuch as Wesleyan has put itself at the forefront of efforts to encourage "diversity" and has demanded that "multiculturalist" perspectives be injected into corner of the curriculum.

Outside the classroom, Wesleyan has been painstaking in nurturing luxuriant and exotic political activities. A partial list of student organizations cited in Wesleyan's official bulletin includes Ahuas Campos (Latin students); Amnesty International; Central American Network; Democratic Socialists for Citizen Action; Gay, Lesbian and Bisexual Alliance; South African Action Group; Students for Reproductive Choice; Students Talking About Relations (against racism, sexism, and homophobia); and Ujamaa (black 255 students). It should not really come as a surprise that this balkanization of campus life has generated more discord than understanding, but Wesleyan's hierarchy does not yet seem to grasp that point.

Yale University
New Haven, Connecticut

Like Harvard, Yale remains at or near the top of the academic prestige hierarchy. And there is no denying the excellence Yale achieves in many of its departments and endeavors. As a research university, it is peerless in some disciplines. As an educator of undergraduate liberal arts, however, it leaves much to be desired and is almost certainly overrated.

One cannot read the Yale catalog without sensing the university's ambivalence about its obligation to liberal education and to its undergraduates. It acknowledges that its graduation requirement of thirty-six courses does not "necessarily make an education." And it uses this pathetically weak definition of a course: ". . . simply a group of students examining a particular subject under the direction of someone who has studied it before." This apparently is to prepare you for all those grad students who stand in for the eminent faculty who *should* be teaching undergraduates but are otherwise occupied. In fact, more than a quarter of all of the people teaching at Yale in a recent year were TAs, filling no fewer than 1,521 slots on the Yale faculty. Yale College, which is what the undergraduate program is called, appears unembarrassed about this, admitting that students "may emerge from college with a collection of miscellaneous information but no wiser than when they entered," although the catalog goes on to stress that that won't happen at Yale, thanks to its insistence on a "rational program of study" which includes a distribution requirement. It is far from a liberal arts core, but then, as Yale says: "One of the distinguishing features of a liberal education is that it has no single definition." (Why does the college keep hedging and fudging?) Well, the consequences of this attitude is that Yale does not actually require . . . It *urges*. Urges what? It urges each seventeen- or eighteen-year-old student to "design a program of study suited to his or her own particular needs and interests." And that's it. Oh sure, Yale—as a "matter of educational policy"—stands behind the *principle* of "distribution," but it *requires* only that a student declare a major "in the later years of college," and the distribution requirement is actually an *anti-core*. What it says is this: Freshmen may do as they wish (a major not being required until sometime in the sophomore year), *except* that they may not put all their eggs in one departmental basket. The actual guidelines read like Internal Revenue Service rules, but the operative words are "Yale does not require prescribed courses in specific subjects." What Yalies must do is take twelve courses (one-third of the number required for graduation) outside the distributional group in which their major will fall. The only requirement per se is the usual intermediate competence in a foreign language.

But the real assault on liberal education comes not in the (non-) curriculum, but in the classroom, particularly in the school's literature departments. Early in the 1980s, Yale was a hotbed of deconstructionism and other attacks on literature. Since then, Yale has been surpassed by places like Duke, but the English and comparative literature departments have been too besotted with post-structuralism to be safely trusted with any reasonably sound piece of literature. (Somehow Yale's classics department escaped infection and remains excellent.) In other respects Yale's record is mixed. When they actually teach, Yale's professors can be excellent. Advising, which is often neglected at big schools, is taken quite seriously by some Yale professors, although it is no substitute for a coherent curriculum.

During the 1980s, the school was the center of heated and dramatic debates over free speech and expression. At one point a student named Wayne Dick was brought up on charges for having the audacity to mock Yale's Gay and Lesbian Awareness Days (GLAD) with posters advertising Bestiality Awareness Days (BAD). Dick's poster advertised one lecture entitled "PAN: the Goat, the God, the Lover." Citing a university regulation against "harassment, intimidation, coercion, or assault, or any other act of violence against any member of this community, including sexual, racial, or ethnic harassment," Yale's faculty placed Mr. Dick on probation for his political incorrectness. This story, however, has a relatively happy ending. When Benno Schmidt assumed Yale's presidency in the mid-1980s, he reopened the case. With support from Yale's law school dean Guido Calabrese and historian C. Vann Woodward, Mr. Dick was acquitted. President Schmidt himself stated the principle clearly in his inaugural address: "To stifle expression because it is obnoxious, erroneous, embarrassing, not instrumental to some political or ideological end is—quite apart from the grotesque invasion of the rights of others—a disastrous reflection on ourselves. There is no speech so horrendous that it does not in principle serve our purposes. . . ." His address was one of the finest moments in Yale's history. And the university seemed to take another huge step toward academic sanity and principle when Donald Kagan, a noted classicist, was named dean of Yale College. How good was Dean Kagan? In 1990, he issued a ringing affirmation of the central place that Western culture should be given in the liberal arts. "It is both right and necessary," he insisted, "to place Western civilization and the culture to which it has given rise at the center of our studies, and we fail to do so at the peril our students, our country, and of the hopes for a democratic, liberal society emerging throughout the world today." That is the sort of talk seldom, if ever, heard anywhere in the Ivy League today. He was, predictably, denounced as a "racist" and a "sexist" by black and feminist groups on campus.

Things began to look even better in 1991 when Yale received a $20 million gift to create teaching positions for courses on Western civilization. Those courses will be offered for the first time in 1993. Unfortunately, both President Schmidt and Dean Kagan have since stepped down—"vomited up by the faculty," as one observer colorfully described it. Although we were greatly heartened by Yale's exceptional good judgment in respect to free speech under President Schmidt and Dean Kagan, we are skeptical that such good sense will survive their resignations. Given the college's lack of a guiding commitment to liberal education, it will likely continue to be prey to the forces of dissolution, division, and deconstruction.

PART III

The Art of Learning

A Guerrilla Guide to the Liberal Arts:

How to Get a National Review College Guide *Education (Without Attending a* National Review College Guide *School)*

You are reading this because, for one reason or another, you are not matriculating at one of the colleges and universities profiled in this book. Fair enough. The question now is: What can you do to ensure that you receive a good liberal arts education wherever you do go to college?

There are ways. And we'll discuss them under three headings: Profs, Programs, and Politics.

Remember this: In higher education, as in life, God helps those who help themselves.

Profs

There are a number of things students can do to find the right professors, and shape an academic program around them. The earliest universities were loose confederations of scholars, and students came not for a university-wide curriculum or even a specific department, but to study with a particular teacher. What's old is new.

Begin by identifying a professor whose work or views you admire. How do you do that? Ask around ("Is there a conservative on the faculty?" "Is there a *moderate* on the faculty?" "Okay. How about somebody who's *not* a socialist?") Look in the library or in departmental offices for a list of books and articles published by the faculty. Look especially for citations of essays appearing in the better opinion journals: *National Review*, of course, and *Commentary, Chronicles, Modern Age, The National Interest, Policy Review*, and even *The New Republic*.

Once you've identified Professor Right, call for an appointment, and when you do, let him know *how* you came up with his name. Even the busiest, most research-oriented professor will be pleased (Well, we mean *flattered*) to know that a freshman has gone to the trouble to read up on his work and seek him out. When you meet, remember to keep the discussion focused (within the bounds of politeness) on *your* curricular concerns. You want to know which are the best professors and courses, and which are to be avoided.

A survey in the *Chronicle of Higher Education* indicates that only 21 percent of college professors are conservative. But many others—including many liberals—have resisted the allure of academic trendiness. (Perhaps this is because of Conquest's First Law—after author Robert Conquest—which holds: *Everyone is a reactionary on the subject he is expert about.*) Any professor, male or female, conservative or liberal, who cares deeply about learning can be a superb faculty "rabbi." Said rabbi ought not to be the counselor assigned to you at orientation. Most of the schools profiled in this guide take advising quite seriously, because they see it as an essential element in their *in loco parentis* responsibilities. But despite the lip service given to faculty-student interaction elsewhere, too many schools do not take advising seriously, and you should seek a second opinion.

Given the money that's being laid down for your education, you have the right to demand the attention of a competent senior professor—but never, never, never make demands in the style of campus radicals. You have interests, but you are not the only one with interests. Look at the whole process as a marketplace, and act entrepreneurially. Trust us: initiative and persistence are almost always rewarded. Respectfully, let the rabbi see some chutzpah.

Ratings

On almost every large campus, and on many small ones too, some student organization publishes a faculty rating guide. College book stores and/or student government offices have copies. Such guides are by nature subjective; why students admire a particular teacher can vary widely, and it's not always pedagogical ability that gets votes. But such guides can be valuable. For one thing, they will let you know which of the most highly experienced faculty are actually teaching lower-division courses.

Another superb list that you *cannot* get would be the one that details all faculty members of the National Association of Scholars. (In this book's first edition we suggested such a list might be available, but it is not.) Things are so bad—because of the more fascistic shades of political correctness—that NAS doesn't dare publish a membership list. But what is NAS? It's an organization of professors dedicated to academic freedom and curricular common sense. Its own informational brochure elaborates:

> The NAS works to enrich the substance and strengthen the integrity of scholarship and teaching, convinced that only through an informed understanding of Western intellectual heritage and the realities of the contemporary world can citizen and scholar be equipped to sustain our civilization's achievements.

Watch for local NAS meetings, and ask your rabbi about NAS membership on campus.

A Few More Tips

Especially if you are taking courses in the sciences, you must be sure who will actually be teaching your section. Necessarily research-oriented, many professors of science turn over lower-form teaching chores to teaching assistants. These TAs deserve a chance. From Einstein to Feynman, many scientists have done much of their best work early, and youth is by no means a disqualification among teachers. But, as we've said before, some TAs have exactly eight semesters more education than their freshman students, and no teaching experience at all.

Inexperience is at least made tolerable by decent English usage. Chemistry is tough enough without having to hear lectures presented in the indecipherable muddle of a heavily accented TA. If you end up with a teacher whose argot is impenetrable, COMPLAIN. If a TA or *scheduled professor* doesn't keep office hours, fails to show up for class, or comes unprepared, RAISE HELL. Tell a dean; write the president; call your congressman; picket the board of trustees. Universities will cheat students only as long as they can get away with it. Don't let them.

And don't kid yourself that business schools are immune from academic nonsense. Scrutinize professors of economics and business administration just as you would teachers in any department.

But remember: If you decide to make waves, you had better be sure your own ship is seaworthy.

And be reasonable. No one should expect to find wonderful, sensible teachers for every course; nor should one expect that every sensible, like-minded professor will be a good teacher. Indeed, you should not pass up the chance to study with *any* great teacher, even if he is a Marxist.

Programs

Discussing the tendency of some curricula to emphasize method over substance, John Silber has remarked: "Thus one does not necessarily learn a science; one learns something about science. One does not really learn a foreign language; one merely studies it for two semesters. This is not education." It is equivalent to the old "grand tour," in which cultivated people of previous centuries spent a few months each in Rome and Paris, and perhaps a week in Constantinople. Dilettantes though they were, they were probably prepared to recognize what they saw in the ruins and the cathedrals, because they were more than likely the beneficiaries of a liberal education.

They may have gone to Yale, where today the denial of a core of knowledge is made explicit. The Blue Book (as Yale's catalog is known) maintains that one of the "distinguishing features of a liberal education is that it has no single definition." Taken literally, this could mean that there are several ways to structure a liberal arts core. But Yale means that there can be no core, which is why it requires nothing of its students (beyond, of course, the departmental demands of their major field). Yale asks only that students take twelve courses (one-third the number required for graduation) outside the distributional group in which the major will fall—and thus suggests that a good time to decide one's major is the first day of the freshman year. Thus students are encouraged to "design a program of study suited to his or her own particular needs and interests," and the Blue Book acknowledges the need for close contact with a faculty counselor. Our research has not been scientific, but we have heard enough on both sides (advising was good; advising was a waste) that we suspect many Yale students are on their own.

But at least the Blue Book is not bloated with silly courses. This is not the case elsewhere. Students need to remember that a college education, at the curricular level at least, is not supposed to be an entertainment. But along with the elimination of requirements elsewhere has come the frequent addition of course offerings of questionable relevance to *higher* education. Most notorious is Rock 'n' Roll Is Here to Stay at Brown University, but similar courses have popped up on other campuses, sometimes with formalistic titles, such as the University of North Carolina at Greensboro's Applied Social Theory and Quantitative Research Methodology—known to students as "Deadhead 101" because the course "studies" the Grateful Dead's followers, who the professor insists are a legitimate subject of sociological study. The University of Illinois offers Pocket Billiards at Dartmouth you can fulfill the humanities requirement with Creative Video. How Fun.

Course Selection 101

No requirements, but lots of dopey diversity. We don't buy it. We think students can in fact do what their academic overseers say is not possible: construct a coherent and intelligent core. And, yes, we think this ought to be true even of pre-professional students. We will not prescribe a single, rigid program for everyone, but we are convinced that the proper scheme of liberal education should include study of the history, literature, philosophy, political thought, ethics, and religions of the West, as well as careful inquiry into the natural sciences and mathematics. Ah, but the temptation to fill your academic calendar with "cheap dates" will be strong: the low road is wide and easily traveled, even if it is crowded. You must pray for strength and repeat after us: proper distribution; solid courses.

Let's begin with the distribution. As noted in the preface, the title of the National Endowment of the Humanities core curriculum report is *50 Hours*. It recommends that not quite half an undergraduate's courses be in a core, and defines the program thusly: eighteen hours in cultures and civilizations (one course in ancient history, two in Western civilization—Athens through the Reformation and the Reformation through the twentieth century—one course in American history, and one in other civilizations); twelve hours in a foreign language; six hours in concepts of mathematics; eight hours in foundations of the natural sciences (with lab work in the physical and biological sciences); and 6 hours in the social sciences and the modern world, which ideally should trace the last two hundred years of development in economics, politics, and psychology. Almost any catalog in the country can yield comparatively satisfactory course along these lines, although only a course syllabus will tell you whether "Western Civilization" is about Homer, Plato, Dante, and Shakespeare, or about "modes of expression." Reading lists are generally available (and you can usually see assigned books in the college bookstore), and we have no hesitation about urging you to run, not walk, away from any course that assigns Frantz Fanon's *Wretched of the Earth* or Howard Zinn's *People's History of the United States*. Go ahead and read the books, but don't eat up academic credits in courses that "teach" them.

Dodging Diversity

Filling in the course for each curricular area is not always easy, since (as
264 noted above) some titles are wolves in sheep's clothing. Naturally, our

readers will avoid "Mad, Bad and Imbruted Women," but let's say you want to study Jane Austen or the Brontë sisters. You should look for traditional courses in the English Department (e.g., Nineteenth-Century English Writers), and steer well clear of Women in Literature, since too often the latter will have more to do with feminist theory than with literature—so much so that you might not even read the great women writers. You will more likely get a snootful of their *interpreters*—and never discover what happened to Emma Woodhouse or Heathcliff.

Similarly, in courses about non-Western cultures and writers, fight shy of any course advertised as advancing "diversity" or the "recognition and affirmation of difference." Good writers can stand on their own without the props of propaganda. Political training is not required for the novels of Chinua Achebe (Nigeria) and Naguib Mafouz (Egypt) to be understood and admired by American undergraduates.

But the right course title and syllabus are not yet the whole story. You can be bilked a number of ways, some of them superficially appealing. For instance, some courses require no papers and no essay exams, all grading is done by computer. If you find yourself in such an automated course (and can avoid it), we suggest you skedaddle pronto, and find a course where scrutiny of your work will be, well, more *organic*, and where more is required of you than just attendance and respiration.

In general, avoid any class titled "The Sociology of . . . ," and definitely steer clear of any class that uses the term "socio-psychological." A good curriculum will employ a minimal number of hyphens.

But of course there can never be complete protection against academic tomfoolery. Imagine the surprise of students in Duke University's English department who take a sensible-sounding course in Shakespeare only to discover that the professor teaches *King Lear* as a critique of seventeenth-century British capitalism.

Finally, we present here a list of Great Books. Make sure you have read many of them before accepting a diploma certifying your education. A great debate rages on about "canonicity," about which books deserve to be called "great," and which ought to be part of a curriculum, or just read by educated people. As you would expect, the argument is only partly about the books. It is also partly (some would say *mostly*) about "greatness," and among the criteria of many who would dump the Great Books concept is the assumption that, since all education is political, greatness can only be measured in a book by its *immediate* revolutionary power. Thus much of what was once considered great becomes the enemy of short-term change—simply because it has endured for so long. If students see why Aristotle's *Ethics* has stood the test of time, they will not easily be convinced to disregard the Western tradition that gradually evolved, in part, from his work.

Here then is the list drawn up early in this century by Columbia University's John Erskine. It is far from being infallible, and critics (then and now) might wonder why Grotius and Hugo make the list while Jane Austen, for instance, does not. Why *Much Ado about Nothing* and not, say, *King Lear*? Why Jeremy Bentham but not Pascal or Hume; Malthus but not Spinoza? Well, you can pick 'em, but for their literary value, *not because of sex or politics*. This list (or the one in our profile of St. John's College, or the one recently revised for the Encyclopædia Britannica Great Books program) is only a guide, a starting point.

The Great Books

Homer, *The Iliad; The Odyssey*
Herodotus, *History*
Thucydides, *History of the Peloponnesian War*
Aeschylus, *Prometheus; The House of Atreus*
Sophocles, *Oedipus Tyrannus; Oedipus Colonus; Antigone; Electra*
Euripides, *Alcestis; Medea; Electra; Hippolytus*
Aristophanes, *The Frogs; The Clouds*
Percy Gardner, *Principles of Greek Art*
Plato, *The Symposium; The Republic; The Dialogues*
Aristotle, *The Ethics; The Poetics*
Lucretius, *De Rerum Natura*
Virgil, *Eclogues and Georgics; Aeneid*
Horace, *Odes; Epodes; Satires; Epistles*
Plutarch, *Lives*
Marcus Aurelius Antonius, *To Himself*
St. Augustine, *The Confessions; The City of God*
The Song of Roland
The Nibelungenlied
St. Thomas Aquinas, *Of God and His Creatures*
Dante, *La Vita Nuova; The Divine Comedy*
Galileo, *Nuncius Siderius; On the Authority of Scripture in*
    Philosophical Controversies; Four Dialogues on the Two Great
    Systems of the World
J. J. Fahie, *Galileo, His Life and Work*
Grotius, *The Rights of War and Peace*
Montaigne, *Essays*
Shakespeare, *Hamlet; Much Ado about Nothing*
Cervantes, *Don Quixote*
Bacon, *The Advancement of Learning; The New Atlantis*
Descartes, *Discoveries on Method*
Hobbes, *Leviathan*
Milton, *Paradise Lost*
Molière, *Les Précieuses Ridicules; Le Bourgeois Gentilhomme;*
    Le Misanthrope; Tartuffe; L' Avare
Meredith, *On Comedy and the Comic Spirit*
Locke, *Essay Concerning Human Understanding*
Montesquieu, *The Spirit of the Laws*
Voltaire, *Candide; Toleration and Other Essays*
S. G. Tallentyre, *Voltaire in His Letters*
Rousseau, *Discourses on Inequality; Confessions*
Gibbon, *History of the Decline and Fall of the Roman Empire*
Adam Smith, *The Wealth of Nations*
Kant, *The Critique of Pure Reason*
Goethe, *Faust*
American State Papers: Declaration of Independence; Constitution
    of the United States; *The Federalist*
Victor Hugo, *Les Misérables*
Hegel, *The Philosophy of History*
Sir Charles Lyell, *The Principle of Geology*

Balzac, *Old Goriot*
Malthus, *Essay on the Principle of Population*
Bentham, *An Introduction to the Principles of Morals and Legislation*
Mill, *Autobiography; On Liberty*
Darwin, *The Origin of the Species; Autobiography*
Pasteur, either *The Life of Pasteur* by René Vallery-Radot; or *Pasteur:*
  The History of a Mind by Emile Duclaux
Marx, *The Communist Manifesto; Das Kapital*
Tolstoy, *Anna Karenina*
Dostoevsky, *Crime and Punishment*
Nietzsche, *Thus Spake Zarathustra; Beyond Good and Evil;* preface
  to *The Dawn of the Day*
William James, *Psychology*

Politics

We don't know if the problem of political correctness on campus is improv-ing or worsening. It would seem to be the kind of dark secret that hates the light, so books such as D'Souza's *Illiberal Education*, Roger Kimball's *Tenured Radicals*, and Martin Anderson's *Impostors in the Temple* ought certainly to be helping things. Still, the revolutionary sensibility of many academics may yet mean that some students, especially feisty conservative students, will find that *their* freedom to speak will not be honored simply because they are not saying what they are *supposed* to say.

In the preface, we quoted Allan Bloom on the subject of diversity—his belief that what is really behind the various restrictions on speech and the numerous curricular diversions is the notion that students are to be affirmed for what they are, not challenged to learn what they do not already know. Such a notion may seem benign at first, until the full implication of its moral equivalency sinks in.

Or do we make too much of this? Surely, you might say, the guardians of political correctness are only out to encourage self-respect and respect for others. Surely they would never attack one student's freedom in defense of another's emotional fragility. Surely they're not scrutinizing every formal text and informal utterance for signs of the isms they abhor.

Surely you're joking.

At Harvard, a dean of race relations and minority affairs (the title alone suggests a siege mentality unwarranted by the realities in Cambridge) called for a ban on 1950s sock hops, because, she said, the fifties were a *racist* decade. Such scrupulosity would be well rewarded in Beijing, but does Harvard really need Red Guards? Throughout academia, this sort of attack on racism—the sort that actually deprives some students of their right to speak—has been justified: as a defense of affirmative action; as a response to inequities in society; as a reaction to campus tensions. At best such actions fail; at worst they exacerbate the problem. And, tragically, many black students—more subject to preferences than any other group—find that their achievements are undervalued by the rest of the community, so strong is the *assumption* that their academic status is earned at a differ-ent, lower standard.

In fact, America *is* a nation of diversity, *is* a multicultural (or more precisely a *multiethnic*) country. The trouble is that many in academia fail 267 to make a true measure of equality. Their idea of diversity, as Shelby Steele has written, "applies democratic principles to races and cultures rather than to citizens, despite the fact that there is nothing to indicate that real diversity is the same thing as proportionate representation."

The Resistance

Few changes in the life of the American university are as troubling as the growth of coercive rules about speech. The tendency to want to fight back is strong, among students and faculties, but the call to battle needs to be tempered by some sensible tactical guidelines. Professor Alan Kors of the University of Pennsylvania has suggested that faculty (and his advice can as easily apply to students) fight back against politicization by facing their leftist colleagues and calmly arguing the case for true academic freedom, and by demanding that they (the leftists, that is) admit that their ends are political, not academic. At a 1990 meeting of the National Association of Scholars he outlined five "talking points".

> First, hold always to your intellectual standards of rigor, evidence, and integrity, but ever remind yourself about the terrible dangers of intolerance. . . .
> Second, hold to [traditional] standards in the classroom. . . . There is no license to avoid logic, evidence, and a base of knowledge. . . .
> Third, take on tendentious or self-indulgent scholarship publicly, encouraging far-ranging, frank, well-informed, [and] honest debate. . . .
> Fourth, build confidence among traditional scholars. . . . Drop your bait, make your jibes, offer appropriate criticisms, reply to nonsense with persuasive argument, and see if it does not embolden those who are faint-hearted. . . .
> Finally, pressure administrators to defend their standards across the whole university: don't let them get away with the sleight of hand whereby they present the culture of science for public consumption, and the culture of the humanities and social sciences for private consumption by the ideologues.

Students should do the same, although at some schools conservative student newspapers provide the opportunity to speak less softly. For information about these papers, including advice about founding one where none exists, write to the Madison Center for Educational Affairs at 1112 16th Street N.W., Suite 520, Washington, D.C. 20005, or call (202) 833-1801.

You may also wish to write to the Intercollegiate Studies Institute at 14 South Bryn Mawr Avenue, Bryn Mawr, Pennsylvania 19010, which publishes several fine journals (*Modern Age, Intercollegiate Review, Campus*) and is a source for information, inspiration, and many fine conservative speakers.

If in the course of building your liberal arts education, and in defense of your First Amendment rights, you encounter difficulties of a legal nature, do not hesitate to call the Center for Individual Rights in Washington at (202) 663-9401/42. It is a public interest law firm "dedicated to the principles of individual liberty, limited government, and the separation of powers," and is especially concerned about issues of academic freedom. Its services are free.

The Editors Choose

We've presented a group of fine colleges and universities, and clearly we encourage our readers to choose a school from among them. But you might wonder which schools *we* would choose—for ourselves; not for our children, since we respect them enough to want them to choose for themselves. Here are our choices.

Charles Sykes
A More Leisurely Sojourn

This exercise assumes that I would actually be on speaking terms with my seventeen-year-old self, a proposition that is problematic at best. Back then, I was a young man in a hurry—rushing through the University of Wisconsin system to graduate in just three years (I was a senior at nineteen). Looking back, I'm not sure what all the rush was about; I would certainly recommend a more leisurely sojourn in the groves of academe. My greatest accomplishment was to graduate with a 4.0 grade point average, a real accomplishment indeed, but one that concealed the gaping holes in my education. And straight A's might also indicate that I was not really challenged. I would try to avoid that the second time around.

My first choices would certainly include St. John's College in Annapolis, the University of Chicago, and the University of the South. I would apply to all three.

As intimidating as it is, I think my seventeen-year-old counterpart would be inspired by the rigor of St. John's. And after a sojourn in Oxford, England, the summer after high school graduation—which I had then and would hope for again—I know I would enjoy the ambience at Sewanee. But, assuming for argument's sake that I could actually get in, I would urge my younger counterpart to choose Chicago, tough sledding though I know it would be. The intensity of the intellectual atmosphere is daunting, but imagine all the things we'd have to talk about!

Brad Miner
Somewhere in Indiana

If I were seventeen again (God forbid!), but knew what I know now, I'd apply to Notre Dame and Wabash, and hope to be counted among the Fighting Irish. Then—when I actually was a high school junior (more than twenty-five years ago)—I applied to just one school, Ohio University, the alma mater of both my parents, and subsequently spent five years there, having too good a time and learning a little. Like many graduates of most universities, my *education* began in earnest after I got my degree. That was then.

Today, my seventeen-year-old alter ego would lean toward Notre Dame because he's Catholic (I converted in my mid-twenties) and a sucker for tradition; toward Wabash because a scholarly, athletic *fraternity* seems the optimal environment for his education. Indeed, were the forty-year-old Miner able to counsel the younger man (as in this hypothesis I guess he is), he'd no doubt recommend all-male Wabash. (Hell, remembering the passions of youth, he might suggest a monastery.) But the kid likes excitement, and he'd probably end up in South Bend, not Crawfordsville.

So I'd do the liberal studies program at Notre Dame: Latin and literature. I'd study hard, too. At least during the week.

Acknowledgments

The editors wish to acknowledge the contributions of the following colleagues: William F. Buckley, Jr., for his encouragement and for his splendid introduction; Wick Allison and Ed Capano, respectively the former and current publishers of *National Review*, for their suggestions and criticisms; Jack Fowler, John Virtes, Paul Marra, and the *NR* library staff, for their help in gathering data; our distinguished board of academic advisers for their invaluable assistance in developing the criteria upon which our judgments of America's liberal arts schools are based (they are: Donald Cowan, Jeffrey Hart, Hugh Kenner, Charles Kesler, and Thomas Short); and Frederic W. Hills of Simon & Schuster, our talented and sagacious editor, for the many suggestions that have made this second edition a better book.

We also wish to acknowledge the many readers, of this book's first edition and of *National Review* magazine, whose suggestions and criticisms have found their way into this new version of the *Guide*. We hope the dialogue will continue, and urge readers of this edition to write to us with recommendations of colleges that ought to be included in the next edition. Thanks in advance for your help.

Please address all correspondence to:

Messrs. Charles J. Sykes and Brad Miner
c/o Fireside Books
Simon & Schuster Building
1230 Avenue of the Americas
New York, NY 10020

About the Editors

CHARLES SYKES, prize-winning journalist, is author of the explosive best-seller *Profscam*, and of *The Hollow Men*, devastating portrayals of the persistent corruption in higher education. His several years of research for those books furnished much of the material for this guide.

BRAD MINER is the former literary editor of *National Review*. A native of Columbus, Ohio, Mr. Miner had a distinguished career in the book publishing industry before joining *NR* in 1989. Like Mr. Sykes, he is the son of a college professor.